This study provides a fresh assessment of Spanish Romanticism through a sympathetic appraisal of its literary theory and criticism. It identifies the origins of Spanish Romantic thought in the theories of German Romantic thinkers, in particular Herder's historicism. The range of reference, from the articles of Böhl von Faber to the judgements made by Cañete and Valera, is counterpointed by the detail of close readings of books and articles published between 1834 and 1844, together with an examination of the ideas which informed the creative work of Fernán Caballero. Derek Flitter's use of the history of ideas offers a corrective to the recent preponderance of political approaches to Spanish Romanticism, countering their stress on its radical and liberal associations with a detailed demonstration that the majority of Spanish Romantic writers derived their inspiration from restorative, traditionalist and Christian elements in their contemporaries' theory and criticism.

Spanish Romantic literary
theory and criticism

Spanish Romantic literary theory and criticism

DEREK FLITTER

*Lecturer in Modern Spanish Language and Literature
University of Birmingham*

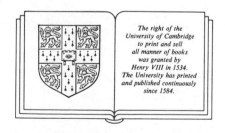

The right of the
University of Cambridge
to print and sell
all manner of books
was granted by
Henry VIII in 1534.
The University has printed
and published continuously
since 1584.

CAMBRIDGE UNIVERSITY PRESS

CAMBRIDGE

NEW YORK   PORT CHESTER

MELBOURNE   SYDNEY

Published by the Press Syndicate of the University of Cambridge
The Pitt Building, Trumpington Street, Cambridge CB2 1RP
40 West 20th Street, New York, NY 10011–4211, USA
10 Stamford Road, Oakleigh, Victoria 3166, Australia

First published 1992

Printed in Great Britain at the University Press, Cambridge

British Library cataloguing in publication data
Flitter, Derek
Spanish romantic literary theory and criticism. –
(Cambridge studies in Latin America and Iberian
literature, no. 5).
1. Spanish literature, 1800–1900 – Critical studies
1. Title
860.9

Library of Congress cataloguing in publication data
Flitter, Derek.
Spanish Romantic literary theory and criticism/Derek Flitter.
p.   cm. – (Cambridge studies in Latin American and Iberian literature: 6)
Revision of the author's doctoral thesis, University of Oxford.
Includes bibliographical references (p. 00) and index.
ISBN 0–521–39068–0
1. Spanish literature – 19th century – History and criticism – Theory, etc.
2. Spanish literature – Foreign influences.
3. Romanticism – Spain.
4. Criticism – Spain – History – 19th century.
5. Literature and society – Spain.
1. Title.   II. Series.
PQ6070.F5   1991
860'.9'145–dc20   90–26853   CIP

ISBN 0 521 39068 0

For my Mother, and in memory of my Father

Contents

Preface

This project first took the form of a thesis presented for the degree of Doctor of Philosophy in the University of Oxford. The text has since been revised, but the essential framework and premises of the work have remained largely unaltered. Further research and revision has been made possible by the award of a Laming Junior Fellowship conferred on me by The Queen's College, Oxford, which enabled me to work in Madrid during the academic year 1986–7. Final work on the manuscript has been carried out thanks to a British Academy Post-Doctoral Fellowship which I took up in October 1987.

My greatest debt is to the guidance and inspiration of Dr Ron Truman, the very best of supervisors. His continual support and encouragement have aided me beyond measure, while the fruitful investigation of many key areas of research stemmed directly from his suggestions. Certain chapters of this study were given in an early form as papers to the Research Seminar in Spanish and Portuguese at the University of Oxford, and I should like to thank members of that seminar for their constructive criticisms of my developing project. I likewise benefited from the discussion session which followed my paper on the ideological construct of Spanish Romanticism at the University of Manchester in 1986. In Madrid, I was able to profit from the wise and authoritative counsels of Professor Hans Juretschke, our most imposing specialist on Spanish Romanticism. To be recalled with pleasure are the hours spent in conversation with Francisco Leal Insúa, a devoted biographer of Nicomedes-Pastor Díaz. I also wish to acknowledge here the substantial help afforded me by staff at the Biblioteca Nacional and Hemeroteca Municipal, Madrid, and especially by don Fernando Grau. In the later stages of this project, I was able to incorporate a number of constructive suggestions made by the anonymous readers of the manuscript for Cambridge University Press, and have been encouraged at every stage in the publishing process by the indefatigable enthusiasm of my editor, Dr Katharina Brett. Lastly, and on a more personal note, I could not write this preface without acknowledging the intellectual mentorship of Dr John Rutherford, as my undergraduate tutor and later as my colleague, and as a greatly valued friend.

In preparing this work, I have silently updated spelling and accentuation except in the case of the peculiar orthography used by Bartolomé José Gallardo. I have endeavoured to reduce the number of footnotes to manageable proportions by citing from *Obras completas* collections in the body of the text.

Abbreviations

BAE	Biblioteca de Autores Españoles
BBMP	*Boletín de la Biblioteca de Menéndez y Pelayo*
BH	*Bulletin Hispanique*
BHS	*Bulletin of Hispanic Studies*
BRAE	*Boletín de la Real Academia Española*
BSS	*Bulletin of Spanish Studies*
CIPP	Colección de Indices de Publicaciones Periódicas
HR	*Hispanic Review*
MLN	*Modern Language Notes*
MLR	*Modern Language Review*
PMLA	*Publications of the Modern Languages Association of America*
Prop. Lib.	*El Propagador de la Libertad*
RABL Barc.	*Boletín de la Real Academia de Buenas Letras de Barcelona*
Rev. Cient. Lit.	*Revista Científica y Literaria*
Rev. Cont.	*La Revista Contemporánea*
Rev. Esp.	*La Revista Española*
Rev. Esp. Ext.	*Revista de España y del Extranjero*
Rev. Lit.	*Revista de Literatura*
Rev. Mad.	*Revista de Madrid*
Rev. Teat.	*Revista de Teatros*
RFE	*Revista de Filología Española*
RH	*Revue Hispanique*
RHM	*Revista Hispánica Moderna*
RR	*Romanic Review*
Sem. Pint.	*Semanario Pintoresco Español*
St. Rom.	*Studies in Romanticism*

Introduction

Interpretation of the word 'Romantic' continues to provide students of literature not only with a fertile source of ideas but also, more disconcertingly, with a bewildering array of contradictory statements. The modern academic meaning is not as exact as we might wish, as the welter of conflicting definitions collected by Lilian Furst in her useful introduction to the European movement amply demonstrates.[1] Unfortunately, understanding of the character and meaning of Romanticism in Spain has been more than usually hampered by problems of definition. Those literary histories published in the nineteenth century offered little analysis of the broader influences which affected the development of Spanish Romanticism, and the first serious assessment of the movement's theoretical bases was provided by the dedicated labours of Edgar Allison Peers. He detected two specific trends: the recovery of national literary tradition and the trenchant opposition to neo-Classical formalism. For Peers, the gestation period of the Spanish movement was long, but the triumph of Romanticism short-lived. A high point was reached between 1834 and 1837, but Romanticism was subsequently rejected in favour of a 'middle way' which he denominated Eclecticism. In retrospect, a major shortcoming of Peers's theory was its failure to take into account the extra-literary considerations essential to a full understanding of Romanticism. Subsequent criticism has in fact dealt principally with the relationship between the literary movement and contemporary ideological and philosophical concerns. Angel del Río, Vicente Llorens, D. L. Shaw, Ricardo Navas-Ruiz, Iris Zavala and José Luis Abellán have at different times linked Spanish Romanticism with liberalism, with spiritual malaise, and with so-called cosmic rebellion. All have sought to minimise the rôle played by Böhl von Faber, Agustín Durán and other critics of the period prior to 1834. This stems from their common premise that 'true' Romanticism finally came to Spain in that year, conditioned by the return of the political exiles. In his recent survey of modern critical responses to the movement, however, Juan Luis Alborg wisely noted that it was the critics of the 1820s, and not the returning political exiles, who were largely responsible for the future orientation of Spanish Romanticism.[2] Alborg also felt that the adoption, by so many modern critics, of what was essentially an a priori definition of Romanticism was ill advised.

In my own view, Alborg's reservations are justified. To begin the analysis of a literary period of immense complexity from a partial first principle is not helpful. Navas-Ruiz's dogged insistence that a person's Romanticism is directly proportionate to that person's liberalism – as he expresses it, 'se es romántico en la medida en que se es liberal'[3] – seems an acute example. Likewise Abellán's view that Romanticism and liberalism went hand in hand.[4] Abellán, in referring to the interpretation of Romanticism adopted by Peers, himself disparaged any wholesale application of a predetermined definition of the term and the exclusion from discussion of material not fitting that definition.[5] To his own readers, however, he betrays a transparent contradiction.

In this assumption that literary Romanticism and political liberalism were interdependent historical phenomena, the significance of Romanticism as a new literary and artistic sensibility becomes subordinate to events tangential to or wholly outside aesthetic formulae and creative endeavour. Susan Kirkpatrick, for example, in opening her recent consideration of Romanticism in Spain's cultural revolution, assures us that 'Romanticism played an important rôle in the evolution of a new way of representing and experiencing inner life that corresponded to the new world of market capitalism and the bourgeois state'.[6] She then predictably accounts for the historical development of Spanish Romanticism with programmatic reference to the social and political spheres: the rise and fall of the Spanish movement she felt to be directly affected by 'the erratic progress of Spain's liberal revolution'; the uncertainty of its hold reflected the equally uncertain progress of the 'bourgeois revolution'; its precisely fixed heyday corresponded to 'the years of greatest liberal activity in pushing forward the first phase of Spain's prolonged revolution'; finally, its attenuation after 1843 is attributed to the political commitment of writers whose primary task was to oppose Narváez's curtailment of liberal advances.[7] This calculated attempt to force a multi-faceted literary movement into inflexible social and political moulds is surely unwise, while the reiterated association of Romanticism with 'liberal revolution' becomes dogmatic. Like Alborg, I feel that any exclusive association of Spanish Romanticism with liberalism and spiritual disquiet is untenable. I have accordingly refrained from adopting any prior definition of Romanticism either as a literary movement or as a wider cultural phenomenon. Nevertheless, I have paid attention to René Wellek's consideration of the term 'Romanticism' in literary theory during the early part of the nineteenth century. Wellek showed that 'Romantic' as a literary designation in the terms formulated by August Wilhelm Schlegel and Madame de Staël was understood and acknowledged all over Europe.[8] By employing Wellek's observation as a point of departure (but not as a rigid or predetermined definition), I believe it possible to chart in a more sympathetic and more fruitful manner the way in which the theoretical bases of Spanish Romanticism developed and expanded. I shall be concerned primarily with an assessment both of the impact, upon Spanish writers, of a framework of ideas deriving from European Romantic theorists and of their response to those ideas. My major contention is that it was the principles of Romantic historicism, stemming from the work of Herder and more fully expounded with reference to literary history by the Schlegel brothers, which dominated Spanish literary theory and criticism during the whole of the period under discussion. Meanwhile, in this rigorous study of Romantic literary criticism the applicability of Morse Peckham's formulations regarding 'positive' and 'negative' Romanticism becomes increasingly perceptible.[9] Peckham considered the view of Romanticism as something indicating spiritual malaise, a view reiterated by recent critics of the Spanish movement. Yet he stressed that this idea of 'negative' Romanticism represented no more than a partial picture. Peckham pointed also to a 'positive' Romanticism, exemplified by the change from a mechanistic, static view of the universe to an organic and dynamic one, accompanied by an emphasis upon the working of the imagination and the creative process. This idea of 'positive' Romanticism, linked to the organic theory of literary history adumbrated by the Schlegel brothers, may profitably be borne in mind during an analysis of the development of Romantic historicism in Spain. One further comment made by Peckham might appropriately be recalled here: 'so much of our difficulty in considering the nature of historical Romanticism has come from assuming its identity with all of the other more or less contemporary revolutions'.[10] Such pitfalls are particularly to be avoided if we are to arrive at a true and impartial estimate of the character and significance of Spanish Romanticism. By approaching the original texts on their own terms, I have instead come to conclude with Northrop Frye that 'The fact of revolution was linked in many poetic minds with the imminence of apocalypse.'[11]

In examining developments in literary theory and criticism in Spain during an extensive and complex period, I have endeavoured to take into account not just the promotion of Schlegelian Romanticism and its further elaboration by Spanish writers, but also the existence of other trends divergent from or hostile to Romantic historicism. However, the reception of Schlegelian ideas and the response to them within this period forms the essential framework of my study, which has been structured accordingly. The continuing presence of certain identifiable trends in literary criticism has attracted the greatest share of my attention, and conflicting sets of ideas have been examined primarily in relation to them. While not wishing unduly to neglect the political background to literary events, I have deliberately refrained from allowing any assessment of political circumstances to become obtrusive. Finally, the chapter on Fernán Caballero may at first sight appear an unjustifiable departure from an essay dealing with literary theory and criticism. I would argue that the unashamedly didactic intention and authorial presence which mark Fernán Caballero's novels and short stories, coupled with the affinities which may profitably be established between her texts and the outlook of contemporary Spanish critics, make the inclusion and examination of material from her creative work appropriate and indeed indispensable to the present study.

I

Böhl von Faber and the establishment of a traditionalist Romanticism

The first systematic exposition of Romantic ideas in Spain was that undertaken by the German bibliophile and scholar Johann Nikolaus Böhl von Faber (1770–1836), a naturalised Spaniard who had settled in Cadiz. Böhl's espousal of Romantic theory was to involve him in a fierce literary polemic with José Joaquín de Mora (1783–1864), a family friend of long standing. Arising as it did in the years immediately following the Peninsular War and therefore in the wake of the constitutional parliament of Cadiz, it was perhaps inevitable that the dispute acquired political implications, an element of the controversy which has just as inevitably coloured later assessments of its nature and significance.

In his presentation of Romantic ideas, Böhl relied upon the principles of historicism. By historicism, I mean the 'historical sense' adumbrated in Germany by Johann Gottfried Herder (1744–1803), who opposed the belief in universal laws and ideals which had formed an essential part of philosophy in the Classical tradition, and instead sought to promote an individualising attitude that placed greater value upon the local and temporal conditions of human existence. The immediate outcome of such a trend was nationalism: a new appreciation of the concept of the nation-state, the idea of the creative forces inherent in the people, of the intimate relationship between individual and national community, and of the organic connection between the present and the past. The ideas of Herder, who was, in René Wellek's words, 'the fountainhead of universal literary history',[1] would provide a rich quarry for all of the German Romantics but more specifically for the brothers Schlegel. Their vision of literary history found definitive expression in August Wilhelm's Vienna lectures of 1808–9 and in those delivered by Friedrich in the same city in 1812.[2] A. W. Schlegel (1767–1845) had already proposed a tentative theory of Romanticism in lectures delivered in

Berlin between 1801 and 1804. These remained unpublished until 1884, and their impact was accordingly less emphatic than that of the later Vienna lectures, editions of which appeared in French (1813), English (1815), and Italian (1817). He differentiated between on the one hand, pagan, sensual and civic Classicism, and, on the other, Christian, spiritual and individualistic Romanticism, each suited to its own historical period and civilisation and possessing its independent values. According to Schlegel, the Christian and chivalresque spirit had been common to all European literature since the Middle Ages, yet the peculiar characteristics of individual nations had also been expressed in their respective literatures. He therefore conceived the idea of a *Kunstgeist*, a spirit of art shaped by the particular milieu of a given nation at a given historical period. Emphasising the dominant role played by Christianity, Schlegel felt that literature had come to depend, to a greater extent than previously, upon imagination and symbol as expressions of its spiritual aspirations. Another concomitant change was that affecting poetic form: while the Classical literatures had been bound by strictly defined 'rules', Romantic literature had reflected the differing characteristics of various nations and peoples, and in each country had acquired a distinctive form. The appearance of French neo-Classicism, pagan in spirit and therefore a modern manifestation of the Classical tradition, had once more threatened European literature with the tyranny of literary precepts: as Classicism was essentially rational and universal in character, it strove towards an unrealistic unity which did not allow for the concept of national differences and, consequently, the right of each people to cultural expression. Crucially, Schlegel's ideas involved the rehabilitation of old Spanish literature, and of Golden-Age dramatists like Lope de Vega and Calderón, condemned by neo-Classicists for their failure to observe the precepts of Aristotle and Horace. It was this section of the lectures which was to be translated and presented by Böhl, whose declared intention was to promote the ideas of A. W. Schlegel in the Spanish literary world. Böhl is widely believed to have been the author of an article dealing with poetics published in Quintana's *Variedades de Ciencias, Literatura y Artes* in 1805.[3] The piece, signed 'A. P. P.', distinguished between man's material and spiritual inclinations and assigned particular characteristics to the literatures of different countries, concluding with a reference to 'German Romanticists'. However, the article which effectively began Böhl's campaign to popularise the ideas of A. W. Schlegel and which gave rise to the polemic with Mora, a direct translation of extracts from the Vienna lectures, appeared in a Cadiz newspaper in 1814.[4]

Böhl was not the first defender of Calderón in a dispute about literary theory. He would himself praise Francisco Mariano Nipho's earlier defence of the Spanish *comedia* in the face of neo-Classicist condemnation. In the 1760s, moreover, Juan Cristóbal Romea y Tapia had responded to attacks upon native Spanish drama made by the neo-Classicist critic José Clavijo Fajardo.[5] Some comments made by Romea y Tapia prefigure the later arguments adopted by Böhl. The former insisted that nations differed in temperament and outlook, in characteristic moral virtues and failings as well as in language, customs and dress; accordingly they must inevitably differ in their dramatic preferences, since the object of the theatre was to depict aspects of human behaviour deserving of an audience's sympathy or disapproval.[6] In Ignacio de Luzán's neo-Classicist *Poética* of 1737 this same basic idea had been given what seemed no more than an accidental passing reference, and subordinated to the overriding premise that there existed a universal Poetics equally applicable in any country and in any historical period; for Luzán, it would be an unacceptable extravagance to seek to attribute to each nation a distinctive literary genius.[7] Romea y Tapia, on the other hand, like Böhl half a century later, employed the idea of cultural pluralism as the starting point for his defence of Spain's dramatic tradition. Yet while the national drama had been vigorously championed by several eighteenth-century writers,[8] Böhl's defence was made under circumstances that were uniquely different. In the later eighteenth century, neo-Classicism had enjoyed official support at the very highest level – from the Conde de Aranda and from Charles III himself – dominating 'approved' literary circles and constituting the only corpus of systematic literary doctrine available to writers. Apologists of Lope and Calderón were continually on the defensive, and more or less forced to recognise the superiority of Corneille and Racine, whatever their assessment of their own country's literary history. By 1814 this was no longer the case. Böhl was able proudly to reiterate a new theory of literary evolution which was rapidly conquering the whole of western Europe. Consistently echoing the principles of A. W. Schlegel, Böhl employed the term 'romancesco' to describe the new movement. He confidently prophesied a return to Spanish traditions, with the creation of a literature which would reflect popular ideals and which would be heroic, monarchical and Christian in character, thus in the tradition of the literature of the *Siglo de Oro*.

This last concept was itself to undergo a radical change. It had existed during the eighteenth century, primarily as a means of asserting a national literary tradition, independent of that of France, which might counter the threat of French cultural dominance. As such, it was elaborated in Antonio Capmany's *Teatro histórico-crítico de la elocuencia española* (1786–94). For Capmany, the sixteenth century in Spain was justifiably regarded as a Golden Age, uniquely rich both in the number and quality of its writers and in the glories of its military conquests.[9] Capmany, who had represented Catalonia in the Cadiz parliament of 1810, would have been an attractive figure for Böhl. An energetic and implacable opponent of the invading French forces despite his advanced years, he would attack Napoleon in works including *Centinela contra franceses* (Madrid, 1808); *Gritos de Madrid cautivo a los pueblos de España* (Seville, 1808); and *Centinela de la patria* (Cadiz, 1810). Capmany's use of the term *Siglo de Oro* thus directly related Spanish literature and empire, but did so with reference to an earlier age than that of Calderón, and so accorded with the more tentative usage of the term by Luis José Velázquez in his *Orígenes de la poesía castellana* of 1754 and by the Jesuit exiles Lampillas and Andrés. For all these writers, a Golden Age in Spanish letters was a concept associated primarily with lyric poetry, beginning with Garcilaso de la Vega (1501–36) and giving way to a period of decadence with the artificial distortions of Gongorine style. Böhl, however, followed A. W. Schlegel in regarding Calderón's drama as the apogee of Spain's literary efflorescence, as the expression both of a distinctive literary genius and of a distinctive set of values.

Religious and ideological preoccupations swiftly complicated the Böhl–Mora polemic. A number of critics have observed that the protagonists themselves appeared to wish a veil to be drawn over its history, probably in view of the fiercely personal tone of some of its documents and the possibility of unwelcome repercussions. Böhl's daughter Cecilia (known to the Spanish literary public by her pseudonym of Fernán Caballero), writing in 1861, confessed that the polemic had led to the trading of personal insults; moreover, since Mora had once more become a close friend of the Böhl family, and since both he and his supporter Antonio Alcalá Galiano had in later years come to admit the Romantic ideas defended by Böhl, it was considered desirable to paper over unpleasant aspects of the polemic. Cecilia was adamant, however, that the dispute had served its purpose in establishing in Spain the reputation of A. W. Schlegel as one of the foremost literary theorists and critics of his age.[10]

Students of the polemic remain indebted to the exhaustive research of Camille Pitollet, who clarified the history of the dispute in his *La Querelle caldéronienne de Johan Nikolas Böhl von Faber et José Joaquín de Mora, reconstituée d'après les documents originaux* (Paris, 1909). Pitollet impressively documents the contributions to Böhl's cause made by his wife Francisca Larrea and by his other collaborators José Vargas Ponce, Juan Bautista Cavaleri and Cristóbal Zulueta. He likewise illustrates the articles written by Alcalá Galiano in defence of Mora. Pitollet's study accorded the dispute its first serious critical consideration, since previous commentators had relied upon Francisco María Tubino's two short articles of 1877.[11] Tubino appears not to have gained access to many of the original documents; moreover, he wrongly states the name of Böhl's adversary to have been Juan José de Mora, and makes obviously inaccurate references to German Romanticism which Pitollet designates 'grossières erreurs'.[12] While Pitollet's study broke important new ground, it made no attempt to link the endeavours of Böhl with later Romantic criticism in Spain. Guillermo Carnero's much more recent research has clarified a previously neglected aspect of Böhl's work by placing it within a historical contextual framework of reactionary thought.[13] Drawing upon important documents from the Böhl family archive now in the possession of the Osborne family at Puerto de Santa María, Carnero has also been able further to illustrate the history of the polemic using material not accessible to Pitollet. However, it is disappointing that this rigorous study does not attempt to link the work of Böhl with the ideas that emerged in later Spanish criticism, especially since Carnero acknowledges at an early stage that the ideological content of Böhl's articles was far from untypical of Spanish Romanticism. He indeed introduces the polemic as a crucial episode in the development of Romantic ideas in Spain, without which it would not be possible fully to comprehend the principal ideological thrust of Romanticism in that country.[14] Juan Luis Alborg has regarded Carnero's preoccupation with Böhl's reactionary stance as an obsessive one, observing that Carnero's energies would have been more profitably employed in an assessment of Böhl's contribution to the future development of Spanish Romanticism.[15] Similarly Hans Juretschke, in a cogent essay, pointed to Carnero's zealous pursuance of the political, rather than literary, aspects of the polemic.[16] Juretschke would later stress that Carnero's approach was deficient precisely because it revealed itself to be rooted in politics.[17] The present study will seek to establish precisely the links between Böhl and later Romantic criticism in Spain while, at the same time, attempting to avoid the kind of partiality detected by Alborg and Juretschke in the work of Carnero.

When Böhl published his Cadiz article above the signature 'un apasionado de la nación española' ('a devotee of the Spanish nation'), his principal concern was the defence of Calderón against the attacks of Classicists. To make this defence he turned to the twelfth and fourteenth lectures of A. W. Schlegel's *Vorlesungen über dramatische Kunst und Literatur*. Although Böhl used only fragments from them, we already perceive the basic premises of Schlegel's brand of Romanticism. Böhl naturally introduced Schlegel's distinction between 'Classical' and 'Romantic' literature, declaring that, as they expressed different values, they ought not to be judged by identical criteria. He went on to state that England and Spain had chosen not to imitate Classical tragedy and comedy; instead they had developed an independent genre which he designated *romancesco*.[18] Unlike that of the ancients, Romantic literature was primarily Christian and spiritual, its themes being those of chivalry. Böhl was, in this respect, swift to echo Schlegel's view of Spain as the Romantic country *par excellence*; if modern, i.e. Romantic, poetry was founded upon religious sentiment, love, honour and knightly valour, then naturally it was in Spain that it attained its highest degree of perfection.[19] It is hardly surprising that we are provided with an idealistic vision of mediaeval Spain as a Christian bastion against the infidel. For Böhl, the 700-year history of the Spanish Reconquest exemplified the chivalric ideal. After the decline of chivalry, he affirmed, its spirit endured in Spain and in Spain alone.[20] Calderón, then, appears as the epitome of Spanish civilisation, embodying in his dramatic production all of the values earlier praised by Böhl. In the same article, Böhl attacked the influence upon Spaniards of eighteenth-century French literature and of Enlightenment thought. Translating from Schlegel, he forecasted that Spanish writers would soon awaken to a realisation of the respective values of the two systems he has outlined; pointedly ignoring 'la crítica bastarda del siglo filosófico' ('the bastardised criticism of the philosophical age'), they will choose to write in accordance with Golden-Age models.[21] Böhl attributes blame more specifically than A. W. Schlegel had done; the more accurate English translation of the Vienna lectures tells us: 'What the Spaniards have hitherto loved from native inclination, they must learn to reverence on clear principles, and, unconcerned at the criticism which has in the interval sprung up, proceed to fresh creations in the spirit of their great poets' (II, 351–2). In addition to outlining aspects of Schlegel's perception of literary history, Böhl also introduced the ideas on poetic composition found in the twelfth of the Vienna lectures. He repeated Schlegel's denial that the failure to observe Classical precepts would necessarily mean the removal of all curbs upon the poetic imagination. A. W. Schlegel wrote: 'The poetic spirit requires to be limited, that it may move within its range with a becoming liberty, as has been felt by all nations on the first invention of metre; it must act according to laws derivable from its own essence, otherwise its strength will be evaporated in boundless vacuity' (II, 94). Works of genius must have a definite form, but one which is organic rather than mechanical in its construction. The former would be innate, depending upon inspiration, an idea which formed an essential part of the expressive theory of literature adopted by Romantics everywhere.

In this early article, Böhl presented his readers with a vision of a Romantic literature centred on nationalism and religion, which glorified mediaeval Spain and which promoted a return to characteristically Spanish literary forms and traditions. These elements, as well as the attacks upon eighteenth-century French literature and philosophy, will assume greater significance when we come to consider later Spanish criticism. However, as Böhl's intention had not been to provide a systematic presentation of the totality of A. W. Schlegel's Vienna lectures, but to vindicate Calderón and early Spanish literature generally, the article constituted only a partial exposition of Schlegel's ideas. Notably lacking was the concept of the different ways of thinking of the northern and southern nations of Europe: the one of a scrutinising seriousness disposed to withdraw within itself, the other impelled outward by the violence of passion (II, 98). Neither did Böhl bring into play the overall perspective of Schlegel's work. As such elements did not form part of Böhl's terms of reference, it was difficult for José Joaquín de Mora to argue against Schlegel's ideas, since he was not able to appreciate their full extension.[22] Mora's reaction to Böhl's article was in fact to publish a rejoinder, based upon Classical precepts. He made reference to 'las reglas eternas del gusto' ('the eternal rules of good taste'), regarding their abandonment as anarchic, as a contagion that encouraged mediocrity.[23] Mora, however, betrays a transparent contradiction, admitting that he did not know of a single Classical drama in which Aristotle's precepts were rigorously observed. At the same time, his article departed from intellectual rigour in what would prove to be characteristic fashion; responding to the designation *romancesco*, the exasperated Mora exclaimed: 'Llámele Vd. como quiera, este género es menester que sea detestable' ('Call it what one will, this genre must necessarily prove abhorrent').[24] A further example is Mora's much later berating of the mediaeval period idealised by the Schlegels. Writing in the *Crónica Científica y Literaria* on 29 May 1819, he insisted that the age of the Enlightenment represented the pinnacle of human achievement, and regarded the supposedly heroic and poetical Middle Ages as a period during which men's only real concern was to clobber each other.[25] His divergence from the ideas of Böhl on a much broader range of issues is implicit in his consideration of Calderón as the prime example of seventeenth-century corruption, of 'la corrupción de su siglo'.[26] While this last phrase places Mora diametrically opposite the Schlegelian perspective, it echoes comments made by Sismondi in his important work first published a year earlier in 1813. Sismondi had viewed Calderón as a product of 'la misérable époque de Philippe IV', of an age which had lost sight of true virtue and grandeur.[27] Böhl, since it suited him not to do so, would fail to draw attention to all of Sismondi's comments on Calderón.

If it was Böhl's defence of Calderón and his attack upon Classical precepts that provoked the polemic, the focus of the dispute soon broadened considerably. When Mora assumed editorship of the Madrid-based *Crónica Científica y Literaria* in 1817, the controversy, perhaps for the first time, would command the attention of a considerable public. The terms of reference of the polemic also grew wider, and Böhl sought more and more to promote the ideas of 'lo romancesco' in general. He was unquestionably well equipped to do so, as he possessed a wide knowledge of recent literary and philosophical trends. While residing at his German country estate at

Görslow, for example, Böhl had published, in 1811, in the *Vaterlandisches Museum*, an article on recent English poetry, dealing with Burns, Southey and Wordsworth. Böhl perceived Wordsworth to be the leader of the new movement in England, the man who had liberated poetry from pedantic rules.[28] When he criticised Mora's assertion that contemporary literature was in a state of decadence and corruption, Böhl pointed to the beauties of the work of Wordsworth, Scott and Southey, as well as to those to be found in the writings of German authors like Goethe, Schiller, Tieck and the Schlegels. The scope of Böhl's acquaintance with Romantic theories is most evident in the third *Pasatiempo crítico* and its appendix.[29] This pamphlet, generally agreed to have ensured Böhl's victory in the polemic, included chapters on the importance of national literatures; on the dramatic unities of time and place, including reference to Samuel Johnson; on the ideas of Sismondi; a translation of the *Edinburgh Review* article on A. W. Schlegel's Vienna lectures; a summary of Madame de Staël's exposition of German Romantic ideas in *De l'Allemagne*, including a translation of the passage in praise of A. W. Schlegel.[30] Böhl thus capitalised on his widespread knowledge of Romantic literature and ideas, and devoted a great deal of energy to the translation, presentation and commentary of important contemporary works. Juretschke has consistently pointed to Böhl's undoubted erudition. While some modern critics have sought to dismiss Böhl as a fanatic, Juretschke has opportunely stressed the breadth of his acquaintance both with current trends in literary ideas and with the general intellectual background of the age.[31] In his formative years spent in Germany, and again during his period of residence at Görslow between 1806 and 1813, Böhl would certainly have become acquainted with, amongst other works, the writings of Herder and of Friedrich Schlegel (1772–1829), younger brother of August Wilhelm.

The task of completing Herder's explorations had fallen upon others; the justifiable view of Germany as a culturally subject nation stupefied by the imitation of French and Classical models, and the denial of Classical precepts as valid criteria for judging individual authors, found more elaborate expression in the work of the Schlegels. However, as Isaiah Berlin emphasises, Herder had also proclaimed the idea of literary nationalism, regarding language and poetry as living organisms whose character was determined by the existing cultural ambiance and by geographical and political conditions. He had encouraged Germans to ignore the inroads made by foreign influences and to return to the unspoilt native sources of the Middle Ages and the sixteenth century. German patriots should seek out the national poetic treasures, the *Nationallieder*, and follow their inspiration, since they alone were genuine and characteristic:

Has a nation anything more precious? From a study of native literature we have learned to know ages and peoples more deeply than along the sad and frustrating path of political and military history. . . . in the former we learn how it [a people] thought, what it wished and craved for, how it took its pleasures, how it was led by its teachers or its inclinations.[32]

All unpolished peoples, claimed Herder, would sing of their deeds; their songs were therefore authentic historical archives. He felt that 'In the works of the imagination and feeling the entire soul of a nation reveals itself most clearly'.[33] Moreover, in the *Fragments* of 1767 Herder had pointed to the regenerative power of folk poetry and had recommended collecting it. Throughout his activity we can detect an all-consuming desire to be the reformer and restorer of German literature, a desire that would be paralleled in the articles of Böhl on Spanish poetry. The sentiments of Herder found renewed expression in Friedrich Schlegel's Vienna lectures of 1812 on the history of literature, where we encounter the perception of literature as the epitome of all the intellectual capabilities and progressive movements of mankind. Friedrich Schlegel wrote:

there is nothing so necessary to the whole improvement, or rather to the whole intellectual existence of a nation, as the possession of a plentiful store of those national recollections and associations, which are lost in a great measure during the dark ages of infant society, but which it forms the great object of the poetical art to perpetuate and adorn. Such national recollections, the noblest inheritance which a people can possess, bestow an advantage which no other riches can supply; for when a people are exalted in their feelings, and ennobled in their own estimation, by the consciousness that they have been illustrious in ages that are gone by – that these recollections have come down to them from a remote and a heroic ancestry – in a word, that they have a *national poetry* of their own, we are willing to acknowledge that their pride is reasonable, and they are raised in our eyes by the same circumstance which gives them elevation in their own. (i, 15)

Schlegel viewed the age of the Crusades, of chivalry, romance and minstrelsy as the cultural spring of the nations of the West. Considering early Spanish literature, he eulogised the Poem of the Cid as a potent example of the spirit of nationality, calculated to exert 'the nearest and the most powerful influence over the national feelings and character of a people', and superior to an entire library of books destitute of that spirit (i, 343). In the same lecture, he described the Spanish *romancero* as not just a collection of popular ballads, but more importantly as true national and heroic poems (i, 346). It is not difficult to perceive how attractive such ideas would have appeared to Böhl, who was himself a tireless collector of popular poetry, and whose *Floresta de rimas antiguas castellanas* was the fruit of twenty years of research.[34] Böhl wished Spanish literature to return to its genuine and characteristic essence, and his articles display an aggressive cultural nationalism. He closely echoed the premise that literary tradition is central to the intellectual life and development of a nation in an article published in 1817 in the *Crónica Científica y Literaria*. Spain's most authentic intellectual achievement or 'verdadera ilustración', Böhl argued, resided in an awareness of all those advantages bestowed upon the country and its people by a beneficent God. Spaniards should strive to cultivate afresh the heroic qualities of courage, loyalty and faith that had characterised their ancestors. He suggested they achieve this by turning to the inexhaustible sources of their literary tradition, where they would find 'cuanto es menester para llenar el corazón de piedad cristiana, satisfacer la razón con sana doctrina, y divertir el entendimiento sin peligro' ('all that is needed to fill one's heart with Christian piety, satisfy one's reason with salutary doctrine, and allow one's intellect harmless recreation').[35] Böhl's assessment of the character of Spanish literature is notably akin to that made by Friedrich Schlegel. The latter had commented:

In this point of view the literature and poetry of Spain are most admirable. Every part of them is penetrated with the noblest natural feeling; strong, moral and deeply religious, even when the immediate subject of writing is neither morality nor religion. There is nothing which can degrade thought, corrupt feeling or estrange virtue. Everywhere there breathes the same spirit of honour, principle and faith.   (ii, 97–8)

There is a marked similarity between the remarks of the two men in both tone and content. Four years later, moreover, when writing to Navarrete about the publication of his *Floresta*, Böhl felt that the work would serve towards the establishment of a new state of consciousness in the aftermath of the political fevers of the day, since only that which was imbued with nationality could truly speak to hearts and minds.[36] Making reference to the work of Bishop Percy in England and to enthusiastic interest in popular poetry in his native

Germany, Böhl appears convinced of the regenerative powers inherent in popular literature. If Herder had viewed himself as the man destined to restore German literature and to promote national cultural expression in that country in the face of the slavish imitation of foreign models, Böhl seemed to consider his own task as a similar one. He condemned what he saw as Mora's unpatriotic desire to subject Spanish literature to French models and precepts; he and his supporters, meanwhile, 'acordes con el impulso sublime de las luces' ('at one with the sublime impulse of enlightenment'), undaunted and single-minded, sought to combat the dominant opinions of the age in order to re-establish true good taste, this despite the prospect of continued attacks from those who were mere minions of the French.[37] Böhl's employment of the term 'las luces' is at marked variance with its more accustomed usage. From the above evidence, I would contend that Böhl was influenced by the ideas of Herder and Friedrich Schlegel to a greater extent than has hitherto been apparent. I therefore find myself in agreement with Juretschke's brief observation that Herder, whose work was directly known to few Spaniards, would indirectly influence much Spanish Romantic criticism.[38] It appears probable that Böhl, at least, possessed firsthand knowledge of Herder's work.

A further reason for Böhl's support for the ideas of German Romantic theorists, as I have already indicated, was that the philosophy underlying their work was very much his own. Indeed, Böhl could confidently point, in the pamphlet *Donde las dan, las toman*, to an intimate connection between enthusiasm for poetry and religious devotion: in Germany, he insisted, the adherents of true poetry and in particular those of Spanish poetry, 'son muy religiosos, muy morales y muy amigos del orden social' ('are devoutly religious, morally upright and lovers of social order').[39] It is on this issue of Böhl's presentation of religious and political preoccupations as inextricably linked to literary ideas that modern critics have written most scathingly of his endeavours. Vicente Llorens condemned Böhl in particularly vigorous terms, highlighting his view of the drama of Calderón as inseparable from Roman Catholicism, a view which meant that attacks upon Calderón's dramatic art were construed by Böhl as profanity.[40] In this assessment of Böhl's endeavours, however, the implicit desire of Llorens to link Romanticism with liberalism may account for his sharp condemnation of the German, who had championed a very different ideological parallel. Llorens claimed that the patriotic character of Spanish liberalism at the time of the struggle against Napoleon might have permitted the acceptance of a strongly nationalistic theory of literary history such as that adumbrated by the Schlegels. Böhl, he felt, had effectively scuppered this opportunity by linking the new ideas with absolutism at a time when many Spanish writers were being persecuted as a result of their liberal opinions.[41] For Llorens, then, the German's efforts were essentially destructive. The Spanish critic does not display a great deal of attachment to Böhl, in the eyes of whom, he comments, the Holy Inquisition would have seemed dangerously liberal.[42] This captious phrase is indicative of the impatience with which Llorens treats Böhl in his studies of the period. Llorens might more profitably have paid attention to the fact that Böhl was not formulating ideas of his own but was expressing Romantic theories largely as they had been conceived and established in Germany: A. W. Schlegel had after all been labelled a reactionary by his detractors. These ideas were attractive to Böhl since they vindicated national popular poetry and Spanish Golden-Age drama, and since the ideological framework which underpinned them was very much his own. It seems difficult justifiably to blame Böhl for the anti-liberal associations acquired by the Romantic movement when he did no more than enthusiastically echo opinions earlier expressed by others. Historical circumstance was largely responsible for the fact that many Spanish writers rejected Romanticism at a crucial time, but at that time the movement was widely recognised as conservative in character; the French Revolution and the Napoleonic wars had been instrumental in creating this perception. Tubino realised that in the early years of the nineteenth century, the combination of 'German' and 'Romantic' was almost tantamount to francophobia, political reaction and Christian orthodoxy.[43]

   D. L. Shaw would later claim that by bringing religious and political considerations into the literary debate Böhl had only confused the issue.[44] For Shaw, 'true' Romanticism was characterised by its revolutionary elements and a specifically contemporary *Angst*. In its application to Spain, this meant that genuine Romanticism arrived with the return of the political exiles after the death of Ferdinand VII in 1833. The presentation of Romantic ideas by Böhl was therefore felt by Shaw to have been misleading. However, he does acknowledge the effectiveness of Böhl's work in directing, especially, the course of literary criticism in the following decade.

Shaw obviously felt that Böhl's theory of Romanticism was incomplete, yet as Alfonso Par, and later Hans Juretschke, have pointed out, Böhl in the course of his articles provided Spaniards with an extensive description of Romantic ideas as conceived at that time.[45] The German cannot be faulted for having failed to bring into his discussion developments which only manifested themselves in later years.

In his pamphlet *Donde las dan, las toman*, Böhl had associated neo-Classicism with the new political order brought about by the French Revolution, and had thus created problems for Mora and Alcalá Galiano by insinuating that they were republicans.[46] In the first *Pasatiempo crítico* of 1817, Böhl claimed that it was not Calderón who was really detested by the supporters of *Mirtilo* (the pseudonym adopted by Mora at the beginning of the polemic in an unsuccessful attempt to withhold his identity, that of a personal friend of Böhl); instead it was the spiritual system intimately related to the dramatist's poetic enthusiasm, his emphasis on religious faith, the limits which he had imposed upon rational enquiry, and his lack of respect for the kind of 'habilidades mecánicas' ('mechanistic skills') which were the only glory of his detractors.[47] It is all too easy to see this kind of bombast as no more than the manifestation of Böhl's own reactionary position. What is certain is that the francophobia displayed so aggressively by Böhl in the polemic with Mora was a long-standing aspect of his character. In a letter written to his wife from Görslow in 1807, Böhl had emphasised that the indefinable qualities of poetry were irreconcilable with reasoning just as the relationship between their respective sources of inspiration – the spiritual and material aspects of human nature – remained mysterious and inexplicable. He used the premise to declare that there could never exist any true poetry in the materialistic and irreligious society of contemporary France, where writers like Bernardin de Saint-Pierre, Chateaubriand and Madame de Staël were subjected to scorn.[48] Böhl's attitude would have made him acutely receptive to the sentiments expressed by Friedrich Schlegel in his lectures on the history of literature. The latter defended Calderón in the name of Catholicism and attacked Voltaire for the Frenchman's atheism, attitudes that probably exerted some influence upon Böhl in the polemic. Friedrich Schlegel associated Calderón with the political and philosophical framework of his day, and similarly linked French neo-Classicism with republicanism and irreligion. René Wellek, for example, encountered in Friedrich Schlegel's Vienna lectures 'a philosophy of history which predicts the ultimate victory of Roman Catholicism over the forces of the Enlightenment and all other forms of secularism'.[49] In the twelfth of his Lectures, Friedrich Schlegel described the Spanish monarchy as historically the greatest and the most splendid in Europe, and the national spirit of Spain as the most developed. Passing on to literature, he observed that 'the stage of Madrid, the living mirror of Spanish life, was the first which arrived at its period of glory' (II, 124). Calderón is described as 'In every situation and circumstance, ... of all dramatic poets, the most Christian, and for that very reason the most romantic' (II, 135). If Schlegel viewed Calderón as representative of seventeenth-century Spanish society, equally he regarded Voltaire as typical of the republican sentiment and irreligion of the France of his day. Not even Böhl, for all his aggressive rhetoric, could have more roundly condemned the French writer. Schlegel attacked Voltaire's irreligion in strong terms, referring to his 'perversity of genius', impious wit and aversion for Christianity, all of which had meant that 'his spirit operated as a corrosive and destructive engine for the dissolving of all earnest, moral and religious modes of thinking' (II, 192–3). Schlegel also had hard words in store for Voltaire when tackling the subject of the French writer's republicanism. Referring to Voltaire's vision of history, he regards it as, in political terms, 'an absurd predilection for the republican notions of antiquity', destitute of any real knowledge of republicanism. Among Voltaire's followers, claimed Schlegel, this notion had become 'a decided and bigoted hatred of all kingly power and nobility, and in general of all those modes of life and government which have been produced by what is called the feudal system' (II, 195–6). We notice here the reference to Classicism: Schlegel saw admiration for Classical literature and admiration for the Classical institutions as inseparable tendencies. It is not surprising, therefore, that he should condemn Voltaire's view that all the modern ages before that of Louis XIV were ages of darkness, and that even in the reign of that monarch, all nations except France were peopled by hordes of barbarians (II, 197). This was exactly the kind of rhetoric used by Romantics against Classicists in Spain in later decades. Schlegel's support for Catholicism and monarchy, as represented by Calderón and seventeenth-century Spanish society, and his condemnation of republicanism and irreligion as represented by Voltaire and modern France, would surely have been borne in mind by Böhl in the latter's vindication of the Spanish Golden Age. If Böhl brought into the polemic political and religious factors that endangered his adversaries, liberals living under the absolutist regime of Ferdinand VII, he probably considered it natural to do so; given the theories which Böhl had adopted from Germany, it was not inappropriate that he should link Calderón with the spiritual and political framework of imperial Spain. Böhl was not merely manifesting personal fanaticism, but reiterating existing views. Particularly helpful in this context is the lucid assessment by José Luis Varela, who recognised that the association of neo-Classicism with republicanism represented a constant in reactionary thought. Varela insisted that in order to make an accurate reading of nineteenth-century textual evidence, we must appreciate the context in which key terms were used: for the reactionary writer, republicanism signified nothing less than anarchy and revolutionary subversion; likewise neo-Classicism was the doctrine of a pro-French faction who promoted a materialistic outlook that had already led to a revolutionary bloodbath, the shock-waves of which were still acutely felt throughout Europe.[50] At the same time, the violent, and often unnecessarily aggressive, rhetoric so often employed by Böhl can be explained by a number of external factors: the ruin, during the Napoleonic invasion, of the commercial house established by the Böhl family at Cadiz, something which would naturally have exacerbated the German's francophobia; the reactionary fanaticism of Böhl's wife, doña Francisca Larrea, which far exceeded that attributed to Böhl himself by the most scathing of modern critics; the fiercely personal tone acquired by the polemic, largely owing to the actions of Mora, who, lacking intellectual arguments, took to publishing doggerel which insulted a certain 'Bolonio' and his followers (Mora even went so far as to mock doña Francisca's limp); finally, the climate of opinion in Spain at the time, particularly conducive to reactionary thought, as both Carnero and Herrero have proved.[51]

If Böhl's position was an understandable one in the circumstances, this is not to say that it is wholly to be approved. Implicitly to accuse his opponents of wishing to introduce republican government in Spain, given the paranoia surrounding such an idea in the reign of Ferdinand VII, was inexcusable, while Böhl's presentation of the ideological associations of German Romantic theories rapidly became all-consuming and dogmatic. It was either personal friction or the ideological thrust adopted by Böhl which initially provoked Mora's opposition. In 1813, the latter had written to doña Francisca from France, where he had been imprisoned, and had enclosed with his letter three *romances* which he had himself composed. These were later forwarded by doña Francisca to A. W. Schlegel. In this same letter, Mora loudly praises the *Romancero*, finding in the old ballads lofty philosophical ideas and cogitations expressed in the most simple and natural language. He appears somewhat surprised that Spain, a country renowned for imaginative qualities of fire and passion, should have produced melancholy sentiments and bleak scenarios more analogous with the mists of the North than with the benign climes of the South.[52] Mora then subscribes to the respective images of northern and southern Europe present in the work of Madame de Staël, the Schlegel brothers and Sismondi; the year of 1813 had seen the publication in French of Madame de Staël's *De l'Allemagne* and Sismondi's *De la littérature du Midi de l'Europe*, both of which elaborate upon this concept. In a further letter Mora praises Shakespeare, describing him as the greatest genius who has ever lived, and deplores Classicist attacks upon the Englishman's work: '¿Qué son las reglas y las *convenances* y las trabas de estos monos junto a sus sublimes arrebatos?' ('For what are the precepts and *convenances* and the shackles of such monkeys alongside his sublime raptures?')[53] The passage was quoted in full by Böhl himself, in the first *Pasatiempo crítico*. Böhl moreover praised Mora's tender and evocative poetic imagination, and commented that he had previously revered the very things which he was now, as *Mirtilo*, decrying.[54] Mora would in fact reaffirm his earlier opinions during his later exile in London. He was led to oppose Böhl's articles, and by extension Romanticism, by personal or ideological, rather than literary, considerations. Having fought in the battle of Bailén and later having suffered incarceration at the hands of the French – he was not freed until 1814 – Mora was unlikely to bear without resentment Böhl's intended lessons in patriotism. Consequently, writing in the newspaper *El Constitucional* in the wake of Riego's *pronunciamiento* of 1820 and the overthrow of absolutist rule, Mora bluntly stated that 'El liberalismo es en la escala de las opiniones políticas lo que el gusto clásico es en la de las literarias' ('Liberalism is, within the range of political opinions, the equivalent of Classical taste in that of literary ideas').[55] Whether or not such a situation may eventually be viewed as misleading or even contradictory, Romanticism had, at an early stage in Spain, acquired ideological associations that Mora, as a committed liberal, found undesirable. Böhl had in fact established a distinctly traditionalist Romanticism centred on premises derived from the Schlegel brothers and from Herder. It involved a powerful cultural nationalism seeking a return to genuine and characteristically Spanish literary forms, and was backed by strong associations with throne and altar. The fact that Böhl was expressing new and, in literary terms at least, revolutionary ideas never before aired in Spain deserves emphatic stress. As Shaw has stated, we find it difficult today to appreciate the revolutionary nature of the fundamental historicist approach: that each country should possess a characteristic national literary tradition which intimately represents the spirit of its people. Shaw perceived the attraction of such an idea for *casticista* critics, and pointed out that Böhl's association of the Spanish literary tradition with Catholicism and monarchy would have lent his premises additional appeal during the reign of Ferdinand VII.[56] If the articles and pamphlets constituting the textual material of the polemic had not reached a wide audience, the dispute did make a mark in the Spanish literary world. For example, Brian J. Dendle has shown Böhl's influence upon Ramón López Soler,[57] and the links between the German and Agustín Durán are well documented. At a later stage in this study, I hope to prove that the brand of Romanticism established by Böhl was reasserted in later decades, and that the characteristics of the movement as perceived by the German proved to be those of the whole of the Romantic period in Spain. In short, we must consider Böhl not as a figure in isolation, but as an important pioneer.

2

The consolidation of Romantic ideas: 1820–1833

Between 1820 and 1823, Spain enjoyed a respite from absolutism during the *trienio constitucional*. As we might expect, there was little promotion of Romantic ideas in these years, when the traditionalist theories of the Schlegels as presented by Böhl would have been unwelcome. The government of the time was engaged in resisting both internal conservative pressures and the external threat of the Holy Alliance, and Schlegelian theory, avowedly antagonistic to the progressive ideals of the Enlightenment and instead intimately related to a trenchant Catholicism, could only have aroused inimical feelings among Spanish liberals.[1]

Evidence of continuing controversy in literary circles is, however, found in the notes added in 1821 by Manuel José Quintana (1772–1857) to his much earlier poem 'Las reglas del drama' (1791). Quintana made reference to current disputes regarding literary preferences, between 'clásico' and 'romántico' or 'romancesco'. His own stance regarding the dramatic unities was an intermediary one: he had abandoned his previous insistence upon rigorous interpretation and observance of Classical precepts, and now saw that there were compelling reasons against, as well as in favour of the unities. English, German and Spanish dramatists, he observed, had all chosen to ignore them, and their work had not suffered as a result; they had indeed been able to produce every appreciable note of dramatic interest and effect.[2] In upholding this last view, in conflict with that of neo-Classical preceptists like Hermosilla, Quintana coincided with Böhl. However, he consistently denied the validity of the term *Siglo de Oro*, especially when applied to the seventeenth-century dramatists, and in broader terms was an ideological opponent of the German. Quintana applauded the French Revolution and, in a Spanish context, looked back to three centuries of unbroken political tyranny and intellectual stagnation imposed by absolutism and the Inquisition. A committed liberal, he was active in both constitutionalist and later *progresista* administrations but, during successive periods of absolutist rule, was imprisoned in Pamplona between 1814 and 1820 and then banished to internal exile in the village of Cabeza de Buey, near Badajoz, between 1823 and 1828.

Writing more specifically of Schlegelian ideas at this time was the versatile intellectual Alberto Lista (1775–1848), a Catholic priest who was at once poet, literary critic and educator of renown. His articles in *El Censor*, a periodical of *afrancesado* opinion published between August 1820 and July 1822, constitute a firm rebuttal of Romantic theory. Lista supported moves to adapt the Spanish stage to Classical forms of drama and opposed the thesis of Böhl. What offended him most was the premise that each nation could forge its own aesthetic, which would reflect its particular outlook and sensibility: an idea he viewed as anarchic. In an important article published in April 1821, Lista was insistent that the ideas propounded in Germany were intended to encourage all over Europe 'la expresión de las pasiones sacadas de quicio y las máximas más peligrosas en materia de moral' ('the expression of deranged passions and, in moral terms, of the most dangerous maxims').[3] If Lista was willing to admit the beauties in the work of Calderón and Shakespeare, his greatest praise was reserved for the elder Moratín, whom he felt had given new life to the Spanish stage through his salutary philosophy and sound precepts. Likewise, for Lista the most admirable figures in modern Spanish literature were the younger Moratín in drama and Meléndez Valdés in poetry. These opinions were to change in the course of the *ominosa década* (1823–33), and Lista's gradual acceptance of Romantic doctrine would come to illustrate the growing popularity and attraction of the new ideas, but it remains the case that Romanticism made little if any progress during the *trienio constitucional*.

The founding in 1823 of the Barcelona periodical *El Europeo*, which coincided with the occupation of the city by the French forces commanded by the Duke of Angoulême representing the Holy Alliance, would at first sight appear to call into question the established connection between Romanticism and reaction, and this at the very time of the restoration of absolutist rule. The manifesto of *El Europeo* inclined towards tolerance and moderation. One of its editors, Fiorenzo Galli, would later describe the aims of the periodical in lyrical terms as a guiding voice of calm which might assuage the political storm and salvage something of value from what was a vast shipwreck: a lone voice, he declared, proclaiming the cause of doomed liberty.[4] In literary terms *El Europeo* sought to mediate in the bitter disputes between Classicists and Romantics – while displaying a marked sympathy for the ideas of the latter – to overcome blinkered nationalisms and, while respecting national traditions, to remain open to European currents of ideas and to encourage wider perceptions of literature's rôle in society. However, in its assimilation of the new Romantic aesthetic, *El Europeo* incorporated tendencies which flew in the face of liberal ideas inherited from the Enlightenment. The association of modern civilisation with the Christian religion, the idealisation of the Middle Ages, the stress upon imagination as superior to reason, and the rejection of eighteenth-century rationalist philosophy, all helped to link *El Europeo* with the character and orientation of the new sensibility.[5]

Of the magazine's young editors, both Luigi Monteggia and Fiorenzo Galli, like their Catalan collaborators Buenaventura Carlos Aribau (1798–1862) and Ramón López Soler (1806–36), were followers of the new Romantic ideas. Aribau would later found, with the publisher Rivadeneyra, the Biblioteca de Autores Españoles. Monteggia and Galli were political exiles who had fled to Spain before the intervention of the Holy Alliance, while their editorial colleague Charles Ernst Cook, born in Alsace, had been similarly expelled from Italy after the revolution of 1821.[6] The second issue of the periodical included Monteggia's article entitled 'Romanticismo'.[7] This contained a purely theoretical consideration of the Romantic aesthetic, any ideological associations that the movement had acquired being suppressed. Neither did Monteggia attempt to link Romantic ideas directly with Spanish literature. What we are left with is a restatement of basic Classical–Romantic distinctions. Monteggia adheres to the outlook of A. W. Schlegel, but with one important difference: if, he argues, Romantic writers are those who successfully and colourfully depict the character of their age in literature, then a number of Greek and Latin authors could be considered to have been Romantics. Monteggia's attempt to rectify Schlegelian categories could really only result in confusion, yet his premise that the immortality of a work lies in its ability to interpret the spirit of its age for future generations might be felt to constitute, as D.L. Shaw has contended, an important recognition of the strictly contemporary character of the Romantic movement.[8]

Immediately evident in the article is the influence of Chateaubriand (to whom Monteggia refers), and of Madame de Staël's *De l'Allemagne*. Following Chateaubriand, Monteggia emphasises the impact of the poetic spirituality of the Christian religion upon literature. Imagination perhaps leads him to excess when he writes of the invasion of southern Europe by the northern tribes, who had brought with them the more lugubrious ideas produced by life in a sterner climate. Monteggia refers lyrically to their propensity for the melancholy songs of bards and druids (34). His imaginative evocation of the northern peoples is reminiscent of Madame de Staël, who had written similarly of their inherent disposition.[9] Although it was not Monteggia's intention to take sides in the literary dispute, it is clear that the spiritual nature of Romanticism made it, in his view, superior. He praises Homer and Virgil, who both enter his category of 'Romantic by the standards of their own age', but regards neo-Classicism as an anachronism based upon outmoded academic conventions rather than genuine inspiration. He therefore points to the gulf separating 'los poetas hijos de las escuelas, que todo lo han aprendido por las reglas aristotélicas' ('poets bred at school, who have learned everything from Aristotelian precept') from 'los inmortales hijos del genio, que todo lo sacan de la naturaleza y del corazón' ('the immortal sons of genius, who take everything from nature and from the heart') (38). Monteggia, then, favours the literary freedoms he associates with Romanticism against the enforced regularity and intellectual rigour of neo-Classicism, typified by the dramatic unities (38–41). He concludes his article by recommending to his readers the work of A. W. Schlegel, Sismondi and Manzoni, as well as the critical articles of the Milanese journal *Il Conciliatore*, which had been instrumental in the dissemination of Romantic ideas in Italy (42). Monteggia was, according to Juretschke, the first critic to use the terms 'clasicismo' and 'clasicista' in Spanish; he would have gleaned them from an editorial in *Il Conciliatore* which stated: 'Noi chiamiamo Classicisti i moderni che imitano superstiziosamente e senza ragione gli antichi' ('We give the name "Classicists" to those modern writers who superstitiously and without justification imitate the ancients').[10] In his treatment of literary themes Monteggia followed in the footsteps of Böhl. Admiring, in terms of aesthetics, the emotional appeal of Christian spirituality, he invited writers to seek inspiration in an idealised mediaeval world. Yet while Monteggia conveyed to his reader a wide vision of European literature, his article sorely lacked reference to Spanish writers.

Monteggia's article was followed, in the seventh issue of *El Europeo*, by López Soler's 'Análisis de la cuestión agitada entre románticos y clasicistas', the aim of which was ostensibly to reconcile warring factions:[11] these continuing allusions to energetically argued critical disputes point to a lively discussion of Romantic ideas in Spanish literary circles. In line with Schlegelian theory, López Soler regarded Christianity as the most important distinguishing factor between the ancient and modern worlds. Essential differences in religion and custom had necessarily led, he felt, to changes in the character and form of literary creation. Christianity had spiritualised poetry and lent it more imaginative expression. As for poets themselves, he asks, in terms reminiscent of Monteggia, could they have been expected to bind their work to narrow formal conventions not found in Nature but learned in the classroom? (51). Instead, they had adopted an organic form of poetry whose inspiration could be considered as innate; here López Soler refers to A. W. Schlegel.[12] As in the case of Monteggia, his impartiality soon gives way to enthusiasm for the new aesthetic, and López Soler gives himself over to the evocation of a lugubrious and melancholy Nature, a scenario which would become increasingly typical in later periods of Spanish Romanticism (47).

Ermanno Caldera has pointed to Schlegel and Schiller, to Madame de Staël and Chateaubriand, as López Soler's sources,[13] but on this question the most compelling evidence has been provided by Brian J. Dendle. The latter amply demonstrates the influence of Chateaubriand on López Soler: in his vision of the Middle Ages; in his stress upon the superiority of the Christian religion; in his affirmation of the importance of emotional feeling. All these aspects of *Le Génie du christianisme* are also to be found in A. W. Schlegel's dramatic lectures, but López Soler repeats one image from Chateaubriand not in the *Vorlesungen*: the allusion to Andromache frenziedly searching for the body of Hector. Similarly, Dendle points to 'Les ruines' as the source for López Soler's article 'Las ruinas'.[14]

In the 'Análisis . . .', and in several other of his literary articles, the young Catalan critic employed the theories of A. W. Schlegel on literary history and on the Spanish theatre. Here Dendle has shown that López Soler's access to the ideas of the German theorist was through the work of Böhl: those themes from the Vienna lectures omitted by Böhl were likewise excluded from López Soler's discussion; Böhl and López Soler employed similar phraseology and imagery in the illustration of their respective arguments; most convincingly, certain changes made by Böhl in his translation of Schlegel were appropriated almost verbatim by López Soler. Dendle is thus led to conclude that 'The Calderonian polemic of Böhl von Faber was of greater importance to Spanish Romanticism than has previously been believed'.[15] I feel that this is not the only instance of affinity between Böhl and Löpez Soler, and that in several articles published in *El Europeo* it is possible to detect Böhl's own ideological preoccupations. For example, in his 'Examen sobre el carácter superficial de nuestro siglo',[16] López Soler bemoaned the lack of respect for religion, the absence of the resolute and heroic cast of mind which had characterised Spaniards in past ages, a widespread degeneracy in behaviour, and a dearth of that salutary pride which had consistently disdained all that did not contribute to cultural progress and achievement. The country had been reduced to a state of nullity, one of weakness, of indolence and of carping criticism which sought to despise a historical past indisputably greater than the present.[17] López Soler's remarks are reminiscent of the outline of 'verdadera ilustración española' as described by Böhl in the *Crónica Científica y Literaria*, in their nostalgic evocation of the past and in their celebration of what are presented as traditional Spanish values.[18] In the same article López Soler praises the labours of mediaeval scholars and writes enthusiastically of the period of Spanish and Portuguese expansion overseas. He subsequently views the period of Louis XIV not as a Golden Age but as one of decadence, and goes on emphatically to stress the pernicious effects of the Enlightenment: 'fueron degenerando las costumbres, el falso talento ridiculizó a la religión, llamó hipocresía a la piedad, y desmoralizando la juventud por medio de una filosofía engañadora desconcertó la armonía del cuerpo político, atrayendo las revoluciones más atroces sobre el mismo país donde cien años antes habían florecido las ciencias' ('the way of life became increasingly degenerate, bogus genius ridiculed religious belief, labelling piety hypocrisy and, by corrupting youth with a deceitful philosophy, upset the harmoniously ordered political system, bringing down the most horrendous scenes of revolution upon a country where a century earlier learning had flourished'). The French Revolution, insisted López Soler, was not a consequence of Enlightenment progress, but, on the contrary, baleful evidence of the degeneracy of the *Ilustración*.[19] In the present, post-revolutionary age he saw affectation, frivolity and superficiality. The solution he proposes is that his own generation seek to promote religious ideals and restore healthy morals. Elsewhere, López Soler repeats the concept of literature as the manifestation of intellectual progress – a concept prevalent in Friedrich Schlegel's lectures and later expressed by Böhl – equating the history of poetry with the history of a nation's progress along the path of civilisation, from its earliest heroes to its most brilliant period of wealth and splendour.[20] Finally, in his article 'Perjuicios que acarrea el olvido de las costumbres nacionales', López Soler attacks the abandonment of national traditions in favour of the imitation of foreign models.[21] Caldera made the important observation that, in this last piece, the Catalan writer was demonstrating an early sense of *costumbrismo*, and furthermore felt that this nostalgic desire for the past and vindication of national tradition made the moderate liberal seem a reactionary xenophobe. He comments that Romanticism, in López Soler's article, almost instinctively takes on a conservative and nationalistic colouring.[22] Alongside López Soler's cosmopolitan vision of the Romantic aesthetic, there is a deep-seated desire to comprehend the authentic Spanish essence, through sympathetic study of the country's history, literature and customs. These characteristics would prove common to both the traditionalist Romanticism already outlined and Fernán Caballero's subsequent brand of *costumbrismo*, affinities of the utmost significance to our understanding of the development of literary ideas in Spain. Again looking ahead, a further indication of López Soler's favourable attitude towards traditional moral values would appear in his prefatory article as editor of the Barcelona newspaper *El Vapor* in 1833. Here he remarks upon the vicissitudes of which Spain has been both setting and victim, and writes scathingly of 'las vanas teorías que han agitado las naciones extranjeras y han querido introducirse en la nuestra' ('the vain theories which have shaken other nations and which have sought to be introduced into our own'). López Soler's reference to the savagery of the Peninsular War and consequent internecine strife is accompanied, crucially, by a swipe at the pernicious philosophy of social revolution emanating from France which he perceives as their cause. Such a philosophy has proved unable to pervert the minds of the majority of Spaniards, but has left behind it 'funestas huellas, vagos principios, aéreos recuerdos que es útil desvanecer' ('baneful traces, vague principles, airy recollections which it is expedient to remove').[23] In the same article, López Soler declares his own adherence to the idea of monarchy, and refers favourably to Capmany, influential in his native Catalonia.[24]

Most modern critics have been too ready to see, in the figure of López Soler, a spirit of liberalism. If he was an opponent of the absolutist régime of Ferdinand VII and a supporter of a greater degree of tolerance and moderation, he was also a stout defender of what he regarded as traditional Spanish values. We know from the evidence provided by Dendle that López Soler became aware of many of the ideas to which he was so passionately attached through his acquaintance with the work of Böhl. I would contend that an affinity between the two men manifested itself not only in López Soler's promotion of the Romantic aesthetic but also in his patriotic spirit and his defence of Christianity and traditional morality in the face of rationalism and materialism. This affinity would largely account for what have been regarded as perplexing trends in López Soler's 'Sobre la historia filosófica de la poesía española'. Both Caldera and Cattaneo point to Alberto Lista's 'Reflexiones sobre la dramática española en los siglos XVI y XVII', from which I have already quoted, as the source for López Soler's article. The influence of Lista is especially apparent in the extravagant praise heaped upon the younger Moratín.[25] However, López Soler, unlike Lista, insists upon the value of popular poetry and, in an impassioned panegyric of Calderón, not found in his source, there is a revealing echo, as it seems, of a turn of phrase employed by A. W. Schlegel. To use an expression coined by a celebrated German man of letters, wrote López Soler, the same could be said of Calderón's drama as of the empire of Charles V; where each was concerned, the sun never set. A. W. Schlegel had written, referring to Spanish Golden-Age drama: 'we may say that in the dominion of this poetry, as in that of Charles the Fifth, the sun never set' (II, 345). Caldera admits to being puzzled by the general perspective of López Soler's article, which did not express the enthusiastic and emotional Romanticism encountered elsewhere in his criticism.[26] This can be attributed to the fact that López Soler was reworking Lista's article; he was not averse, as we have seen, to appropriating material from other authors. Moreover, Lista was acknowledged to be one of the leading critics of the day, and was an obvious candidate for such imitation. Nevertheless, López Soler did not refrain from displaying his own literary preferences in the two examples cited. I prefer to see this as evidence of López Soler's strong inclination towards Romanticism rather than to view the article as a whole as evidence of the critic's supposed eclecticism.

A salient feature of the literary articles published in *El Europeo* was admiration for the work of Walter Scott. Cattaneo felt that Scott's novels met a specific need, itself arising from the resurgence of interest in Catalan history in the early nineteenth century, together with a keen regionalist spirit and a desire for the recovery of the values of tradition.[27] Scott received abundant mention in a series of 'literary notices', which formed a regular feature of the periodical. The mediaevalism that has been apparent throughout this consideration of literary criticism in *El Europeo* culminated in the editors' determination to embark upon a translation of the complete works of Scott, a venture frustrated by the censor. Fuller evidence of the influence of Scott would re-emerge with the publication of López Soler's historical novel *Los bandos de Castilla* in 1830.

If *El Europeo* appeared for only five months, and probably did not reach a large number of readers, it nevertheless played a significant rôle in promoting Romantic ideas in Catalonia. If the cosmopolitan nature of the periodical and its avowed moderation meant that the strident cultural nationalism and the ideological crusade so evident in the work of Böhl were not so vehemently repeated, the Romantic aesthetic as outlined in *El Europeo* depended, nonetheless, upon the same sources that had influenced the German and were advanced by him in his literary polemic. Böhl's influence is seen in the articles of López Soler, and we encounter a marked coincidence in the views of the two men in ideological, as well as aesthetic, terms. In addition to the specific evidence adduced by Dendle, my examination of previously neglected articles points to a broader concordance. Furthermore, it would be López Soler, upholder of many conservative values, who would go on to play a further part in the development of Spain's traditionalist Romanticism. As Juan Luis Alborg has observed, what the periodical lacked most was an experienced and learned critic who could have effectively directed the course of its literary criticism (López Soler, for example, was only seventeen at the time of the publication of his 'Análisis . . .').[28] Nevertheless, *El*

Europeo did play an important pioneering rôle in drawing the attention of Spaniards to the new aesthetic, and as such can be seen to have prepared the way for later Romantic criticism.

While Schlegelian Romanticism had gained ground through the dissemination of its fundamental set of ideas in *El Europeo*, the text-book of rhetoric, *Arte de hablar en prosa y verso*, published in Madrid in 1826, tenaciously espoused the most rigorous tenets of neo-Classicism.[29] Its author was José Mamerto Gómez Hermosilla (1771–1837), an *afrancesado* who had been forced to emigrate to France between 1814 and 1820 and who had later collaborated with Lista in the publication of *El Censor*. In the *Arte de hablar*, art is defined as a set of invariable principles founded upon the inherent nature of man, a postulate which constitutes an unqualified rejection of any theory of historicism. Hermosilla revealed his unwillingness to countenance abandonment of Aristotelian precepts in his judgement of Lope de Vega, contending that 'Lope es la prueba más irrefragable de que el hombre de mayor talento, aunque sea también muy sabio y erudito, no hará jamás una composición literaria perfecta, si ignora o quebranta voluntariamente las reglas' ('Lope himself constitutes irrefutable proof that a man of the highest genius, even though he be also erudite and learned, shall never produce a perfect literary composition so long as he ignores or wilfully breaks with the precepts').[30] His treatise was the most inflexible to have appeared in Spain for generations, more intransigent by far than Luzán's *Poética* of 1737. Blanco García felt that Hermosilla, who had worked with Lista on *El Censor*, did not share the latter's intellectual tolerance but instead adopted a fiercely doctrinal approach based exclusively upon Aristotle, Horace and Boileau. For Blanco García, the *Arte de hablar* revealed an 'antithetical combination' of subtle critical observations and insufferable doctrinal pedantry.[31] The work was soon attacked by writers who regarded it as retrograde: Bartolomé José Gallardo labelled it 'Arte de hablar disparates' ('The art of speaking nonsense'), and it was likewise condemned by Lista and by Agustín Durán. These three men, commented Menéndez y Pelayo, effectively limited the harmful effects of Hermosilla's outmoded and narrow work, which had appeared when the triumph of Romantic ideas was virtually guaranteed; he described the three as learned and loving supporters of Spain's literary tradition and as champions of an incipient Romanticism.[32] Although the *Arte de hablar* went into many subsequent editions as a university text-book, it found little favour among Spanish literary critics of either its own or succeeding generations.

Those who had considered Hermosilla's work to be retrograde would presumably have regarded Francisco Martínez de la Rosa's neo-Classicist *Poética* of 1827 as equally anachronistic. The verse text had been composed while Martínez de la Rosa (1787–1862), imprisoned on the orders of Ferdinand VII, was incarcerated at the Peñón de la Gomera between 1814 and 1820. A deputy in the Cadiz parliament, he had briefly served as prime minister during the *trienio constitucional*. As one of the *anilleros*, moderate liberals who wished to rewrite the constitution of 1812 so as to render it less unpalatable to the monarchy, he had made bitter enemies of the radicals, and had been forced to resign from office. The prose annotations and appendices, of greater interest to the literary historian than the verse text of the *Poética*, were written after 1824 in Paris, where the author lived in enforced exile between 1823 and 1831. Here Martínez de la Rosa reveals his commitment to neo-Classicism, praising both the treatise of Boileau and that of 'the sensible Luzán', whom he considered to have been the great restorer of Spanish verse; in his turn, Luzán had been aided by other humanists of good taste.[33] Typically neo-Classicist also are the author's discussion of the propriety of language in poetry and drama, his later assessment of the dramatic unities and, above all, his reference to French theatre as 'el más arreglado de Europa' ('the most ordered in Europe') (II, 356). The employment of the term 'arreglado' in this sense provides a strong link between the *Poética* and eighteenth-century neo-Classical literary criticism.[34] The only hint of a break with the Classical tradition occurs in Martínez de la Rosa's observation upon the Greek idea of Fate: the different religious and ethical beliefs of modern society no longer allowed for such a curious idea (II, 368). The remark does suggest some acquaintance with Schlegelian theory, and the appendix dealing with the Spanish *comedia* reveals the author's familiarity with the new literary ideas. Martínez de la Rosa twice mentions A. W. Schlegel in writing of the influence of Golden-Age drama upon European theatre and of its recent popularity in Germany. Since the new literary grouping had put down stronger roots in Germany than elsewhere, and since the study of Spanish literature had long been cultivated in that country with greater eagerness and reward than anywhere else in Europe, it was not surprising that the Spanish dramatic tradition had lately acquired there such renown (242). This enthusiastic reception he contrasted sharply with its condemnation by French neo-Classicists. Martínez de la Rosa remarks with a suggestion of aggrieved patriotism that the severity and intolerance of French critics resulted in their vituperation of Spanish Golden-Age drama (III, 242–3); he specifically attacks Boileau's harsh judgement (III, 245). Taken as a whole, however, the *Poética* shows little indication of the changes which would shortly afterwards affect Martínez de la Rosa's literary ideas and which culminated in the composition of his Romantic drama *La conjuración de Venecia* in 1830. The *Poética* impressively displayed the broad scope of its author's literary knowledge, but it appeared when the tide of opinion in literary circles was turning decisively against neo-Classicism and in favour of Schlegelian Romanticism. In 1827, a work which pedantically discussed the range of vocabulary appropriate to poetry and the exact number of hours available within the confines of the unity of time in drama was hopelessly out of date. The theoretical works of Hermosilla and Martínez de la Rosa represented the swansong of a movement which, in Spain at least, had produced little of creative worth – the comedies of the younger Moratín and the tragedies of Quintana being honourable exceptions – and which had never gained popular appeal. The years of 1828 and 1829 would see a definitive shift towards the new historicist theory, one which would bring Spain somewhat closer into line with developments in literary ideas.

In 1828, the nationalistic spirit so prevalent in the articles of Böhl manifested itself in no uncertain terms in the work of a fellow bibliophile who shared the literary tastes of the German. Agustín Durán (1789–1862) had trained as a lawyer but was more interested in collecting manuscripts of Spanish *comedias*, and would devote the greater part of his life to books, not only as collector and publisher but also as director of the Biblioteca Nacional in Madrid.[35] The declared aims of Durán's major contribution to the critical debate, the *Discurso sobre el influjo que ha tenido la crítica moderna en la decadencia del teatro antiguo español y sobre el modo con que debe ser considerado para juzgar convenientemente du su mérito peculiar* were quite specific.[36] He wished to demonstrate the independence of the Spanish theatre, in character and origin, from that which imitated Greek models; to prove that, being dissimilar, these types of drama should not be forced to adhere to identical precepts; to justify the claim that

Spanish drama, inherently more poetic, required greater freedom of form and ought to be judged by more flexible criteria (55). In this long article he largely followed the overall plan of A. W. Schlegel as adapted by Böhl. Durán thus repeats Schlegel's idea of world history falling into two phases, that of the ancients and the modern or mediaeval period, the latter being imbued with the spirituality of the Christian religion and of chivalry. The new religion and the different social structure of the Middle Ages, he affirms, had brought important changes: they had provided new directions for men's thoughts and imagination and had opened up fresh possibilities for poetic creation, itself founded upon an essentially spiritual outlook (78–9). In literary terms we then encounter the familiar distinction between Classical and Romantic. Durán repeats the premise that while Classicism fixed upon the physiological aspects of man, Romanticism depicted the aspirations and preoccupations of his spiritual nature. He writes: 'el teatro romántico procede de las costumbres caballerosas adoptadas en la nueva civilización de los siglos medios, de sus tradiciones históricas o fabulosas y de la espiritualidad del cristianismo' ('Romantic drama has its origin in the chivalric way of life adopted by the new civilisation of the Middle Ages, in its history and legend, and in the spirituality of the Christian religion') (85). Durán acknowledges his sources, praising the efforts in this field of erudite German critics. For all these reasons, he denies the validity of Classical precepts for modern Spanish literature, since they represented the expression of a wholly different civilisation (83).

The first part of the *Discurso* comprises a defence of national cultural expression in the face of Classicist attacks. Durán consistently stresses the need of each nation to produce a literature of a spirit akin to its own traditions, customs and values; he thus disavows the concept of universal literary 'rules'. Like Schlegel and Böhl, he declares Classical drama to be unsuited to modern Europe, preferring instead that the theatre should represent in each country 'la expresión ideal del modo de ver, juzgar y existir de sus habitantes' ('the idealised expression of the views, judgements and existence of its inhabitants'), a phrase which he frequently repeats in the course of the *Discurso*. Given the tendency of French neo-Classicism to deny national differences, Durán displays a degree of francophobia akin to that so prevalent in the articles of Böhl. For example, he condemns those French neo-Classicists who had contemptuously regarded the enthusiastic preference for Shakespeare and Calderón over French drama in England and Spain as evidence of the barbarous state of those two countries; Durán accuses the French of a sickening degree of cultural snobbery (70). He goes on to write of the independence of the stage in England, Spain and Germany, but the *Discurso* was not really intended to have a European perspective. As the title suggests, it centres on the defence of traditional Spanish dramatic forms. Just as both August Wilhelm and Friedrich Schlegel had done, Durán directly links the apogee of the Spanish theatre with military dominance and empire, and sees the breakdown of both as contemporaneous. The result, he feels, was the cultural dominance of France in the age of Louis XIV. In this period, France had attained a degree of splendour which had allowed her, in both political and cultural terms, to dominate the rest of Europe, offering her theatre as a model of perfection and good taste (58). Durán consistently praises the dramas of Racine and Corneille. He certainly cannot be regarded as a fanatical anti-Classicist. What he passionately condemns is the judgement of Spanish dramatists by neo-Classical criteria. Durán concedes that the French, whom he designates the Greeks of modern times, were able to adapt, and in some cases to better, Classical models. Yet he passionately condemns all attempts to impose the imitation of French neo-Classicism on the Spanish stage. In his opinion, Montiano and Luzán had been either unable or unwilling to recognise the beauties of Golden-Age drama as a spontaneous, genuine and independent national form. This failing had led them to impose a dramatic theory incompatible with the traditions and beliefs of Spaniards. Following his defence of national cultural expression, Durán declares that each country must possess a characteristic literature imbued with its own national spirit or 'espíritu nacional'.[37] Like Böhl, Durán felt that Spanish drama and poetry reflected the Christian and monarchical character of the nation.[38] Spanish drama successfully synthesised elements of the national spirit, instinctively recognised by popular audiences; this is a concept which is particularly close to the spirit of the 'return to the people' encountered in the work of Böhl. It will assume greater significance when we come to consider the ideas of Fernán Caballero later in this study.

Durán sought to vindicate Golden-Age drama on the grounds that it was original and characteristic, permeated with the true national spirit of Spain, and was therefore invested with consider-able poetic grandeur. He actively counselled a return to such forms of dramatic expression and to the *castizo* ideals of religion and monarchy as sources of inspiration.[39] If Durán advocated the regeneration of the Spanish stage in accordance with such ideas, he was outlining what he genuinely understood Romanticism to involve. In his view, Spanish Golden-Age drama was eminently Romantic. His overall vision of literary history was inherited from the German Romantic theorists, as was the idea of the supremacy of the creative imagination and the concept of *Volksgeist* as a spiritual force in national literatures.

Caldera felt that Durán had been encouraged to write the *Discurso* by the appearance of Martínez de la Rosa's *Poética* and Hugo's famous preface to his play *Cromwell*, both in 1827. The same critic has also observed that the fierce *casticismo* of the *Discurso* would have attracted many supporters, given the political climate of the period in which it appeared.[40] What is clear is that the *Discurso* gained immediate popularity and provoked considerable reaction: Gies states that the first edition sold out as soon as it appeared, and furnishes impressive evidence of the popularity and acclaim gained by both the *Discurso* and Durán's later *Romancero* (1828–32).[41] In the wake of an unfavourable Classicist review of the *Discurso* in the *Correo Literario y Mercantil*,[42] Böhl von Faber wrote to Durán expressing his support; he admired the *Discurso*, which championed the same principles that he himself had vigorously defended for five years against José Joaquín de Mora. The German felt that Durán had clarified these ideas in eloquent fashion, and had so enhanced their appeal.[43] Meanwhile, news of Durán's work soon reached England, where *The Athenaeum* would welcome his determination to free Spanish drama from the influence of French neo-Classicism. Here we encounter the following approbation of Duran's endeavours: 'Having established the assertion that the stage is the representation of the national character, he traces with a skilful hand the circum-stances which had acted in Europe generally, and Spain in par-ticular, to create the particular character of his country, and to give birth to its drama. His reflections on the difference which the spiritual religion of the modern world has made in the nature of its poetry, are very good.'[44] Assessment of Durán's work by modern critics has been varied. Shaw, in his cogent presentation, is perhaps harsh with Durán in regarding the *Discurso* as representative of a 'timid, early, Christian and medieval orientated sector of the [Romantic] movement in which the Spanish bourgeoisie saw its comfortable religious and traditionalist ideas reflected with no dangerous tincture of radicalism or *criticismo*'.[45] While not denying the efficacy of the work in directing trends in Spanish drama, Shaw felt that its influence was largely negative. He regarded Durán's interpretation of Romanticism as inadequate, and based upon mistaken suppositions. While Durán had followed the ideas of the German Romantic theorists, and had thus indissolubly linked the Spanish *comedia* with Romanticism, the *Discurso* had failed to portray the other side of Romanticism, as the expression of a new and anguished sensibility. This 'contemporary Romanticism', viewed by Shaw as the authentic manifestation of the movement, would only emerge in Spain during the following decade, typically in the poetry of Espronceda and in the character of the eponymous hero of the Duque de Rivas's *Don Alvaro* (1835).[46] However, as David Gies affirms, Durán's failure to include such a theme stemmed not from inability, but from a determination to exclude from discussion something which he viewed as dangerously subversive – and, it is important to note, as something alien to genuine Romanticism.[47] The Spanish critic would in later years consistently reject the 'manía melodramática, que exagerando las pasiones los [poetas] conduce a una afectación insoportable, que algunos confunden con el bello y sublime romanticismo' ('mania for melodrama, which, with its exaggerated portrayal of the passions, induces in poets an unbearable degree of affectation, confused by some with the beauty and sublimity of Romanticism').[48] While Durán's theory of Romanticism may seem deficient to modern readers, Gies prudently reminds us that, although literary criticism with the benefit of hindsight can be near perfect, 'by defining romanticism in 1828 he [Durán] cannot be faulted for not defining correctly whatever eventually came to be called romanticism in the decade and century which followed him'.[49]

As we can gather from a reading of the *Discurso*, Durán was interested not only in Golden-Age drama but also in early Spanish poetry. The greater part of his endeavours was devoted to the collecting of ballads for publication in his various *Romanceros*.[50] The national character, which found magnificent expression in the Spanish *comedia*, likewise resided, claimed Durán, in such poetry. The *romances* bore impressive testimony to the unique character of

Spanish poetic expression and embodied the inherent characteristics of the nation itself. Prefacing the first volume of the *Romancero caballeresco* of 1832, Durán affirmed that in the old ballads we could find depicted with greater clarity than in historical texts

las costumbres, las creencias, las supersticiones de nuestros mayores, y la idealidad con que el pueblo concebía el heroísmo, la lealtad y el valor: allí se ve también el modo esencial y original de existir propio de aquella sociedad, con los progresos y retrocesos que experimentaba la civilización según las vicisitudes y circunstancias de cada época.[51]

(the way of life, beliefs and superstitions of our ancestors, and the idealism with which the common folk conceived of heroism, loyalty and valour: there we see also the essential and original features of that society's existence, including the improvement or decline experienced by that civilisation according to the changing circumstances of each age.)

These comments, a concise summary of the earlier German Romantic approach to popular literature, afford an obvious link with the ideas of Herder, Friedrich Schlegel and Böhl, and provide notable evidence of a further consistent trend in the development of Spanish Romanticism. The five volumes of the *Romancero* published between 1828 and 1832 were well received and gained Durán lasting fame. Reviewing the collection, the *Boletín de Comercio* agreed with Durán that no other poetic form cohered so well with the linguistic features of Castilian Spanish or accorded so impressively with the essential character of the nation.[52] Böhl and Durán soon entered into an enthusiastic correspondence.[53] The former had sent copies of the *Romancero* to friends in his native Germany, and the *Magazin für Literatur des Auslandes* in Berlin, reviewing the last volume in the collection, praised Durán's recognition of the beauties of this lost literature of Spain.[54] This determination to restore and to vindicate traditional Spanish literary forms transcended ideological divisions. Bartolomé José Gallardo, noted – and often persecuted – for his radical ideas, wrote to congratulate Durán on the publication of the *Romancero*. Gallardo's letter moreover suggested that Durán had played some part in ensuring the appearance of a second edition of Böhl's *Floresta*, published in Hamburg in 1827.[55] Throughout the 1820s we see a great deal of mutual help between those writers interested in early Spanish literature. While preparing the *Romancero*, Durán kept in close contact with Quintana, Moratín, Lista, and especially Böhl, in order to facilitate the exchange of views and materials.[56]

It appears to me unnecessary to insist further on the links between Durán and earlier Romantic ideas as expressed in Spain. The aggressive tones of the *Discurso* and his devoted labours in the compilation of the *Romancero* helped to reveal the inspirational qualities to be found in Spain's national literature. The direction taken by Spanish poetry and drama in the following decades would indicate that the efforts of Durán and others in this field were successful. If Durán did not possess Böhl's erudition, his work commanded a larger readership and so had a more considerable impact. Meanwhile, Durán not only made an exposition of Romantic ideas consistent with existing trends, but also, in his assessment of the Spanish character as displayed in national literature as eminently Christian and monarchical, followed the broader thrust of the movement. On a more personal level, Durán exercised a strong influence upon both the middle-aged Alberto Lista and the youthful Juan Donoso Cortés. In the 1820s, Lista was becoming increasingly interested in the history of Spanish literature. Responsible for the education of many young men who would later become Romantic writers, he had been Durán's intellectual mentor, and it was he who Durán wished could have undertaken the defence of the *comedia* which eventually found expression in the *Discurso* of 1828.[57] The two had met while Durán had been studying Law in Seville. Both Juan Eugenio Hartzenbusch and Nicomedes-Pastor Díaz would later underline Lista's importance in Durán's intellectual development.[58] Juretschke details Lista's education in Classicist and Enlightenment thought and goes on to show how he modified his critical stance under the impact of Schlegelian theories. The younger Lista saw the beginnings of Spanish poetry in the introduction of the Italian hendecasyllable by Garcilaso de la Vega; neither the earlier Spanish poets nor the popular poetry of the *romances* held any interest for him.[59] While Lista followed Meléndez Valdés and Quintana in praising the *romance* form, like them he did so with reference to Lope de Vega and Góngora. At this stage, Lista's admiration for the Classical authors was unbounded, and his vision of literature largely determined by his enthusiastic reading of Horace. Thus Lista valued finely wrought artistry and erudite imitation more highly than originality and spontaneity, and admired the qualities of a dignified and cultured poetic style rather than the natural simplicity of popular verse.[60] A change in Lista's position is nevertheless evident by 1828. In his *Discurso sobre la importancia de nuestra historia literaria,* he would praise A. W. Schlegel for his efforts to revive interest in the Spanish literary tradition.[61] Given the fact that Schlegelian ideas were strongly associated with Roman Catholicism and monarchy, and given also Lista's own involvement in both constitutional and absolutist administrations, the change in tone between 1821 and 1828 could be attributed to political expediency. However, as Juretschke has noted, Lista's letter to Félix José Reinoso in 1829 appears to show that he sincerely accepted some of the ideas to be found in A. W. Schlegel's Vienna lectures. The Greeks, wrote Lista, depicted in their literature the men of the forum, the only men known to their particular religion, customs and social structure. In the Middle Ages, on the other hand, spiritual life was intensified by a religion which stressed intimacy between mankind and Creator God, so that human sentiment took on the kind of spirituality bred both by religious beliefs and solitary contemplation.[62] In the same letter, Lista applied A. W. Schlegel's principles to the history of modern European drama, distinguishing English, German and Spanish theatre from that of France and Italy, and arguing in favour of the relaxation of the dramatic unities in the case of the former grouping. With regard to Spanish drama of the Golden Age, in an article in the *Gaceta de Bayona* in the previous year, Lista had already recognised that it expressed a characteristic national genius.[63] The article reviewed a project in which Durán, aided by Eduardo de Gorostiza and Manuel García Suelto, reprinted at least 118 *comedias* from his personal collection, in instalments published between 1826 and 1834.[64] This change in Lista's critical position is at least partly attributable to the influence of Durán. Caldera, for example, affirms that Lista's change of heart respecting Lope de Vega stemmed from a reading of Durán's *Discurso*, a view in which I would concur.[65] We must also bear in mind the high regard which the two men felt for one another and the fact that they would often discuss literary ideas together. Here we can cite Lista's glowing reviews of Durán's *Discurso* and *Romancero*.[66] In a letter to Durán dated 1829, the young Cuban writer Domingo del Monte, describing his recent visit to Madrid, commented that Lista had recommended that he read the *Discurso*.[67] Lista came to consider seriously the poetry of the *Romancero* only after the publication of Durán's collection. Through the influence of Durán and his own wide reading, Lista modified his position of total opposition to Romantic ideas and rejected the limits imposed by neo-Classicist doctrines. By 1831, he could state, in a letter to Durán, that the recent work of Moratín (on the origins of Spanish drama) and Martínez de la Rosa (the *Poética* of 1827) suffered from a cardinal error: 'haber estudiado su asunto con preocupaciones y ojos clásicos y querido por fuerza violentar a una nación a recibir una literatura que estaba en pugna con su creencia, espíritu y costumbres' ('that of having approached their subject with the perspective and preoccupations of a Classicist, and of having sought to force a nation unwillingly to accept a literature in conflict with its beliefs, spiritual values and way of life').[68] Böhl's letter to Durán dated 28 December 1830 likewise censured Moratín's judgements in the 'Discurso histórico' which had prefaced his *Orígenes del teatro español* (published posthumously in Paris in 1830). Böhl felt that Moratín's judgements had been inevitably distorted by his 'infatuation' with literary precepts.[69] Moratín regarded the Poem of the Cid as 'deforme' ('misshapen') and lacking the 'regularity' of cultivated verse, while he lamented Lope de Vega's failure to reverse the increasing corruption of good taste prevalent in the Spanish theatre of his day.[70] Lista would himself go on to adopt a sociological approach in which the writer necessarily became a representative of his age. He followed A. W. Schlegel and Böhl in his vindication of the house of Austria, and recommended the use of the term *Siglo de Oro*, a designation still rejected by Quintana.[71] Most important of all, Lista accepted that Schlegelian theory *was* Romanticism and, when later attacking the excesses of certain Romantic works, never admitted that what he saw as immoral and subversive elements deserved the name of Romanticism. It was crucial for the growth and appeal of what Juretschke designated 'historical Romanticism' that a critic as influential and respected as Lista should accept its basic premises and not reject them.

Another important figure attracted to the historicist approach in the late 1820s was the young Juan Donoso Cortés (1809–53). When Donoso had first come to Madrid from his native Estremadura in 1828, he had been recommended to Durán by Quintana, and the author of the *Discurso* became Donoso's close friend and mentor. Durán had first met Quintana at the latter's famous *tertulia*, meeting-place for liberal intellectuals in Madrid in the early years of the century, and the men were to remain lifelong friends. Quintana would have come to know Donoso while in internal exile in the province of Badajoz; he was himself allowed to return to Madrid in 1828. Quintana's warm letter of recommendation described Donoso as a young man of precocious talent backed up by a commanding intellect and impressive erudition.[72] Evidence of the impact upon Donoso of the ideas we have been discussing is clearly to be found in his own *Discurso* pronounced at the Colegio de Humanidades at Cáceres in 1829.[73] Donoso had recently been appointed to a professorship there, a post originally offered to Quintana, who declined it in favour of Donoso. The aim of this speech was to distinguish the character of modern civilisation from that of the ancients. At an early stage, Donoso makes a historical résumé of the social and ethical revolution which overtook the Classical world, and fixes upon the differences in character and ideas between this period and the mediaeval world, or between ancient and modern civilisation. In his adoption of the historicist approach, evident in his introductory remarks on Greece, Donoso declares that the country's literature had followed the path prescribed by its historical circumstances and necessities (1, 27). Here Donoso can clearly be seen to be following Durán. In a later apostrophe to Greece, he begs understanding for his own literary preferences, which were for the lugubrious poetic world of Ossian rather than the more tranquil scenes of Greek verse (1, 27–8). We are reminded of the similarly emotional celebration of the new sensibility found in López Soler, a feeling reinforced by Donoso's affirmation of the superiority of 'sentimiento' ('feeling') over 'raciocinio' ('rational analysis'): an idea that had found expression in Durán's *Discurso*. Having again followed Durán in contrasting the 'outer man' of Classical literature with the 'inner man' of the Middle Ages, Donoso seeks to explain the melancholy and lugubrious literary scenario which had been produced by the age of sensibility, finding the answer in the character of spiritual contemplation which was a consequence of the Christian faith. Having established the familiar distinctions between the two civilisations, Donoso rejects, as A. W. Schlegel had done, the validity of the unities of time and place on the modern stage, and proposes that unity of action be replaced by 'unity of character'. He sums up these differences in individual character and collective culture by remarking upon the chasm separating the scale of values operative in ancient Greece from that of modern Europe, seen as an inexorable consequence of the relentless march of time (1, 32). Donoso similarly repudiates the idea of literature as the imitation of eternal unchanging Nature, providing us instead with a definition of poetry very much in line with Romantic expressive theories. He insists that 'lo que se siente se expresa, y que la poesía no es otra cosa que la expresión enérgica de las sensaciones' ('that which is felt is expressed, so that poetry is no more than the energetic expression of sensations'); the history of poetry is therefore the history of our sensations (1, 33). However, these feelings or sensations will change with the character of the age, since each revolution in sensibility necessarily produces a similar revolution in its portrayal (1, 33). If Donoso may appear to be attempting to reconcile the 'sensation-alism' of Locke with the conceptual pattern of the Romantic theory of poetry, we are clearly meant to understand 'sensaciones' to signify experienced emotions. The heightened capacity for spiritual contemplation and the melancholy sensitivity which he earlier identifies with the change in the character of man in the mediaeval period had led, for Donoso, to the new aesthetic exemplified by Ossian, which he feels to be superior to that of the Greeks. Meanwhile, Donoso's emphasis upon the vehement passions of the author and of the writer's response to conceptions which are awe-inspiring, point to Longinus and to Burke, both of whom were greatly influential upon the development of pre-Romantic sensibilities (Burke's *A Philosophical Enquiry into the Origin of our Ideas of the Sublime and Beautiful* had been translated into Spanish by Juan de la Dehesa and published at Alcalá in 1807). His idea of poetic composition, furthermore, is one of an organic process such as that described by A. W. Schlegel. It is worth stressing that Böhl, López Soler and Donoso all emphasised the organic nature of poetic inspiration and composition; organic analogies formed a key part both of Herder's philosophy and of the historicist theory of literary history which developed from it. Donoso certainly appears well aware of the complex developments in thought and response that eventually led into Romanticism. Later in the *Discurso*, he refers to the philosophical theory of the sensations, naming Bacon, Locke, Condillac and Helvetius, condemning it in no uncertain terms as sterile and absurd. For Donoso, any theory of sensations which are necessarily fixed and determinate must be insufficient to explain ideas, which are imprecise and defy rational analysis (1, 40). This is a further indication of Donoso's adherence to the new sensibility. He later praises the poetry of Byron for its presentation of the kind of mysterious and sublime melancholy described in earlier parts of this *Discurso* (1, 44).

Giving an indication of what would later become his major preoccupation, Donoso insists at length upon the importance of

Christianity as a spiritual and civilising force, a section of the *Discurso* in which the influence of Chateaubriand is evident, and goes on forcefully to attack philosophical rationalism and religious scepticism. He also reveals to his audience the influence of Durán upon his thought, and dedicates a lyrical eulogy to his mentor (I, 41). Not surprisingly, this follows praise for the work of Shakespeare, Lope de Vega, and particularly for that of Calderón. Donoso views Spanish drama of the Golden Age as especially robust and genuinely inspired, expressive of the splendour, majesty and valour which characterised that historical period (I, 41). In contrast to the originality of such playwrights, Donoso felt that French philosophers of the eighteenth century had lost all sense of individuality, and had acquired instead a superficial spirit. This assertion would be often repeated by Donoso in succeeding years. Finally, he praises the invention and determination of Madame de Staël in her pioneering work on Germany. In this *Discurso*, Donoso provides us with clear evidence of his literary and philosophical inclinations; he was to retain this perspective when publishing his well-known works of the 1840s.

Further support for the imaginative reconstruction of history exemplified by Walter Scott was to arrive in 1830, the year after Donoso's Cáceres speech. Prefacing his historical novel *Los bandos de Castilla*,[74] López Soler declared it to be a conscious adaptation and imitation of the style of Scott. In the prologue to *Los bandos de Castilla* López Soler professed his impartiality regarding Classicism and Romanticism, yet the piece is often cited as his Romantic manifesto, since it bears the mark of his emotional response to the new ideas. López Soler in fact reveals, as well as an enthusiastic commitment to the new aesthetic, ominous signs of the extravagant treatment which many impressionable young writers would dedicate to certain kinds of literary scenario: treatment which would lay the Romantic movement open to attack and result in the ridicule later heaped upon the kind of graveyard Romanticism labelled by Mesonero Romanos 'romanticismo de tumba y hachero'. The series of lugubrious imitations prompted by Espronceda's mysterious poem 'El canto del cruzado' would be a good example, and in 1831 Madrid witnessed the publication of Agustín Pérez Zaragoza's *Galería fúnebre de espectros y sombras ensangrentadas*, a collection of particularly gruesome tales.

López Soler's *Los bandos de Castilla* was to initiate a stream of novels dealing with turbulent periods in Spanish history, a trend which would continue uninterrupted until after 1850. Five translations of works by Scott had already appeared in Spain, and four more would be published in 1830, excluding the numerous Spanish translations of the Scottish writer that had been published abroad.[75] In the prologue to his translation of *The Lady of the Lake* (1830), the young writer Mariano de Rementería declared that the scenes depicted by Scott in this work were illustrative of qualities sadly lost to present society: they impressed the mind with evocations of religious faith, loyalty and chivalry that had been stifled by more recent 'progress'.[76] This comment reveals, as well as a coincidence with the vision of the mediaeval period so common among Spanish critics of the period, a nostalgia for the spiritual certainties and the valuable qualities characteristic of a past age. Three years later, in 1833, an anonymous reviewer in *El Vapor* commended Scott's presentation of values which he felt would be beneficial to modern society in a period of political tumult and civil strife.[77]

The pages of José María Carnerero's *Cartas Españolas* provide further evidence of the pervasive influence of Romantic historicism during this period. 'El literato rancio', in two articles published in the magazine in February and March of 1832 under the title 'Sobre clásicos y románticos', sought to denigrate the new school, basing his arguments entirely upon neo-Classical formalism.[78] There had always been, declared the author, innovators of varying degrees of talent who had sought to overthrow salutary principles, and who had on many occasions briefly captured the allegiance of the public; however, he went on, Classicists had always reasserted their dominance over the delirious ravings of their antagonists.[79] The articles provoked a swift response from a writer signing himself 'El consabido', who declared himself astonished by the news of a supposed Romantic movement whose principal characteristic appeared to be unqualified contempt for any form of cultivated artistry or guiding principle. 'El consabido' went on to reveal his own acquaintance with a different school, that described and defended, he tells us, by Schiller, Schlegel and other erudite Germans, well versed in the Classics and seeking to distinguish between Classical and Romantic literature in order to facilitate the examination and analysis of the works of each.[80] The author then proceeded to give a concise summary of Schlegelian theory, perceiving the origins of Romanticism in the literature of the Middle Ages, in works of all genres representative of a new conception of the poetic ideal bred in a social and religious climate entirely different from that of the ancient world.[81] 'El consabido' strongly recommended Durán's *Discurso* to other readers of *Cartas Españolas*, and, in words reminiscent of Durán himself, asserted that 'la voz Romántico o Romancesco expresa el género de literatura y poesía que tienen su base en el modo de existir y pensar político y religioso de la edad media o siglos caballerescos' ('the term "Romantic" describes the type of poetry and literature founded upon the framework of religious and political life and thought belonging to the Middle Ages').[82] As Gies reminds us, Carnerero himself had published a favourable review of Durán's *Discurso* in the *Gaceta de Madrid* in 1828;[83] could the magazine's editor have himself been responsible for the efforts of 'El consabido'?

What is certain is that men like Durán, Lista and Donoso had popularised Romantic historicism, which would dominate literary criticism in Spain in the years ahead. When Martínez de la Rosa, after his return from France in 1831, published his volume of *Poesías* (1833), the battle for Romantic ideas had effectively been won. Martínez de la Rosa's prologue meanwhile expounded the same doctrine of a 'justo medio' which had first appeared in his 'Apuntes sobre el drama histórico', published in Paris in 1830. In the earlier work he had opted for this happy medium in the acrimonious conflict between opposing literary camps (I, 291). Martínez de la Rosa would carry the same idea into politics when appointed prime minister in 1834. Abjuring the intolerance which he regarded as inevitably pertaining to any extreme position, Martínez de la Rosa declared himself disinclined to serve either Classicist or Romantic cause (II, 145). While the author remained adamant that certain artistic principles are immutable, the change in his ideas since the composition of the *Poética* is pointedly illustrated by the way in which he qualifies the assertion: 'mas no por esto se infiere que no estén sujetas a mudanza, al sabor de los siglos y de las naciones algunas reglas prescritas por los maestros del arte' ('but it should not be inferred that those literary precepts formulated by learned masters of the arts are not subject to change in accordance with the general flavour of ages and nations'); the Classical masters had themselves, he reminds his readers, devised their precepts from contemplation of the models of their own time (II, 145). A further indication that the author has moved away from his previously rigid Classicist stance arrives in the following paragraph, where he counsels an ample degree of licence for the poetic imagination, which ought not to be forced to follow step by step the tracks of the ancients (II, 145). In these comments, Martínez de la Rosa employs terms which might be considered appropriate to the author of a play like *La conjuración de Venecia*. Yet while he recognised that the new school possessed many distinguished authors and brilliant ideas, in the next breath he does not hesitate to recommend Horace's exhortation to follow Greek models (II, 146). He is firm in his belief that admiration and respect for Classical models is not necessarily incompatible with the broader range demanded of nineteenth-century literature. The poems in this collection testify to his reluctance to abandon previous models: virtually all are identifiably inspired by Classical themes and practices. Despite his apparent move towards Romanticism in *La conjuración de Venecia*, it appears that Martínez de la Rosa's inclinations were still towards neo-Classicism. The arguments in his prologue to the *Poesías* are tortuous, and it is tempting to conclude that the widespread acceptance of Romantic ideas and their triumph over neo-Classicism, both in France and in Spain, rather than personal convictions, led Martínez de la Rosa to professions of impartiality and moderation.

To sum up, the abundant evidence considered in this chapter reveals the dissemination, in Spain in the 1820s and early 1830s, of a coherent historicist theory of Romanticism. Based upon Schlegelian principles, it was characterised by a stress upon the spiritual power of Christianity, by an idealised vision of the Middle Ages, and by the vindication of Golden-Age drama and popular poetry. There was substantial critical agreement during the period on the question of what Romanticism really involved, and the 'Fernandine critics' settled upon a position very much in accordance with that defended by Böhl in the previous decade. The establishment of the Parnasillo in the last years of the reign of Ferdinand VII was another important step in the diffusion of the new ideas among both respected literary figures and hopeful young writers. At the same time, the popularity of foreign authors like Walter Scott, Chateaubriand and Ossian had helped to create a powerful impression for the new movement, and even before 1833 the first Romantic works written by Spaniards were beginning to be published within Spain. Despite the restrictive censorship in force during the *ominosa década*, which had led to the suppression of Antonio Gil y Zárate's historical tragedies *Rodrigo, rey de los godos* and *Blanca de Borbón* and of Larra's drama *Macías*, Schlegelian Romanticism was able to gain considerable ground.

With the advantage of hindsight, it is all too easy to perceive the deficiencies of such a brand of Romanticism. Numerous modern critics, directly linking literary Romanticism with political liberalism, have urged that 'true' Romanticism only came to Spain with the return of the political exiles in 1834. However, the evidence already adduced in the present study confirms the validity of Schlegelian Romantic historicism as a widely accepted theory of Romanticism. I therefore feel that it would be more constructive to assess impartially its development from this period, rather than to judge the movement adversely in the light of critical developments not apparent in Spain in the 1820s. What must be avoided at all costs is the pitfall of approaching the whole subject with presuppositions regarding the nature of the term 'Romanticism'. The most influential critics of the *ominosa década* defended what was then perceived as Romantic literary theory. This historicist approach should not be viewed as timid; in its own time it was innovatory and, in purely literary terms, revolutionary. The importance, for all these Spanish critics, of national history and traditions was to assume heightened significance in later years, with the incorporation of an increasingly sociological approach into literary criticism, a further consequence of Romantic thought. It would be Lista, Durán and Donoso, not Hermosilla and Martínez de la Rosa, who would continue to exert an influence upon Spanish literary ideas in the late 1830s and 1840s.

3

The exiles, liberal Romanticism and developments in criticism

The historical Romanticism that gained ground during the reign of Ferdinand VII can only in part explain the literary events of 1834 and 1835. The background to the emergence of plays like *La conjuración de Venecia* and *Don Alvaro*, and poetry like the *Canciones* of Espronceda, is to be found in the experiences of the political exiles in England and France. Martínez de la Rosa and the Duque de Rivas wrote their respective dramas for French audiences accustomed to the dramatic spectacle of works like Hugo's *Hernani* and Dumas *père's Antony*. Espronceda, meanwhile, had seen at first hand the street barricades of the July Revolution of 1830, and had formed part of Joaquín de Pablo's abortive attempt to restore constitutional government in Spain, a subject he was to commemorate in an effusive poem. In this respect, Alfonso Par, as early as 1935, shrewdly indicated the divergent characteristics of these two types of Spanish Romanticism. Par observed that the movement's early phase owed its inspiration to Germany; the returning political exiles brought with them very different elements pertaining to what he described as a 'second Romantic phase'.[1]

Statements on literature and aesthetics made by the exiled Spanish writers are illuminating. Firstly, the enthusiasm for early Spanish literature displayed by José Joaquín de Mora during his residence in London appears striking, not least since he was to make a number of assertions and comments that openly conflict with his previous position in the polemic with Böhl. Mora settled in London when forced to flee Spain in 1823, and remained in England until his departure for South America in 1827. Between 1824 and 1825 he published, in *The European Review*, a series of three articles on Spanish poetry.[2] Assessing mediaeval Spanish verse, he points to two possible ways of approaching early poetry: firstly, that of the erudite and dedicated literary historian; alternatively, the more intuitive approach of 'The man who trusts more to his sensations than his knowledge, who seeks in poetry only the poetic spirit, and who connects this spirit with the manners and characters of the nations among whom it is developed.'[3] Throughout these articles, Mora remains faithful to the principles of Romantic historicism. For example, he regards the differing climate, religion and customs of individual nations as 'the circumstances that determine the prevailing character of poetry'.[4] For Mora, the Spanish poetic type had been determined by the growth of the nation during a long period of religious wars, and had thus become characterised by patriotism and religion. These qualities were admirably evident, he felt, in the old *romances*, faithful in their representation of nature and truth, and genuinely inspired by vehement passions: 'by the admiration always excited by great actions, by the love of country, by confidence in the Divinity'.[5] This last is a comment which equally suggests a Classicist evaluation of Greek literature. Mora, however, does more than enthusiastically praise the creative inspiration and spontaneity of the old ballads; he hopes for a regeneration of Spanish literature in just such a natural and imaginative style and feels that new writers would be better influenced by England than by France. For Mora, 'The English style, free, natural, energetic, sometimes gloomy, but always independent, is much better suited to Spanish poetry than the poverty, slavishness and uniformity of the writers of the court of Louis XIV.'[6] His position is now almost diametrically opposed to that which he sustained against Böhl. Further confirmation is found in a passage in which he commends the investigations into Spanish literature made by German writers: 'Schlegel and Bouterwek, though often overlooking the respective merits of authors, penetrate into the spirit that inspired them, and know how to appreciate the striking beauties of their first attempts'. Mora declared that he would pursue this kind of empathetic course in his study of early Spanish poetry, laying aside Horace and Boileau and following instead the dictates of the heart and the imagination.[7] These comments would lead Vicente Llorens to recognise that Mora was here judging the *romances* in an even more Romantic manner than Böhl.[8] If Mora's volte-face at first appears remarkable, it is less surprising when we bear in mind the content of his earlier letters from prison in France.[9] If Mora had then favoured the *romance* form in the face of Classical precepts, he now displays a substantially greater knowledge and recognition of the Romantic aesthetic as formulated in

Germany. Llorens suggested that Mora was influenced, during his residence in England, by the ideas of Blanco White; Blanco's mediaevalism would have held none of those ideological associations, unwelcome to Mora, so prevalent in the work of Böhl. Llorens was also of the opinion that Blanco's ideas on literature influenced Antonio Alcalá Galiano, although he was unable to find any evidence of personal contact between the two men (in this case political differences would have intervened).[10] Alcalá Galiano (1789–1865) had left Spain under sentence of death, since he had proposed the famous declaration of Ferdinand VII's incapacity to govern. In the polemic with Böhl, he had not adopted a position as uncompromising as that of Mora, and had won the respect of the German for his moderation. Alcalá Galiano possessed an impressive command of the English language. During his years in exile, he became well acquainted with English literature, and his own literary ideas were markedly influenced by contemporary English writers. In 1828, he was appointed Professor of Spanish at the University of London, and from his introductory lecture we are able to gather some evidence of his gradual move towards acceptance of Romantic ideas. Here Alcalá Galiano reveals himself to be little disposed towards the poem of the Cid and other examples of the earliest Spanish literature. In this respect he was following Blanco, and indeed refers to 'the Rev. Blanco White, a very good judge in literary matters, though often very hostile to his own country'.[11] More significant, however, is his reference to the dramatists of the *Siglo de Oro*: 'At the head of these is Calderón, whom the critics of a very enlightened nation have made an object of unbounded admiration and applause, in which sentiments I am ready to concur.'[12] Alcalá Galiano was here alluding to the German Romantic theorists; while still himself unwilling to express such unqualified approval of the work of Calderón, he had by this time moved away from his earlier condemnation of what he had regarded as that dramatist's excesses. Much firmer evidence of the change in Alcalá Galiano's position is apparent in the prologue, written five years later in 1833, to his great friend Angel Saavedra's narrative poem *El moro expósito*.[13] This prologue was written while both Alcalá Galiano and Saavedra (1791–1865), who would in the following year succeed to the title of Duque de Rivas, were residing in France, and has been viewed by a number of critics as the authentic manifesto of Spanish Romanticism. Several of its premises were echoed by Larra and taken up by other Spanish writers.

As in many other statements on literary ideas made during the Romantic period in Spain, we encounter a superficially eclectic protestation of impartiality on the part of Alcalá Galiano. He declares that 'Classical' and 'Romantic' are terms that defy adequate definition and expression, and goes so far as implicitly to commend English writers for their refusal to recognise such a dichotomy (121, 125). However, since Saavedra's poem was itself a product of Romantic ideas, the author of the prologue must seek to explain them; the prologue in fact takes up and echoes a large number of the ideas of the first Romantic generation. In a passage apparently influenced by Madame de Staël's *De l'Allemagne*, Alcalá Galiano differentiated between the cultural heritage and traditions of the Germanic nations and those of the Latin world, indicating that it was in the former that Romantic ideas first cohered (109).[14] For Alcalá Galiano, the Germans had proved the existence of more than one path to perfection in literary terms; he therefore rejects any universal theory of art and accepts instead the idea that the literature of each nation will possess its particular character. More specifically, he felt that Spain possessed a genuinely national literature in the *Romancero* and also, although less perfectly, in the drama of the *Siglo de Oro* (113). For this reason, Alcalá Galiano generously praises Meléndez Valdés for having sought in his own time inspiration in traditionally Spanish poetic forms, although he does not hesitate to utter harsh condemnation of what he regarded as the ludicrously artificial qualities of Meléndez's pastoral verse. Meléndez, by converting Jovellanos into 'el mayoral Jovino' ('Jovino the head shepherd') and himself into 'Batilo el zagal' ('Batilo the shepherd boy'), had failed to respond to genuine poetic inspiration; instead he had slavishly followed established patterns and had sacrificed to them all traces of spontaneity (118–19). Poetry, Alcalá Galiano stressed, should be 'natural y nacional', and we are left in no doubt that 'natural' is to be understood as original and spontaneous: a consistent feature of the prologue is the condemnation of imitation wherever it occurs in literature. Literary forms may change from age to age, but originality and spontaneity are essential components of any good poetry. Thus writers may follow Classical models when it is appropriate to do so, yet poetry should always be the expression of genuine emotion. Assessing events in Spain in the later years of the eighteenth century, Alcalá Galiano recognises that the *restauradores* were correct to seek to end what they saw as a period of sterility and decay. However, he regards their attempt to impose French neo-Classical taste and standards as erroneous, since it amounted to imitation at second hand. As a result of the actions of the *restauradores*, Spain was still bound to Classical precepts. Other nations, meanwhile, had successfully broken free from them, and Spain was virtually alone in Europe in continuing to submit to the limits imposed by foreign theorists and, within its own borders, by Luzán and his followers (122–3). Moratín and Martínez de la Rosa are severely censured for studiously ignoring the new ideas as if they had never come into existence (this is a criticism repeated in Alcalá Galiano's articles for *The Athenaeum*, written in the same year).

There are undoubted similarities between aspects of Alcalá Galiano's prologue and attitudes that had emerged in Spain through the work of Böhl and Durán: the rejection of universal models and insistence upon cultural pluralism; the identification of a characteristically Spanish spirit in the *Romancero* and in Golden-Age drama; the condemnation of the *restauradores* for their attempt to introduce unsuitable foreign models to the Spanish stage; the promotion of the idea of poetic composition as organic, the product of the creative powers of imagination and inspiration, and true to the artist's experience. Whilst the above ideas resemble those of early Romantic theorists, Alcalá Galiano places an increased stress upon the perception of literature as the expression, in a given country, of its contemporary age (114–15). Beginning from this premise, he is led to a number of conclusions. Firstly, he views French neo-Classicism not simply as a stilted imitation of Greek and Latin models but as the inevitable product of its age, when taste inclined towards the Classical (115). Similarly, Dante was not a mediaeval Romantic, but rather a man of his particular age or 'un hombre de su siglo' (111); this last observation marks an important difference between Alcalá Galiano and A. W. Schlegel, since the latter had viewed both Dante and Shakespeare as Romantic writers. In the case of Spain, Alcalá Galiano links literature and society in describing the period of decadence under the later Habsburgs. *Culteranismo* is regarded as the inevitable effect of the stifling of creativity and philosophical inquiry (115). A number of Alcalá Galiano's assertions appear intended to rectify what the author felt to be misconceptions in A. W. Schlegel's overall perspective; thus, for example, the view that mediaeval writers could not consciously have been Romantics since the movement was strictly contemporary.[15] A further break with Schlegelian categories occurs in the declaration that Golden-Age drama, if nationalistic in spirit, nevertheless preserved several characteristics associated with Classicism. Alcalá Galiano here specifies artifice in versification, mythological allusion, and the elevated style employed by all except the *gracioso* (108–9). Yet the author's preceding observations regarding Golden-Age drama lead in a markedly different direction. Pointing to its non-observance of the dramatic unities, its mixture of comic or festive style with passages of a tragic or elevated tone, its frequent treatment of mediaeval themes, and the chivalresque colouring given to Classical or mythological plots, Alcalá Galiano reaches the affirmation that 'bien hay razón para darle el nombre de romántica, y para considerarla como sujeta a las condiciones del actual romanticismo' ('it can with good reason be called Romantic, and be regarded as subject to the terms of contemporary Romanticism') (108). While these comments are later qualified in the manner indicated, the characteristics that Alcalá Galiano attributes to Romanticism are not far removed from those earlier advanced by other Spanish critics. As they had done, he consistently regards the products of inspiration as necessarily superior to works that displayed only hollow imitation. He therefore concludes that the creation of a new literature in many countries of Europe represented a return to the achievements of ancient Greece: to the expression of past memories together with emotions aroused by the immediate present; to an imaginative expression which was vehement and sincerely felt, neither a slavish reworking of sources nor a task made irksome by the rigid prescriptions of a dogmatic body of criticism (125). For Alcalá Galiano, as for A. W. Schlegel, the Greeks were imaginative creators of a spontaneous national literature.

The most novel aspect of the prologue was undoubtedly its stress upon actuality; Spain must have an original and spontaneous literature which would embrace the national spirit and at the same time adequately embody the tastes and preoccupations of contemporary society. One possibility, felt Alcalá Galiano, could be to promote a modified version of the justifiably admired Golden-Age drama, which would provide a robust and genuinely national genre (123). He did not wish Spanish writers to follow the lead of the new French Romantic drama, which he disdained as mere affected anti-Classicism (120–1). It is easy to imagine the confusion that some aspects of the prologue would have caused in Spain. Alcalá Galiano refuted several Schlegelian ideas which had gained increasing acceptance in the country during the previous decade; most prominently, he asserted that Golden-Age drama, which earlier critics had praised as the Romantic creation *par excellence*, incorporated elements indicative of Classicism. Despite the divergences of perspective between Alcalá Galiano's prologue and documents such as Durán's *Discurso*, however, it would be unwise to pass over the fact that the author was effectively reaffirming Herder's historicist approach to developments in literature, and was echoing ideas regarding cultural nationalism, inspiration and spontaneity earlier asserted in both England and Germany. The prologue constituted a considered and broad-minded promotion of literary ideas on the part of its author, yet it fell very much into a void. Llorens felt that the failure of the prologue to make any immediate impact can be partly explained by the confusion resulting from its discussion of Golden-Age drama, but more by the fact that, with the exception of Byron and Scott, all of those contemporary English writers praised by Alcalá Galiano were unknown in Spain.[16] At the same time, *El moro expósito* itself received scant critical attention until examined some eight years later by Enrique Gil y Carrasco.[17]

If Alcalá Galiano had viewed Romanticism as a specifically contemporary movement, there is little indication in the prologue of that new and anguished sensibility, usually described as the *mal du siècle*, which several modern critics have felt to be characteristic of 'true' Romanticism. There is no mention of the metaphysical crisis so evident in the work of Byron and Shelley (the total exclusion from consideration of the latter is less forgivable than that of Keats, whose work had not yet really come into prominence). Neither is any mention made in the prologue of the efforts of Böhl and Durán. However, both the polemic and Durán's *Discurso* are discussed in Alcalá Galiano's articles, also written in 1833, for the English magazine *The Athenaeum*.[18] Here he makes an impartial presentation of the Böhl–Mora polemic, acknowledging that his own views have since changed, but writes dismissively of Durán's *Discurso* and appears unaware of the popularity it had already achieved.[19] He repeats his wish that Spain follow the literary ideas of England, and also renews his condemnation of what he saw as the excesses of French Romantic drama. While, in his insistence upon the desirability of a 'natural and national' literature based on history and popular tradition, Alcalá Galiano was anticipating the future direction of historical Romanticism in Spain, he still chooses to describe the theories of A. W. Schlegel as 'more ingenious and fanciful than just'.[20]

A great deal of significance has been attributed to the return to Spain of political exiles like Alcalá Galiano, Espronceda and the Duque de Rivas; it has often been argued that they brought with them ideas and experiences without which Romanticism would never have triumphed in that country. Courtney Tarr, however, writing as early as 1939, argued persuasively against the idea that the return of these exiled writers somehow represented 'the signal for the immediate triumph of a romanticism they were supposed to have brought back in their baggage'.[21] There is indeed justification for Tarr's contention that 1834 was not a decisive year in the fortunes of Romanticism. Martínez de la Rosa's *La conjuración de Venecia*, staged in April, set no recognisable standard or model for subsequent Romantic drama. At the same time Larra, whose Romanticism was never doctrinal, refused to ascribe *Macías* – first performed in October 1834 but, like Martínez de la Rosa's play, written some time earlier – to the influence of any one literary school. Historical novels in the Romantic fashion, meanwhile, had been published by López Soler, Patricio de la Escosura and others during the reign of Ferdinand VII. In the field of literary criticism, the returning exiles were not to play a leading role, since Martínez de la Rosa (allowed back in 1931), Alcalá Galiano and the Duque de Rivas would all dedicate the greater part of their energies to politics. The author of *La conjuración de Venecia*, no longer a radical, was appointed prime minister in 1834 and was the architect of the new 'conservative constitutional settlement', as Raymond Carr described the *Estatuto Real*.[22] The constitution of 1812 had been discredited and, after the outbreak of the Carlist war, concessions had to be made to those royalists grouped around the Queen Regent. Martínez de la Rosa and other moderate liberals accepted power on terms that excluded the *exaltados*, who were not amnestied until Christmas 1834. The Duque de Rivas, meanwhile, would serve in the cabinet of the *moderado* Istúriz; now a declared enemy of *progresistas*, he was forced to flee to Portugal to escape persecution after the sergeants' revolt at La Granja in 1836 returned power to a radical government. These are indications, buttressed by further evidence that will emerge in the course of this study, that the equation of literary Romanticism with political liberalism breaks down under careful scrutiny.

The most eminent critic of the day had in fact lived in Spain during the *ominosa década* and had been involved in the *Parnasillo*; this was, of course, Mariano José de Larra (1809–37). I shall not attempt to examine all the complexities of Larra's personality and literary output, but will assess his attitudes to certain aesthetic and literary possibilities and highlight those aspects of his work which have especial bearing upon later Spanish criticism. Larra grew up under the influence of eighteenth-century French ideas; his father was an *afrancesado* who left Spain as a doctor in the defeated French army. As a child, he came to speak French as his first language, and would preserve his faith in many of the ideals of the Enlightenment throughout his short life. In accordance with his intellectual formation, Larra initially adopted, in terms of literary ideas, a Classicist position. His early articles, for example, are headed by epigraphs from Horace and Boileau. However, if he was never openly to espouse the Romantic cause, his literary principles would develop considerably under the influence of certain Romantic ideas and creative works. In his first critical article, a review of a melodrama by the Frenchman Victor Ducange entitled *Trente ans, ou la vie d'un joueur*,[23] Larra ridicules the extravagances of that genre, especially the abuse of the unity of time. Here he reveals himself to be well aware of the dispute between Classicists and Romantics, to which he makes passing reference, and lambasts Ducange from his own markedly Classicist position (i, 16). Yet at least part of Larra's opposition to this kind of melodrama stemmed from his strong *casticismo*; despite the bantering tone of the article, he is embittered by the fact that Spain should always follow French models to a ridiculous degree, to the extent that 'el que no ha estado en París está dispensado de tener sentido común' ('he who has not seen Paris is exempted from possessing common sense') (i, 17). Aware of the irony of a situation in which the French should introduce Romantic melodrama to Spain after Boileau had condemned Golden-Age drama for its abuse of the unities, Larra tells us that the French did not want to hear of Lope's *comedias* for it was then too early for Romanticism to be discovered. We Spaniards, he commented sarcastically, are very contrary souls; we do everything back to front (i, 17).

Larra was never entirely to forswear the Classicist principles upon which his early articles are grounded, but, in the course of his critical career, came to accept important elements of Romantic thought. For example, he lavished praise upon Agustín Durán's historicist approach to literary history in his review of the *Discurso*.[24] The fact that the latter work was being serialised in *La Revista Española* in 1833 is another indication of its popularity and influence. Larra opened this article by linking Spanish literature and empire, associating the decline of Spain's military and political fortunes with the contemporaneous decline of its literature (1, 206). He lamented the decadence of Golden-Age drama, and condemned those *preceptistas* who had failed to distinguish between the great playwrights of the *Siglo de Oro*, described as 'the fathers of Romanticism', and later dramatists like Valladares and Comella (1, 206). He further attacked the *refundidores* who had in his view maltreated and distorted many Golden-Age plays, and went on vigorously to support the idea of a theatre reflecting differing moral necessities and ways of life in different nations. Larra approvingly cited Durán's premise that canons of taste could be traced in each country to 'su modo de ver, sentir, juzgar y existir' ('its own form of seeing, feeling, judging, and living'), and concluded that the issue of Classicism and Romanticism should not be viewed in absolute terms but in relation to a country's particular needs (1, 207). Larra was undeniably impressed by the ideas expounded by Durán, whom he praises in the most fulsome terms. He regarded the *Discurso* as the work of a master and warmly recommended it, not least since he felt it to revive interest in the extraordinary beauties of a national dramatic tradition sorely neglected at home while the object of justifiable admiration throughout the rest of Europe (1, 207). Several ideas put forward by Larra are similar to those expressed independently by Alcalá Galiano in the same year. The change in Larra's position in the years between 1828 and 1833 is a notable one.

From this point on, Larra would consistently employ a historicist approach in his own literary criticism. While admiring the beauties of Martínez de la Rosa's *Poesías*, for example, he felt obliged to express reservations about the author's cultivation of the Anacreontic ode in the contemporary age.[25] The light touches of Anacreon belonged to a youthful and vigorous society, while the state of contemporary Spain required instead the kind of profound spiritual questioning of a Lamartine or a Byron, since societies which were intellectually spent demanded more powerful stimulation (1, 274). In a subsequent review of Juan María Maury's *Espagne poétique*, Larra again referred to the decadence of Spanish literature and society, and to the upsurge of French cultural dominance under Louis XIV.[26] Although viewing neo-Classicism as a product of its age, he regarded it as ill-founded, since French taste had inspired a literature excessively burdened by 'la influencia regularizadora, acompasada, filosófica del siglo' ('the regularising, measured, philosophical influence of the age'). A multitude of *preceptistas*, misinterpreting the words of Horace, had sacrificed Lope and Shakespeare upon this neo-Classical altar, with the result that good taste had been established over the ruins of genius (I, 378–9). We could be excused for believing the above passage to have come from the pen of Durán, or even that of Böhl. In the same article Larra writes of the *Siglo de Oro* much in the spirit of the other two men, evoking a glorious epoch of military, political and literary achievement; it had been the zenith of a nation blessed by providence, and during it Spain had acquired a degree of splendour which neither she nor any other country was likely to equal (I, 378). Larra's view of the Spanish *Siglo de Oro* therefore squares with that earlier adumbrated by the Schlegel brothers and professed by Böhl. The fact that he expresses it is, I feel, once more indicative of the increasing level of acceptance which had been attained by historical Romanticism during the decade leading up to 1834; despite the political differences separating Larra from Böhl and Durán, such ideas would have appealed to *Fígaro*'s sense of patriotism. In his review of *La conjuración de Venecia*, which appeared on the following day,[27] Larra wrote approvingly of the 'independent genius' of the Golden-Age dramatists, particularly regarding their development of the historical drama, and viewed Martínez de la Rosa's play as a fresh example of it (I, 384). Here Larra expresses the important Romantic idea that drama should have a broad scope and not be bound by the character conventions of the Classical age; this dramatic genre, he affirmed, was a faithful representation of life in which nobility and populace, important public figures and humble folk shared the stage. In the same article, he had already criticised the desire of unimaginative preceptists to limit the possibilities of dramatic composition to the Classical models of tragedy and comedy: with changes in religious belief, custom, and social order, such rigid definitions were no longer applicable (I, 384). In his later review of Martínez de la Rosa's *Aben-Humeya* for *El Español*,[28] Larra would go further, and affirm that 'el drama histórico es la única tragedia moderna posible, y que lo que han llamado los preceptistas tragedia clásica, no es sino el drama histórico de los antiguos' ('the historical drama is the only possible modern form of tragedy; what preceptists have called Classical tragedy is no more than the historical drama of the ancients') (II, 225). Dramatic composition then presented two immediate possibilities: the comedy of manners, designed with the instructive purpose of correcting vice; alternatively the historical drama or Classical tragedy, a form which had varied not in order to satisfy whimsical literary creeds but in accordance with profound historical change. Differences in philosophical concerns and religious beliefs, in ways of life and legal systems, had made such a process of literary change inevitable (II, 225). Larra again condemned the *refundidores* who had attempted to adapt Golden-Age dramas to fit the demands of the Classical precepts. The *refundidores* had also been criticised by Alcalá Galiano in the course of his articles in *The Athenaeum*. The views of the two men further approximated in their promotion of a specific type of literature especially suited to contemporary Spanish society; in this respect, Larra was much more of a radical than Alcalá Galiano, and also more forthcoming in his exposition of the kind of literature he desired. It was precisely this emphatic vision of a literature which would reflect contemporary social change and political progress that separates Larra from the spirit of the works of most European Romantic theorists. The cult of mediaevalism and the revaluation of institutionalised religion did not appeal to *Fígaro*'s rationalist spirit and faith in the Enlightenment ideal of progress. José Luis Varela felt that elements of eighteenth-century rationalist optimism clearly underlie Larra's support for the Romantic aesthetic in his review of *La conjuración de Venecia*.[29] If Larra enthusiastically accepted Durán's historicist exposition of literary theory, his intense social awareness led him to seek its formulation in strictly contemporary terms. This preoccupation had emerged in Larra's article of 1833 which reviewed *La extranjera*, a translation of D'Arlincourt's melodrama. All of those themes and situations appropriate to Classical comedy had, he declared, been exhausted. Meanwhile, the minds of men had recently been almost exclusively engaged by 'la funesta sucesión de revoluciones políticas y grandiosas que han trastornado en nuestros tiempos el orbe' ('the lamentable sequence of grandiose political revolutions which has in our times unhinged the whole world'). Therefore, continued Larra, contemporary writers must seek new directions if they were successfully to cater for the desires and needs of a reading public weary of the monotony attendant upon strict observation of literary 'rules'; 'sensaciones fuertes' ('powerful sensations'), professed Larra, had come to replace the delicate sensitivity and sparkling wit of Racine and Molière (I, 183). This recognition of the necessity for radical thematic change in drama is tinged with a regret stemming from Larra's own Classicist formation, and shows that *Fígaro* was far from oblivious to the disagreeable aspects of a period of social transition. Moreover, it antedated by some two years Espronceda's savage indictment of Classicism for its failure adequately to represent the condition of contemporary society, argued along similar lines if couched in more violent and scornful terms.[30] In principle, Larra viewed the modern drama as a 'bastardised genre', dangerous in the sense that it allowed mediocrity to capture the stage. *Fígaro* obviously found it difficult to accept such a production, yet felt its development to be inevitable: the character of contemporary society demanded it. Early in 1835, in dealing with a different genre,[31] he protested that Spanish poetry had not even begun to swim abreast of contemporary currents. Despite Larra's teasing reference to the artificial conventions of the pastoral lyric – murmuring streams, turtle doves 'y otras fantasmagorías por este estilo' ('and other such forms of phantasmagoria') (I, 456) – he was making the serious point that writers of this kind of escapist and trivial verse were in 1835 either hypocritical or hopelessly out of date: they wrote poetry in which neither they nor their public could believe. *Fígaro* himself desired a new literature which would be investigative, philosophical and progressive. If this was a desire representative of those Enlightenment ideals so dear to the author, it also reflected the influence on Larra of the ideas recently expressed in France by Victor Hugo.

Larra's proposals for Spanish literature found their most eloquent promotion in his article 'Literatura', which, as the sub-title declared, constituted a profession of faith.[32] Larra bemoaned the lack of 'un carácter sistemático investigador, filosófico; en una palabra, útil y progresivo' ('a systematic character, investigative and philosophical; in a word, useful and progressive') in the literature which flourished under the absolutist Habsburgs (II, 131). In this article, he made the well-known definition of literature as 'el termómetro verdadero del estado de civilización de un pueblo' or barometer of a nation's cultural standards (II, 130). Bonald's celebrated formula 'La littérature est l'expression de la société' was widely accepted at this time in France, and was leading writers not only to reflect, but also to seek to modify, contemporary society in their creative work.[33] Larra used the assertion as a starting point for his rapid evaluation of Spanish literature. If the Golden Age had engendered considerable brilliance, Spanish literature ought to have changed in character along with the European climate of ideas, but had been prevented from doing so by the obscurantist attitude of the Church, which had baulked progress. Here Larra is once again close to the position of Alcalá Galiano. In the same article, Larra insisted that the analytical and positivist spirit of the nineteenth century was not necessarily detrimental to literary creativity. In his clarion call for artistic freedoms, he strongly echoed the words of Victor Hugo; in the preface to *Hernani*, Hugo had written: 'Le romantisme, tant de fois mal défini, n'est, à tout prendre, et c'est là sa définition réelle, si l'on ne l'envisage que sous son côté militant, que le libéralisme en littérature. ... La liberté dans l'art, la liberté dans la société ...'.[34] Similarly, Larra would proclaim: '*Libertad* en literatura, como en las artes, como en la industria, como en el comercio, como en la conciencia. He aquí la divisa de la época, he aquí la nuestra, he aquí la medida con que mediremos' ('*Liberty* in literature, in the arts, in industry, in commerce, in individual conscience. Here is the motto of the age, here is our motto, our critical yardstick') (II, 134). However, these freedoms would be best employed in a specific and constructive manner, so that literature would not consist of mere fantasy and adornment but would serve an important utilitarian purpose in declaring significant moral truths. This promotion of 'useful truths' was far from new in Spain, and had formed an important part of the philosophical framework of the ideas of Jovellanos. As such, it represents a further link between Larra and the Enlightenment. Meanwhile, Larra took the historicist argument to what he felt to be its logical conclusion, declaring that any literature contributing to the effective presentation of the developing characteristics of a nation and period must necessarily be worthwhile. This assertion in turn led on to a genuinely eclectic profession of impartiality between Classicism and Romanticism. Larra refused to take sides in the Classical–Romantic controversy and affirmed, in a much-quoted passage, that his library would contain Virgil and Ariosto, Racine and Calderón, Molière and Lope de Vega; Shakespeare would be there, as would Schiller, Goethe, Byron and Victor Hugo along with Corneille, Voltaire,

Chateaubriand and Lamartine (II, 134). Earlier historicist perspectives as outlined in Spain are at a far remove from Larra's insistence upon a literature born of human experience, scrutinising, analytical and philosophical, accessible to the uncultured masses. It was to be 'apostólica y de propaganda; enseñando *verdades* a aquellos a quienes interesa saberlas, mostrando al hombre, no *como debe ser*, sino *como es*, para conocerle; literatura, en fin, expresión toda de la ciencia de la época, del progreso intelectual del siglo' ('apostolical and propagandist; communicating *truths* to those interested in learning them, revealing man not *as he ought to be* but *as he really is*, in order to know him; literature which is, in short, the complete expression of the knowledge of the age, of the intellectual progress of a new century') (II, 134). Susan Kirkpatrick felt that both Larra's earlier adoption of the historicist approach to literature and his formulation of the above criteria were not only inspired by outside influences but also fortified by his personal experience of life in a period of transition. In her view, Larra came to regard Romanticism as an essential corollary of social and political progress.[35] This judgement tends, however, to underestimate the influence upon Larra of the principles of Romantic historicism. After all, those ideas which Larra had so enthusiastically praised in his review of Durán's *Discurso* were dominant in Spanish literary criticism at this time. Nevertheless, it was only when events in France showed that Romanticism could reflect a new and radical perception of the world, incorporating both positive and negative aspects of social change, that Larra felt able to lend such ideas his wholehearted support.

If Larra saw literature's aim as the communication of important moral truths relevant to contemporary society, he declared on more than one occasion that Alexandre Dumas had set out to fulfil exactly such a useful mission. For Larra, *Térésa* had been directed towards a moral end, and *Catherine Howard* contained a moral message in its depiction of the corrupting power of ambition in women, despite the lurid spectacle of Ethelwood's terrible vengeance. Larra would later condemn similar scenes in *La Tour de Nesle* because he saw no food for thought in the play, only dramatic spectacle; Dumas's aim had been to develop a terrifying plot by even more terrifying means (II, 276).[36] However, Larra goes on to argue that the theatre could not be held responsible for moral degeneracy, asking rhetorically whether gory Romantic dramas were the cause of social revolution or one of its consequences (II, 278). He himself opted for the latter perspective, insisting that literature was no more than the expression of its age. In short, drama could reflect, but not guide, contemporary morality (II, 278). Larra also drew attention to the frequent employment of horrific scenes in Classical tragedy, a point reiterated by Alberto Lista (II, 278). He had earlier provided a rather more precise indication of what he felt the rôle of the theatre to be in an article entitled *Teatros*,[37] which carried the blunt statement that 'El teatro, pues, rara vez corrige, así como rara vez pervierte' ('The theatre, then, is only rarely a corrective and equally rarely does it pervert') (II, 157). Neither as exemplary nor as prejudicial as opposing factions had depicted it, it was, quite simply, the most cultivated form of public entertainment. Despite indications to the contrary, Larra did not go so far as to negate any constructive moral purpose in theatre; drama, if unable to cure vice, could at least attenuate the problem (II, 157). He soon realised that Dumas's *Antony* was one of those rare examples of a play which could do just the opposite: corrupt minds and pervert moral standards. Larra was swift to join the chorus of outrage provoked by the performance of the Spanish translation. The sub-heading of the first of his two articles on the play significantly referred to the inappropriateness of such dramas on the Spanish stage.[38] Much has been made of Larra's condemnation of this play which portrayed a situation very similar to his own, yet the critic's objections were partly based upon the premise that the destructive philosophy of the plot was particularly close to real life. For that very reason, argued Larra, it was especially dangerous; here in fact resided the 'grande inmoralidad' of a drama which was uncomfortably compelling and which possessed too many morbid attractions (II, 253). If he was to lend considerable support to the ideas of what came to be termed liberal Romanticism, since they largely approximated to his personal philosophy of social and political progress, *Fígaro* was deeply shocked by the nihilism of *Antony*. He felt that Spanish literature had graduated from the previous marasmus created by the forces of political reaction and the restrictive Aristotelian principles, and had adopted the impulse of progress and reform. On the other hand, the philosophy of modern French drama, the product of contemporary innovation, appeared to be 'show a man a corpse and so encourage him to stay alive!' The adoption of such plays on the Spanish stage would signify a movement into decadence without the experience of a period of transition. Larra desired a literature that would promote exemplary and dynamic models of human progress; instead, certain plays imported from France presented a horribly pessimistic vision of the future path of mankind, a vision which he likened to a 'grito de desesperación, al encontrar el caos y la nada al fin del viaje' ('cry of desperation at encountering only chaos and nothingness at the end of the journey') (II, 247). Larra would of course have been peculiarly susceptible to the terrors of such a vision, as his faith in the possibilities of progress and reform gradually deserted him in the face of disillusion. In his literary criticism, increasing support for the premises of historicism and for several other Romantic elements would be balanced, in his later articles, by condemnation of some of the movement's excesses, exemplified by his review of *Antony* in 1836. His profound concern at encountering 'la *desorganización social*, personificada en *Antony*, literaria y filosóficamente' ('*social disorder personified in Antony*, in both literary and philosophical terms') (II, 248) was something shared and echoed by many others. Spanish critics were already formulating systematic distinctions between what they regarded as, on the one hand, acceptable and, on the other, deplorable new trends in both creative literature and literary ideas, as I hope to establish in the following chapter of this study.

Indicative of the passions of the moment is the prologue written by Jacinto de Salas y Quiroga (1813–49) to his first volume of poetry. It contains an idealistic vision of uncorrupted freedom and inspiration in poetic composition, and Salas y Quiroga echoes Alcalá Galiano's assertion that there exists more than one path to perfection in literary creation.[39] He who did not dare to write a line without seeking the approval of Horace, Boileau and Martínez de la Rosa, commented Salas y Quiroga, could never be considered a great poet.[40] Significant here is the pejorative reference to Martínez de la Rosa's *Poética* as well as to the work of more established theorists. Salas y Quiroga on the other hand praises the sublime and terrible beauties of Hugo's *Lucrèce Borgia*. Although he pays lip service to neo-Classicism in his praise of Racine,[41] the author feels that literature should display more variety; unconvinced by the concept of a 'happy medium' (Martínez de la Rosa again), he casts aside all that smacks of convention in his abandonment to the ideals of genius and inspiration. Salas y Quiroga felt something akin to idolatry for Hugo: he would later publish in *El Artista* a long and extremely lyrical article which described a visit to the great French writer.[42] He nevertheless viewed with sadness the tendency to imitate French writers, and counselled Spaniards to seek inspiration in the work of Cervantes, Lope, and Calderón; these, along with Tirso and Moreto, ought to be the subjects of literary study. What is more, Salas y Quiroga felt the best way forward to be 'resucitar su ya olvidada escuela' ('resurrect their forgotten school'), even with its 'sublime ravings'.[43] The sentiments are familiar ones, and express the kind of cultural nationalism so prevalent in earlier criticism. Durán's *Discurso*, we are tempted to assume, had influenced Salas y Quiroga more positively than had Martínez de la Rosa's *Poética*. As we shall see in chapter 5, Salas y Quiroga's closing comments were to prove prophetic.

In the same year, Pablo Alonso de la Avecilla published his *Poética trágica*, a work clearly influenced by Madame de Staël.[44] Avecilla voiced his own support for the historicist approach by affirming that climate and social mores, religious and philosophical belief, all shape the changing nature of human feelings, so that 'En diferentes latitudes, en diferentes tiempos, distinto será el carácter de la poesía y distinta la idoneidad del hombre para los varios géneros poéticos' ('In different climes, in different ages, the character of poetry will vary, as will man's aptitude for the various poetic genres').[45] This passage exemplifies the climatic theory of literary creation and development adumbrated by Herder in the *Ideen zu eine Philosophie der Geschichte der Menschheit* (1784–91). Avecilla in effect promotes a geographical theory of literary history: mist and overcast skies would lead writers to display a melancholy spirit and to depict terrible and brooding passions, while sunshine and tranquil beauty would inspire more picturesque and less gloomy writing. He concludes that a writer born in the serenely beautiful land of Granada could never possess the 'tragic sublimity' of one bred in the lugubrious mountains of Scotland.[46] This is a rather lyrical presentation of ideas prevalent in *De l'Allemagne*, and it is to that work that Avecilla later turns for his long definition of Romanticism.[47] Meanwhile, he applies to dramatic practice the historicist criteria outlined above, claiming that to be successful both as a literary spectacle and as a means of moral instruction it must necessarily follow historical changes in collective behaviour and thought. On the other hand, a poetical framework conceived many centuries past could not be applicable in its original form to a different nation and a different age.[48]

The historicist approach was clearly being widely adopted by

Spanish critics. In 1835, however, a less coherent and more bombastic presentation of literary ideas appeared. The Spanish press became the scene of a fierce dispute between Classicists and Romantics, in which serious consideration of literary ideas became submerged in a sea of dialectic. The standard-bearer of the Romantic cause was the magazine *El Artista*, edited by Eugenio de Ochoa (1815–72), which ran from January of 1835 to April 1836. In his introductory article which headed the first issue, Ochoa unequivocally proclaimed the Romantic idea of an aristocracy based on sensibility, a quality that he believed to reside in a few privileged souls. Ochoa stressed the superior qualities of emotion, and, establishing a dichotomy between *positivo* and *ideal*, insisted that Man is not just a rational being but a sublime creature bearing the imprint of his Creator.[49] Although he did not spurn Larra's view of *lo positivo* as an essential feature of contemporary literature, his approach was noticeably different from that of *Fígaro*. Ochoa went on confidently to assert that great artists would emerge out of the social and political turmoil besetting Spain at this period – he recognised that society found itself in a period of transition – also enunciating what he saw as the necessary conditions for such a process: when Spaniards, united by the sacred ties of love and fraternity, abandoned feelings of mutual discord. They must act in accordance with the superior gifts that a prodigal Nature had bestowed upon them and attempt to emulate the glorious history of their forebears.[50] It is a passage reminiscent of Böhl von Faber and López Soler which points also towards the concept of 'regeneración', a characteristic feature of later criticism.[51]

El Artista stridently proclaimed the Romantic cause, and Ochoa himself made several febrile denunciations of Classicism; the pejorative term 'clasiquista' was applied to men considered boring and outdated, men who thought that anything really important had already been said or done by the time of Aristotle.[52] Such dialectic was, of course, meaningless. However, Ochoa's idealistic description of a Romantic is more significant; he writes of a soulful youth who wished to see the recovery of 'las santas creencias, las virtudes, la poesía de los tiempos caballerescos' ('the sacred beliefs, the virtues, the poetry of the age of chivalry'); a man more deeply impressed by the deeds of Spanish heroes than by the feats of the ancient Greeks; who preferred Jimena to Dido, el Cid to Aeneas, Calderón to Voltaire, and Cervantes to Boileau; for whom Christian cathedrals were more poetic than pagan temples; for whom nineteenth-century man was no less sensitive to emotion than his predecessor of the age of Aristotle.[53] Ochoa then proclaimed the Romantic cause from a position of exalted patriotism, seeing the essence of the school in its mediaevalism and religious spirit and choosing to subordinate writers and literary figures belonging to the Classical tradition to those whom he regards as their Spanish Romantic counterparts. Even in this tirade, we can find strong evidence of the principles of historical Romanticism, a view that is confirmed when we assess the thematic content of *El Artista*. The reader immediately notes an extensive preoccupation with the defence of Golden-Age drama, especially of Calderón. An early review of Agustín Durán's *Talía española, o colección de dramas del antiguo teatro español* (1834) stressed the arbitrary nature of the unities of time and place, making reference to A. W. Schlegel's observations on Aristotle.[54] In the fifth issue of the magazine, Ochoa provided his readers with a long article in which he accorded Calderón high praise and defended the drama of the *Siglo de Oro* against Classical precepts.[55] In the same issue, an article by the Conde de Campo Alange similarly undertook to defend the theatre of the *Siglo de Oro*, and condemned attempts to introduce foreign models to the Spanish stage. The author highlighted 'un carácter nacional, generoso, altivo, osado y caballeresco en sumo grado' ('a national character, generous, proud, adventurous and chivalrous in the highest degree'), exemplified by a national litera-ture rich in poetic imagination, universally admired and slavishly imitated by the French.[56] For Campo Alange, the *restauradores* were correct to rid Spanish literature of the degenerate taste that had sullied it in the second half of the eighteenth century. He felt, however, that the Spanish stage should not have followed the models of French neo-Classicism but should instead have returned to the style of Lope and Calderón.[57] Campo Alange went on to praise the efforts of German critics and translators who had helped to rehabili-tate Golden-Age drama, naming both Herder and the Schlegel brothers. Ochoa himself, in a later issue of *El Artista*, regarded neo-Classicism as unsuited to modern society, not just because of the pagan mythology that informed it but also because it was the expression not of a Christian and monarchical society but of an idolatrous democratic one; in other words, he continued, because it was founded upon false values.[58] At the same time, he vigorously defended the Christian religion against the disdainful sarcasm with

which he felt it had been disgracefully treated by pseudo-philoso-
phers in the eighteenth century.[59] If these are comments reminiscent
of Böhl and Durán, we frequently discover, in the pages of *El Artista*,
themes and preoccupations much akin to those evinced by earlier
critics. The nationalistic spirit of historical Romanticism as outlined
in Spain in the course of the previous two decades is certainly
evident, and a definite critical position can be seen to emerge out of
what was very often, on both sides of this literary dispute, no more
than wearisome harangue. González García and Calvo Serraller, in
their introduction to the recent facsimile edition of *El Artista*,
emphasised this defence of the Spanish dramatic tradition and
viewed it as an example of the influence increasingly exerted by the
work of Durán.[60] Yet while *El Artista* voiced stalwart support for the
tenets of historical Romanticism, the magazine contained, on the
whole, less than unqualified enthusiasm for more radical Romantic
works. Campo Alange, for example, began his review of Rivas's *Don
Alvaro, o La fuerza del sino* in markedly cautious terms: *El Artista*, he
stated, had not doubted that the play would meet with stout resist-
ance from many men of letters; such reservations had not been
unfounded, although the audience had treated the play more
benignly than had been expected.[61] He noted, however, the negative verdict on the play which had already appeared in the newspaper *Eco del Comercio*. Like other Spanish critics, he found *Don
Alvaro* difficult to understand: its structure was felt to depend upon
too many arbitrary events and coincidences, and its philosophical
concept of fatalism or 'sino' regarded as unsatisfactory. At the same
time, Campo Alange regarded the play as unwieldy, and better
suited to the novel; some scenes, he stipulated, should have been
shortened, and others omitted altogether. Notwithstanding these
reservations, a large part of Campo Alange's piece is given over to
the defence of *Don Alvaro* against possible Classicist attacks, yet his
lukewarm praise contrasts sharply with the encomium often
accorded Golden-Age and Romantic works reviewed in *El Artista*.
Leopoldo Augusto Cueto, later analysing the same play for *El
Artista*, echoed the reservations – and perplexity – of Campo Alange.
For Cueto, the appearance of *Don Alvaro* on the Madrid stage had,
since it was a refreshingly original Spanish play, predictably caused
a degree of surprise; this effect had however been heightened by
reaction to what he described as the drama's curious structure.[62]
This last phrase provides an indication of the bewilderment which

seems to have been the first impression made by the play in the minds of critics. In a biographical sketch of Rivas, Ochoa referred to the work as 'obra indefinible', while Cueto himself described it as 'Eco a un tiempo de nuestro teatro antiguo y del romanticismo moderno, e hija de una inspiración cuyo origen no se conoce' ('At once an echo of our early theatre and of modern Romanticism, born of an inspiration whose origins are unknown'), as a 'composición singular'.[63] Like Campo Alange, Cueto felt that *Don Alvaro* contained too many diverse incidents to be able to function altogether satisfactorily within the confines of drama. His warmest defence of the play likewise stemmed from a desire to stave off formalist critiques of the work. It is surely no coincidence that Rivas's indebtedness to the Golden-Age dramatists and his 'local colour' scenes were the features of the play which elicited greatest critical approval. They were perceived as elements of a national cultural tradition that neo-Classicism sought to deny, and support for them intimately connected with *El Artista*'s vociferous promotion of historical Romanticism. The philosophical aspects of the play did not attract detailed comment. While Campo Alange evidently felt the idea of 'sino' difficult to understand, Cueto described the play's climactic ending as one of an unfamiliar new taste but of extraordinary effect.[64] It perhaps seems contradictory than *Don Alvaro*'s violent denouement should not have provoked the kind of invective later levelled against *Antony*, a play felt, even by a critic as progressive as Larra, to constitute a systematic threat to orthodox morality and values. After all, Don Alvaro's frightening suicide after his proclamation of himself as an emissary of Hell and 'demonio exterminador', together with the apocalyptic paraphernalia of the play's final scenes, effectively rival the French dramatists' conspicuous predilection for the terrible. Larra himself had in fact left Madrid, on a journey which would take in Lisbon, London and Paris, before the play's performance, and so was not present to give his verdict. We can only conclude that *Don Alvaro*, appearing early in 1835 before the staging in Madrid of the first French Romantic dramas, may have been saved to a degree both by its novelty and by its characteristically Spanish features. René Andioc's exhaustive investigation provides valuable evidence regarding the reception of Rivas's play. Out of a morass of conflicting data, Andioc is eventually able to show that *Don Alvaro* was given nine performances between 22 March and 4 April 1835, the latter date marking the end of the theatrical season in Madrid. Andioc's collation of material indicates that the principal reaction to the play was one of bewilderment. *Don Alvaro*, he commented, through its novelty and capacity to shock, was for many people 'inclasificable'.[65]

Iris M. Zavala points to *El Artista*'s support for Victor Hugo; she links the magazine with literary revolution, describing it as a staunch and prominent supporter of French Romanticism.[66] Zavala quotes Ochoa's comment in the third issue of *El Artista* on the triumph of 'La revolución literaria que empezaba a formarse cuando salió a luz este periódico, y que nosotros abrazamos con entusiasmo y convicción' ('The literary revolution which was incipient when this periodical was first published, and which we wholeheartedly and sincerely embrace'). However, Ochoa's words describe the triumph of Romanticism over Classicism. Zavala's equation of one kind of revolution with another is precarious, and the implicit assumption, in this chapter of her study, that the Romantic revolution in literature was associated with the growth of democratic socialism, is difficult to justify. The favourable review given to *Notre-Dame de Paris*, cited by Zavala, appeared early in 1835, before any French Romantic dramas had been performed on the Spanish stage. The first to do so was the Spanish version of *Lucrèce Borgia*, in July of 1835. When Ochoa came to review it he was forced to admit, despite the admiration which he himself felt both for this play and for the work of Hugo and Dumas in general, not just that its success was still in doubt but that it was clearly impossible for the play to succeed in Madrid.[67] Ochoa, himself an enthusiastic translator of Hugo, hoped that the Spanish public would eventually come to appreciate such drama; this was not to be. *El Artista* itself had ceased to be published by the time of the furore surrounding Dumas's *Antony* (translated by Ochoa) and *La Tour de Nesle* in 1836, which hastened the demise of this kind of play on the Spanish stage.

Meanwhile, in Catalonia, the youthful Manuel Milá y Fontanals was to celebrate what he saw as the undisputed triumph of Romanticism. In his first published article 'Clasicismo y romanticismo', which appeared in *El Vapor* on 7 August 1836, he proclaimed that Europe had decided in favour of the new school; instead of the attractive but outdated world of Classicism, it had chosen one which more nearly reflected modern beliefs and contemporary needs and thus possessed greater emotional appeal.[68] For the young Manuel

Milá, Classicism represented 'poetry of the senses', while Romanticism constituted 'poetry of the spirit'.[69] The influence of Schlegelian ideas is clear. In December of that same year, and again in the pages of *El Vapor*, a young writer named Illas similarly voiced support for historical Romanticism while condemning the artificiality of Classicism. Writing of literary criticism in *El Vapor* in the years from 1836, Ramón Silva commented: 'Save for the confused and inconsistent "professions de foi" of Fontcuberta not a single extensive article advocating "extreme" romanticism appears nor is any attempt made to refute the anti-Gallic champions of mediaevalism.'[70] Elsewhere in literary criticism, further support for the idea of Spain's early literature as the embodiment of characteristically national values came from Bartolomé José Gallardo. Reviewing Böhl's *Teatro español anterior a Lope de Vega* (1832), he looked on Golden-Age drama as a faithful representation of the character of the Spanish people. Its salient features, he claimed, were precisely those which typified Spanish genius:

el jenio, labrado al influjo del clima benigno de España y de los trances varios de la guerra de siete siglos que le dejó por herencia un Rei desastrado. Valiente, pundonoroso, leal e ingenuo el Español es esencialmente caballeresco, es el Paladín de Europa por ecscelencia. El temple particular de su injenio ... en nada se echa más de ver, que en el Teatro.[71]

(a genius developed in Spain's benign climate and in the various critical junctures of the seven centuries of war that were the legacy of a single wretched king. Valiant, honourable, loyal and candid, the Spaniard is inherently chivalrous, the European paladin *par excellence*. The special temper of his genius ... is nowhere better seen than in the theatre.)

Gallardo's patriotic approach makes both the tone and content of the above passage strongly reminiscent of those earlier employed by Böhl, while the assessment of Spanish national character and genius links closely with that delineated in Böhl's early translation of A. W. Schlegel.[72] This effusive patriotism represents a constant element in the critical writing considered in this chapter: from Mora to Alcalá Galiano, from Larra to Ochoa, Salas y Quiroga and Campo Alange, all point to a characteristic national literature, and all do so approvingly. Another point upon which we can detect considerable agreement is that of the promotion of a new literature imbued with the genuine national spirit, perhaps in the style of the *Siglo de Oro*. Golden-Age drama was defended, more or less vigorously, by all the

above critics. In literature as in politics, however, steady renewal
was not possible. The hopes placed by many in the *Estatuto Real*,
described by Larra as the keystone for the regeneration of Spain (1,
386), were soon to be disappointed. The year of 1836 saw a Carlist
army at the gates of Madrid in June, and a radical ministry forced
upon the country by the revolt at La Granja, the *sargentada*, in
August. Spanish society was further divided by Mendizábal's expro-
priation of ecclesiastical assets, which outraged a powerful body of
Catholic opinion – it was these measures, for example, which were to
provoke Donoso's resignation from political office. The country
went increasingly in fear of a violent revolution, one which those
more disturbing Romantic works were widely felt to portend. The
condemnation of extravagance in literature, as Larra's critique of
Antony made clear, was at least partly motivated by the threat of
grave socio-political consequences.

In strictly literary terms, the fierce battles in the press between
Classicists and Romantics were effectively to render any extreme
position impossible: the impact of Romantic ideas had made a
return to strict neo-Classical practice out of the question, while a
furious reaction against certain plays considered to be pernicious
and immoral would swiftly end the brief vogue enjoyed by Hugo
and Dumas, making the position of their Spanish followers untenable. The unsuitability of Classicism in nineteenth-century Spain,
and its inability adequately to respond to the needs of contemporary
society, had been devastatingly ridiculed by Espronceda.[73] Equally,
Romantic excess would be hilariously caricatured by Ramón de
Mesonero Romanos in his famous piece 'El romanticismo y los
románticos' of 1837.[74] Literary critics in many reviews soon declared
their impartiality in the conflict, and disavowed partisanship in
favour of either school. While the tenets of Schlegelian Romantic
historicism had been established before 1834, the performance of
some controversial plays in 1835 and 1836 had now reawakened
trenchant Classicist attacks and appeared to threaten the Romantic
triumph. As we shall see in the following chapter, a process of
clarification in the literary debate would effectively overcome this
danger and allow historical Romanticism to survive the reaction
against alleged immorality and excess. Meanwhile, Alcalá Galiano
and, more specifically, Larra, were to bequeath an enduring legacy
to later Spanish criticism. Their emphasis upon the intimate links

binding literature to contemporary society would bear considerable fruit in the following decade. This, indeed, would prove to be the principal development in Spanish literary criticism established by liberal Romanticism.

4

Condemnation and clarification in the literary debate

Edgar Allison Peers regarded 1837 as the year of the failure of the Romantic movement in Spain, pointing to the triumph of a literary school which he denominated Eclecticism.[1] According to this theory the Eclectic ideal involved a self-consciously reconciling criticism or *juste milieu*, in evidence since approximately 1820, which was able to triumph because of the ineffectiveness of the Romantic movement. Peers felt that the success of Eclecticism stemmed partly from the desire of Romantics to preserve features of the 'Romantic Revival' and partly from the vehement Classicist objections to the revolutionary elements of the 'Romantic Revolt'. In his view Eclecticism, although not specially created as a compromise, satisfied most writers by rendering any extreme position impossible, so that by 1840 it had become the accepted literary mode of the day. A crucial element in Peers's theory was the disavowal of literary partisanship by a number of critics. He first quotes from an article, published in the recently established *Semanario Pintoresco Español* in 1836, in which José de la Revilla refused to countenance exclusive allegiance to either of the opposing schools: instead, a staunch supporter of beauty, he would enjoy with equal pleasure its charming effects in the works of Sophocles and in those of Victor Hugo, in the works of Shakespeare just as in those of Molière.[2] Revilla's comment was only one of many, and Peers goes on to cite several more.[3] I believe, however, that he is too ready to lend unqualified acceptance to these statements, and does not allow sufficient consideration to other specific critical trends displayed during the period, or on occasion in the same articles from which he quotes. Revilla, for example, in the very same article, further observed that works of literary creation were inevitably shaped by 'las costumbres e índole religiosa y política de los pueblos y siglos a que pertenecen' ('the ways of life and the religious and political ethos of the peoples and ages to which they belong').[4] This comment furnishes a clear indication of historicism; if Revilla enjoyed reading Sophocles and Molière, he would presumably expect nineteenth-century Spanish literature necessarily to differ from such works.[5]

If Peers was too willing to accept at face value these claims of impartiality, it is not difficult to perceive why they should be expressed. Critics and creative writers alike must have been growing weary of the partisan diatribe often seen in previous years, while controversy surrounded the performance of plays like Joaquín Francisco Pacheco's *Alfredo* (1835), Alexandre Dumas's *Antony* (1836), and Antonio Gil y Zárate's *Carlos II el hechizado* of 1837. All of these were sometimes regarded as examples of simply 'el romanticismo', with no attempt made to discriminate between them and historical Romanticism. The same situation applied to some rather gruesome narrative poems and short stories published in various magazines. Yet to insist upon the idea of an Eclectic triumph simply because certain elements designated as 'Romantic' were under attack is surely unwise. There was a considerable difference between, on the one hand, the historicist theory consistently expounded in literary criticism and, on the other, the dramas of Hugo and Dumas and the Spanish plays which they inspired. The term 'romántico' was frequently applied indiscriminately to both. Many influential critics, however, distinguished between different forms of Romanticism. It was a trend that had begun before the arrival of French Romantic drama in Spain, but which became more pronounced in the wake of the furore aroused by the more violent plays of the period. It would come to direct the course of Spanish literary criticism in future years, and its leading exponent was Alberto Lista. As early as 1834, Lista, who had come to accept the principles of Romantic historicism in the 1820s, began a determined attack upon French Romantic drama, before the works concerned had appeared on the Spanish stage; he was in fact to become the inveterate enemy of what he termed 'el romanticismo actual' ('modern-day Romanticism'). Writing on contemporary French literature in *La Estrella* in January of 1834, he pointed to what he regarded as the perversity of many Romantic works, singling out Hugo and Dumas. On the other hand, he excepted Chateaubriand from such allegations.[6] Just a week later, Lista published a further article in the same paper under the heading 'Del romanticismo'. Here he distinguished between two different Romantic currents.

Linking historical Romanticism with the etymology of the word 'romantic', Lista stressed its mediaeval and Christian associations in terms reminiscent of the Schlegels. This he contrasted with the recent emergence of a 'monstrous' literature: 'Los espectáculos dramáticos reducidos a cuadros inconexos, la decencia y la moral holladas en las descripciones de amores adúlteros y de malvados que se esfuerza el autor en hacer interesantes; el lenguaje furibundo; la naturaleza, en fin, sacada de su quicio, esto es lo que ahora se llama romanticismo' ('Dramatic spectacle reduced to a series of unconnected sketches, moral decency trodden underfoot in descriptions of adulterous love and wickedness which the author strives hard to make interesting; frenzied language; in short, the natural order of things entirely unhinged, that is what is now called Romanticism').[7] Citing *Antony* as a prime example of this tendency, he insisted that nothing could be less Romantic than this kind of depravity. Lista renewed the same charges in his lectures on Spanish literature delivered at the Ateneo in 1836, alleging the respectability given to prostitution in Hugo's *Angelo*, decrying *Antony*'s glorification of murder and adultery, and pointing disgustedly to Dumas's portrayal of royalty in *La Tour de Nesle*.[8] He returned to the attack in 1839, in a series of articles published first in Cadiz and subsequently in Madrid.[9] Here, however, he also reiterated his historicist interpretation of Romanticism, seeing the origins of the movement in a grand social revolution brought about in the world by 'la ruina de la religión gentílica y la abolición del gobierno republicano' ('the fall of a heathen religion and the abolition of republican government') (II, 36). Fundamental changes in the character of society, religious belief and morality made concomitant changes in literary creation essential. The new literature constituted a form of expression suited to the values and aspirations of a Christian and monarchical society. For Lista, this was the only authentic definition of Romanticism as a literary phenomenon. In an article published in Cadiz and then Madrid in 1839, he argued that the plays of Shakespeare and Lope could be regarded as Romantic if that word was understood not in the ridiculous sense it had lately acquired, but rather in its only acceptable sense: 'entendiendo por *romántico* lo perteneciente a la literatura cristiana y monárquica, propia de nuestra civilización actual' ('if we understand "Romantic" to describe attributes of the Christian and monarchical literature characteristic of our modern civilisation') (II, 64). Lista ended the same article by stressing that

Shakespeare and Calderón had nothing in common with Hugo and Dumas (II, 67). As for contemporary French drama, commonly supposed to be Romantic, it depicted a grotesque morality in which man must either satisfy his every desire whatever the human cost or else turn despairingly to suicide. As such, it was contrary to the sentiments of modern society and could be no more than a passing vogue (II, 42). In Lista's view, this drama was characterised by moral depravity, horrific and bloody spectacle, deliberate falsification of history and a number of other more dangerous anti-social tendencies. Nothing could be further removed from a literature reflecting the character and needs of a society founded on Christianity and monarchy, and, by implication, from genuine Romanticism. His condemnation of French Romantic drama therefore did not constitute a rejection of Romanticism *per se*.

Lista's acceptance of historical Romanticism and condemnation of liberal Romanticism was to become a representative stance in Spanish literary criticism. In January 1834, the same month in which Lista had published his two articles in *La Estrella*, there appeared in the Barcelona newspaper *El Vapor* a review of Hugo's historical drama *Marie Tudor*. The reviewer, in an agitated tone, pointed to an ominous surfeit, in all literary genres, of 'curses against humanity and Heaven'. These, he felt, were often boldly expressed but indicative of a diseased mind at work.[10] In a later review of Dumas's *Catherine Howard*, published in *El Vapor* in July of the same year, the reviewer bluntly declared that contemporary drama had reached the most dangerous extremes of violence and outrage; 'ya no pueden hollarse más descaradamente los fueros históricos, dramáticos, sociales y literarios' ('never can any form of authority – historical, dramatic, social or literary – be more shamelessly trodden underfoot').[11] These are sentiments very similar to those so forcibly expressed by Lista, again linking violent elements in drama with subversion on a much wider scale. A further series of two articles on modern drama published in *El Vapor* during the same month reinforces the comparison. In the first of these, the still unnamed reviewer affirmed that each country had developed its own drama according to national character and taste.[12] Turning in his second article to post-revolutionary France, he vividly depicted a degenerate society lacking in personal values and public spirit and devoid of any form of morality; this setting was to produce the '*nuevo género de romanticismo*' ('new kind of Romanticism') represented by Hugo and

Dumas.[13] The key phrase here is that which I have cited; it enunciates a distinction between the French dramatists and earlier Romantic ideas. It is worth noting that the editor of *El Vapor* at this time was Ramón López Soler, who had championed Schlegelian Romanticism in the previous decade. In a short study of the literary articles published in the paper under the editorship of López Soler, Ramón Silva observed that dramatic criticism was 'marked by a strongly conservative tone, a condemnation of Gallic excesses and a keen enthusiasm for the dramatists of the Golden Age'.[14]

When editorship of *El Vapor* passed to Andrés Fontcuberta, there followed a marked change in tone in its literary articles. Fontcuberta was a fiery radical who had in the previous year begun to edit a paper named *El Propagador de la Libertad*. He distinguished between two kinds of Romanticism as other critics had done, although this time from a different standpoint. Fontcuberta regarded the movement's first generation as retrograde, preferring the innovations of the French Romantic dramatists. In the first of a series of articles on German literature (published under the transparent pseudonym 'A. de Covert-Spring'), Fontcuberta identified Romanticism with the movement described by Madame de Staël in *De l'Allemagne*, which he regarded as entirely different from the French school lately designated 'Romantic'.[15] In the last of these articles, Fontcuberta returned to the beginnings of Romanticism, seeing its origins in Germany in the work of the brothers Schlegel.[16] He viewed Schlegelian ideas as 'una doctrine impotente' ('an impotent doctrine') since they looked towards the past and not the future. As a progressive liberal, he opposed their conservative philosophical framework. Hans Juretschke has drawn attention to the fact that these articles are a plagiarism of Heinrich Heine's *Die Romantische Schule* of 1833. He highlights both Fontcuberta's attempt to invalidate the theories of the Schlegels and Madame de Staël and his distinction between German-inspired historical Romanticism and French Romantic drama.[17] Fontcuberta in fact wished to stress the disparity between the first and second Romantic generations just as strongly as did his ideological opponents. Political ideology was itself a dominant factor in his literary criticism; as Juretschke observed, the term 'romántico' seemed to Fontcuberta a hollow one, devoid of specific meaning and intrinsically unacceptable to a man whose stance was always determined by socio-political considerations, never aesthetic ones.[18] This explains why Fontcuberta continued to employ

'Romantic' to describe Schlegelian ideas; for the new dramas, he preferred the term 'moderno'. As editor of *El Vapor*, he would salute Pacheco's *Alfredo* (1835) as 'el segundo grito de alarma dado en España, a la literatura fósil de nuestros retrógrados' ('the second call to arms delivered in Spain against the fossilised literature of our reactionaries'). It seems likely that Fontcuberta would have regarded *Don Alvaro* as the first such clarion call. He at any rate appeared supremely confident of the success of this 'sublime mission' detected in the work of 'modern' dramatists – the term 'Romantic' is not used.[19]

Fontcuberta was in a minority. Similar distinctions to those made by Lista and similar fierce attacks upon dramatic excess were becoming increasingly frequent, both in Barcelona and in Madrid. Juan Donoso Cortés, in his own review of *Alfredo*, repeated his insistence upon the organic nature of civilisation which had formed an important part of his *Discurso* at Cáceres in 1829.[20] While Donoso continued to accept the Schlegelian definition of Romanticism, he rejected the revolutionary elements of what for Spain was the movement's second generation. Donoso had especially harsh words for those who, ignorant of the true nature of Romanticism, claimed to follow its banner while profaning its heaven-sent gift of inspiration. This last phrase led into a piece of strident rhetoric in which Donoso fulminated, in language characterised by savagely graphical metaphor, against excess. The muse of certain literary practitioners, he wrote, was a murderous, dagger-wielding phantom clad in rags, whose blaspheming mouth thirsted for blood, whose feet trod only on corpses and mire, whose forehead was branded with the words 'incesto' and 'profanación' (1, 172–3). Surprisingly, Donoso did not specifically condemn *Alfredo*, a drama widely attacked by contemporary critics, but instead detected a serious and coherent underlying philosophy in the play. This benevolent attitude is perhaps explained by Donoso's close friendship with Pacheco, which dated from their student days in Seville. Donoso's censorious tone, like that finding expression in the articles of Lista, was motivated by underlying preoccupations reaching beyond aesthetics. His later attack on the radical liberal politicians, the *progresistas*, reveals marked similarities – in tone, content and imagery – with his consistent vituperation of what he considered outrageously immoral and dangerously pessimistic literary works. In an article entitled 'La religión, la libertad, la inteligencia', published in *El Porvenir* in 1837,

Donoso blamed the *progresistas* for the political uncertainty of the day, accusing them of inciting unrest and thus accelerating political dissolution. He had recourse to graveyard imagery, likening the actions of radicals – the 'party of imbeciles' – within society to the lugubrious preparations for a funeral (1, 378). This morbid evocation tallies with the imagery adopted in Donoso's earlier condemnation of literary excess. In 1838, when the theatre-going public had become sated by the violent aspects of many plays by Hugo and Dumas and by several Spanish imitations, Donoso would bitterly complain that 'el mundo . . . para los dramaturgos de nuestros días es un horrible desierto sin vegetación y sin verdura; en medio de su soledad se levanta un cadalso, y al pie de ese cadalso suele haber un verdugo que amenaza y una víctima que gime' ('the world in the eyes of modern-day dramatists is a desert devoid of any vegetation or verdure; in the midst of this desolation there is raised a scaffold, and at the foot of this scaffold there is usually the threatening figure of an executioner and a groaning victim') (1, 406). While the scaffold and executioner were features that had become associated in the public mind with the wilder dramas, Donoso's stark tone assumes a quality of prophetic warning couched in macabre terms.[21]

The ferocity of many attacks upon Hugo and Dumas was not only the product of righteous indignation. Critics realised that the two men possessed consummate dramatic artistry; for this very reason their plays were especially dangerous. An anonymous reviewer wrote in the *Eco del Comercio* after the performance of the Spanish translation of *Antony*: 'el pensamiento dominante en este drama es eminentemente antisocial, si vemos en él preconizado el adulterio y completamente hollados todos los principios conservadores de la moral y de la sociedad' ('the philosophy which dominates this play is anti-social in the extreme, for in it we see adultery commended while every principle aimed at the conservation of moral and social order is trodden underfoot').[22] The review appeared just one day after the first of Larra's two scathing articles on the same play in *El Español*; this was rapidly becoming a familiar protest on the part of an outraged – and clearly unsettled – body of critical opinion. Yet as the reviewer states, although the play's irresponsible doctrine ought surely to provoke universal alarm, Dumas was a writer of genius whose talents could neutralise feelings of indignation. Thankfully, in the eyes of the reviewer, such talent did not extend to making the world-view of *Antony* a palatable one, but the same article reveals an apprehension that the excesses of certain works could discredit Romanticism, something which its author was determined to prevent. Those, like himself, who wished to see Romanticism effectively acclimatised in Spain, ought to ensure that the public at large did not form a false idea of the school, a real danger when 'uno de sus principales apóstoles predica la inmoralidad y la relajación de todos los vínculos sociales' ('one of its most prominent apostles preaches a doctrine of immorality and the relaxation of all social ties and obligations'). Everything pointed to the success of the new school, he felt, but its fortunes could be reversed if writers did not show more caution.[23] It is of some import that, in common with numerous other critics, he refutes the identification of Romanticism with plays that appeared to threaten the existing social order and prevailing moral code. The reviewer felt it to be a further part of his duty, moreover, to counter 'la mala inteligencia en que muchos están respecto del *fin del romanticismo*, y que desde luego achacamos a la exageración de algunos de sus sectarios' ('the erroneous notion shared by many concerning the *end of Romanticism*, the cause of which we can of course ascribe to the extravagances of some of the move-ment's adherents'). These are forthright and revealing comments. Excesses, chiefly in the drama, were making 'Romantic' something of a dirty word and were understandably causing confusion. The very real danger that works of an extreme radicalism could discredit a movement which, ironically, they did not truly represent, helps to explain the appearance, at this crucial stage in the literary debate, of several calculated attempts at clarification. In the first issue of his magazine *No me olvides* in May 1837, Jacinto de Salas y Quiroga distinguished between disparate trends. He and his collaborators were determined, he professed, to defend the Romantic movement against the widespread calumny that had been directed at it, a calumny which had led to misinterpretation of the school's methods and aims.[24] Salas stressed that by 'Romanticism' he was referring neither to 'esa ridícula fantasmagoría de espectros y cadalsos' ('that absurd phantasmagoric set of ghosts and scaffolds') nor to 'esa inmoral parodia del crimen y la iniquidad' ('that immoral parody of iniquity and vice'), sure references to French Romantic drama and its Spanish imitations; he condemned such abuse of literature as loudly as anyone else.[25] Instead, he viewed genuine Romanticism in an entirely different fashion, as a means of moral improvement closely bound up with spiritual revival.[26]

Salas y Quiroga's article was followed a week later, in the second issue of *No me olvides*, by Fernando Vera's 'Verdadera poesía'. Vera also rejected any association of genuine Romanticism with the more violent aspects of recent literature. He found it surprising that some people had been stupid enough, as he put it, to seek in squalid and offensive works the true sources of a Romanticism which they ridiculed simply because they had failed to understand its meaning. Vera was adamant that 'La misión del romanticismo es santificar al hombre, no desmoralizarlo' ('The mission of Romanticism is to sanctify man, not to corrupt him').[27] Again in *No me olvides*, the twenty-year-old Ramón de Campoamor differentiated between the conflicting interpretations of 'Romantic':

Aunque impugno aquí el *romanticismo*, no se crea que impugno el *romanticismo* verdaderamente tal, sino ese *romanticismo* degradado cuyo fondo consiste en presentar a la especie humana sus más sangrientas escenas, sueños horrorosos, crímenes atroces, execraciones, delirios y cuanto el hombre puede imaginar de más bárbaro y antisocial: esto no es *romanticismo*, y el que lo cree, está en un error; el *romanticismo* verdadero tiende a conmover las pasiones del hombre para hacerle virtuoso; el *romanticismo* falso que usurpó este nombre y es el que he expuesto anteriormente, sólo tiende a pervertir la sociedad, y éste es justamente el que yo trato de impugnar.[28]

(Although I am here impugning *Romanticism*, it should not be felt that I am impugning *Romanticism* in its true manifestation, rather that debased form of *Romanticism*, the nature of which is to exhibit to humankind its bloodiest scenes, most nightmarish visions, atrocious crimes, execration and frenzy, every kind of anti-social barbarism that it is possible for a man to imagine. This is not *Romanticism*, and he who believes that it is labours under a delusion; genuine *Romanticism* is given to stirring man's passions to inspire him with virtue; the false *Romanticism* that has usurped its name, the kind which I have earlier described, is given solely to perverting society, and it is precisely the latter that I wish to impugn.)

Campoamor summarises then the issues at stake. Perceiving less authentically Romantic works as anti-social, he employs characteristic vocabulary: 'sangriento', 'crímenes atroces', 'execración', 'delirio', 'pervertir la sociedad', all become familiar terms upon a close reading of critical articles directed against alleged immorality. This kind of vocabulary is an indication both of the strength and ferocity of the critical reaction and of the real and unsettling threat that disruptive works were felt to pose. They seemed genuinely to have undermined what might be described either as moral confidence or as complacency. Significantly, however, Campoamor also moots the idea of a positive mission that historical Romanticism, with its stress upon nationalism and religious faith, appeared well equipped to fulfil, an idea that will be further explored in chapter 7.

The same type of distinction continued to be made in future years. In 1839, Manuel Milá y Fontanals would censure the negative and disruptive tendencies of many modern novelists, naming Hugo, Soulié and George Sand. Milá's article in fact distinguished in its title between Walter Scott and 'la escuela escéptica' ('the sceptical school'); Scott himself is loudly praised as a truly Romantic writer.[29] Subsequently, in the appendix to his *Principios de literatura general*, Milá pointed to two opposing tendencies which had from the start been apparent in the new school: the first was one of spirituality and restoration; the other of individualism, vanity and religious scepticism.[30] Hans Juretschke has consequently regarded Milá as an enthusiastic representative of a profoundly conservative historical Romanticism.[31]

All of the evidence adduced here shows that Spanish critics were able to distinguish between the divergent trends the new movement had engendered; while some of its features were warmly accepted, others, belonging almost without exception to a handful of more radical works and considered an affront to morality, were virulently condemned. There was a marked tendency to dissociate the extravagant nature of these works from what was perceived as authentic Romanticism. Such a disavowal of violent elements in literature helps to explain both the ultimately superficial protestations of impartiality and the caution with which the term 'Romantic' would subsequently be used. Condemnation of excess, meanwhile, was virtually unanimous, and came eventually to constitute a vehement protest against what were perceived as the exaggerations of Romanticism in France. The dramas of Hugo and Dumas rapidly disappeared from the Madrid stage: performances of plays by Hugo in Madrid numbered nineteen in 1835 and again in 1836, but only four in both 1837 and 1839; there were none in 1840 nor in 1841.[32] The popularity of Dumas likewise suffered a sharp decline: in 1836, five of his plays were given a total of thirty-two performances; in 1837 this became two plays given on a total of nine occasions, and in 1838 his two plays were given only seven performances.[33] Nevertheless, the attack upon extravagance and alleged immorality was still being maintained. In 1841, Salvador Bermúduz de Castro wrote in his *El Iris* of the falsification of history so deplorably evident in the wilder

Romantic dramas: playwrights had been prodigal, he felt, in staging gory vendettas replete with daggers and poison in order to achieve what was euphemistically called 'local colour' and dramatic interest.[34] During the following year, Fermín Gonzalo Morón added his weight to the attack, which was not usually directed against Romanticism as such, but more specifically against certain dramas inspired by France. He lamented the fact that Gil y Zárate had, in *Carlos II el hechizado*, chosen to imitate the ill-fated school of Hugo and its injurious moral vision.[35] Gonzalo Morón similarly objected to Hartzenbusch's *Doña Mencía* (1838), labelling it 'drama francés, género exagerado y asaz violento' ('a French drama, an exaggerated and overly violent genre').[36] At the risk of offending men of poor taste, he declared his desire to see it banished from the Spanish stage. On the other hand, Gonzalo Morón would describe Gil y Zárate's subsequent historical dramas and Hartzenbusch's *Los amantes de Teruel* (1837) in a markedly different fashion, as plays inspired by Spain's national literary tradition.[37]

Nevertheless, some fierce and unqualified attacks upon Romanticism continued to be made by Classicists. In 1842, Ventura de la Vega (1807–65) used his inaugural speech as a member of the Real Academia Española to censure the Romantic movement.[38] After recalling his own Classicist education, Vega referred to the 'Vandal invasion' championed by Hugo.[39] He voiced especial condemnation of the preface to *Hernani* and the inflammatory gesture contained in the maxim that literary Romanticism was the equivalent of political liberalism.[40] The end of censorship in Spain, by providing new freedoms, had opened the way to this Romantic torrent from France which had flooded Spain and brought with it a contagious pestilence.[41] We swiftly become aware that Vega's remarks are directed against the kind of Romanticism which had likewise been condemned by historicist critics. The greater part of his attack is confined to the dramas of Hugo and Dumas and their Spanish imitations. All of the plays mentioned by name are Spanish translations of works by Hugo or Dumas: *Lucrecia Borja*, *Teresa* (which, incidentally, had been translated by Vega himself!), *Antony*, *Angelo*, *Angela*, and *La Torre de Nesle*. There are no references to Spanish Romantic plays which represented a reworking of Golden-Age themes.

Vega's reliance upon Horace's 'vos exemplaria graeca nocturna versate manu, versate diurna', which he quotes with relish, does not square with the position adopted by the majority of Spanish critics. It is interesting to compare Vega's reliance upon these lines with Jaime Balmes's comments in his essay 'De la originalidad' of the same year. Balmes felt that Horace had been at his most impressive when he had himself neglected to follow that same instruction.[42] On the other hand, Vega's unqualified rejection of the French and French-inspired dramas is more typical. Their design, he states, was to pervert society; as Vega saw it, 'su plan de destrucción era completo; los tiros se asestaban a la cabeza y al corazón, a la inteligencia y a la moral' ('their aim was one of complete destruction; their fire was directed at hearts and minds, at moral feeling and intellect').[43] At the same time Vega was able to claim that the Spanish theatre-going public now found such 'dramas patibularios' ('dramas of the gallows') repugnant.[44] Their demise was a development viewed with satisfaction by virtually all critics, the great majority of whom continued to support Schlegelian Romanticism, and Vega's vituperation of anti-social tendencies in drama links closely with much earlier comments made by Lista and others. The body of evidence to be assessed in the following chapter of this study will clarify the process. Where Vega radically differs from almost all other contemporary critics is in his desire to witness a rebirth of neo-Classical tragedy on the Spanish stage, and in his detrimental references to Dante and Lope de Vega. Dante's *Divina commedia* is characterised, for Vega, by its disorganised structure and extravagant style (11), and whilst the dramatic unities had in no way inhibited Molière, the author of *Tartuffe* and *Le Misanthrope*, the abandonment of those unities had certainly not aided Lope de Vega, whose thirty-volume legacy might have been beneficially reduced to three tomes worth their weight in gold (8). This implicit subordination of a Spanish Golden-Age dramatist to a French neo-Classicist would have been unthinkable for most of Vega's Spanish contemporaries. Together with his tenacious adherence to the precepts of Horace, such opinions demonstrate that Vega's was a dissenting voice representative of a minority. Crucially, his most strident condemnation was directed specifically against French Romantic drama. Works exemplifying the premises of Romantic historicism escaped his attack.

The outrage provoked by the French dramas was concerted, and Hugo was consistently the target for critical brickbats. In 1840 José María Quadrado was led to protest that Hugo had somehow come to be seen as the leader of some kind of Jacobite clique, as the patron of some hellish anarchic school, and inevitably-held responsible for any kind of literary extravagance: daggers and poison, graveyard lyrics, all were laid at his door.[45] Quadrado's comments hint at a far-reaching consequence of critical reaction against Romantic excess. While some hair-raising plays contained what was no more than gratuitous indulgence in violent effects, the fury of the backlash which they provoked came to constitute a wholesale rejection of anything that smacked of pessimism or unorthodoxy. The successful move to stifle degeneracy perhaps inevitably led to the suppression of a passionately expressed metaphysical *Angst*, such as that encountered in Don Alvaro's memorable soliloquy in Rivas's play and in Espronceda's *Canciones*, *El estudiante de Salamanca* and *El diablo mundo*. Among numerous modern critics who have written of this aspect of Spanish Romanticism, Richard A. Cardwell has provided a remarkably lucid assessment of its potent presence in the above works.[46] After 1837, however, Espronceda was the only established writer consistently to express the profound spiritual questioning found in serious examples of this 'rebellious' Romanticism. His almost mythical status and the quality of his work were together enough to stave off or at least, as in the case of Enrique Gil's critique, to attenuate possible censure.[47] Young poets like Nicomedes-Pastor Díaz and Salvador Bermúdez de Castro would meanwhile soon abjure the pessimistic tones of their early verse, while the sheer weight of the critical reaction would deter emerging writers from 'negative' attitudes. Certain aspects of the Romantic movement had undoubtedly disturbed Spanish critics, and there was to be no future for works that displayed any kind of excess. It is a situation which has prompted the misinterpretation of events by some modern commentators, who have seen in this critical reaction the rejection of the Romantic movement itself. In view of the evidence brought forward here, Salvador García's contention seems more justifiable: in his assessment of literary ideas in the 1840s, García felt that the vituperation of the wilder dramas implied no more than the rejection of certain elements of the new school. He chose, on the other hand, to highlight evidence of the profound assimilation of the historical Romantic aesthetic, to the point where writers considered it part of an organic tradition and entirely separable from excesses that had taken place in the mid-1830s.[48] Something not given full weight by García is the link between this later criticism and the earlier work of Böhl, Durán and others. In fact, Lista, Durán and Donoso, all of whom had promoted the historicist approach in the previous decade, were in the forefront of the attack upon the disruptive aspects of what came to be known as liberal Romanticism.

It is not difficult to account for this process of rejection. The appearance in Spain of plays like *Alfredo* and *Antony* was too abrupt for them to succeed; as Larra laconically observed in his March 1836 review of Dumas's *Catherine Howard*, in a single year Spain had moved from Ferdinand VII to a constitutional parliament and from Moratín to Alexandre Dumas (II, 186). Likewise, the furore that certain plays provoked brought discredit upon the school. Despite the genius of a critic like Larra, so long as the only works which seemed to approximate to his vision of a new and dynamic literature were such as these, his hopes could not be realised. Neither did these works constitute what most people felt Romanticism to be. French Romantic drama, which had directly inspired both *Don Alvaro* and *Alfredo*, was very different in character and spirit from the Schlegelian Romanticism consistently expounded in the reign of Ferdinand VII. Lista and many others were therefore led to regard the French dramas as a distortion of authentic Romanticism. In addition, the radical vision of the new works, which appeared to deny Christian teaching and to portray the entire gamut of moral depravity and vice, could not prove acceptable. Again, the new works were inspired by France, and seemed to perpetuate the kind of ideology that had contributed to the French Revolution. Not only supporters of political reaction and Catholic orthodoxy, but also liberals such as Larra attacked them. After the reception accorded *Antony* and *Carlos II el hechizado*, it was next to impossible for extreme works to flourish. The failure of some of them, including García Gutiérrez's *El paje* (1837), was clearly due as much to public disapproval as to critical condemnation. This play was felt by N. B. Adams to be consciously inspired by Dumas's *La Tour de Nesle*, itself translated by García Gutiérrez as *Margarita de Borgoña* and staged in 1836.[49] Others fell victim to the authorities: the *Junta de Lectura* banned García Gutiérrez's *Magdalena* (1837), which was consequently never staged, while *Angela*, a translation from the French put on in 1838, was removed after just one performance. An illuminating report can be found in the *Eco del Comercio* for 20 March 1838. It stated that the play was, in strictly artistic terms, an admirable one, yet after its first performance it had been suspended, apparently for its immorality. Certain situations, the report continued, could not be depicted on the stage without offending public morality, even if the object of the dramatist was to censure them; from the third act on, the plot of *Angela* turned on a situation of precisely this kind.

This rejection of allegedly immoral works, principally in drama, did not constitute the failure of Romanticism. Attacks were levelled almost exclusively against the kind of 'graveyard Romanticism' labelled by Mesonero Romanos 'el romanticismo de tumba y hachero'. Meanwhile, critics emphasised the positive aspects of historical Romanticism. Alongside condemnation of disruptive tendencies there was a coherent effort at clarification, so that there was nothing to prevent the reassertion of Romantic historicism in Spanish literary criticism after the years of bitter controversy. The Romantic cause was aided by the opportune appearance of Hartzenbusch's majestic drama *Los amantes de Teruel* in January of 1837. The play demonstrated the potential of historical Romanticism to create a new type of recognisably Spanish drama, and appeared just as the immediate impact of Hugo and Dumas was fading in the face of controversy. *Los amantes de Teruel* has been felt to share with Rivas's *Don Alvaro* a common world-view, dominated by the concept of love as the supreme vital support amid the uncertainties of an often burdensome existence: deprived of this 'existential' principle, to which all other material and spiritual considerations are subordinate, the lovers in these plays inevitably die. In Hartzenbusch's play, however, Isabel dies reconciled to God and in a spirit of Christian resignation, in scenes which contain orthodox religious imagery, while the climactic scene of *Don Alvaro* is not without satanic undercurrents in vocabulary, stage direction and gesture. Hartzenbusch's trend-setting drama did not exclude spiritual questioning, but showed a crucial dilemma confronted (if not satisfactorily solved) in terms of Christian morality. This distinction pointedly illustrates both divergent trends in Spanish Romanticism and the position of Hartzenbusch's masterpiece within the movement's main stream. After all, the deaths of Diego and Isabel were the culmination of a story known to all Spaniards and already brought to the stage by Tirso de Molina and Montalbán.

The year of 1837 can therefore be regarded as an important turning point rather than as a year of conclusive failure. This is borne out by researches made by N. B. Adams, who highlighted the decline in the fortunes of Hugo and Dumas on the Madrid stage and conversely stressed the growing popularity of original Spanish Romantic dramas.[50] In 1837, French Romantic plays were given on about two dozen occasions. Some were being restaged after appearing in previous years but *Antony*, which had attracted such adverse criticism, did not reappear; the play had a first run of just four performances in June 1836, and was revived for one more performance only, in August of the same year. On the other hand, stated Adams, 'The native drama which can be called Romantic, including plays with varied historical, melodramatic and sentimental elements, shows considerable progress in 1837'; original Spanish Romantic plays were in fact given 115 performances in the same twelve-month period.[51] Adams points out that García Gutiérrez's *El trovador*, after twenty-five appearances in 1836, was given on a further seventeen occasions in 1837, while *Los amantes de Teruel* had fourteen performances in its first year. Finally, important in the present context is Adams's detection of a broad and increasing tendency to employ specifically Spanish subjects and themes and to draw on national history and legend. Zorrilla would prove to be a typical case. Prefacing *Cada cual con su razón* (1839), he declared his indignation at the invasion of the Spanish stage by 'los monstruosos abortos de la elegante corte de Francia' ('the monstrous abortions of the elegant French court'), a reference carrying a strong degree of scornful irony. He had himself, he stated, sought in Calderón, Lope and Tirso de Molina dramatic inspiration of a kind markedly different from that which had produced *Hernani* and *Lucrèce Borgia*.[52]

Adams's evidence of trends in the theatre dovetails with my own assessment of developments in the critical debate and reinforces earlier conclusions. If the essence of Romanticism was constituted by revolutionary elements indicative of both social and metaphysical crisis, then the school cannot be said to have been firmly established in Spain. A very different and no less valid manifestation of Romantic tendencies, however, would prove to be a more enduring phenomenon in that country.

5

Reaffirmation of Schlegelian principles in literary criticism

While Edgar Allison Peers had viewed Romanticism as a purely literary phenomenon, Angel del Río felt that this limited perspective necessarily rendered Peers's interpretation of events untrustworthy.[1] He based his own analysis upon a distinction between liberal and conservative romanticisms, regarding the former as the only genuine manifestation of Romanticism in Spain. Del Río claimed that this authentic Romanticism constituted a sudden and total reaction in the early 1830s. He saw the survival of a conservative Romanticism after 1840, with its restoration of the literature of the Golden Age and embodiment of the national tradition, as evidence of an enforced change of direction in the face of reactionary external pressures, as a break with the movement's origins caused by 'the impossibility that the new ideas, the new interpretation of the world, the new revolutionary and unorthodox philosophy of romanticism, could take root in the orthodox and catholic soil of Spain'.[2] D.L. Shaw would subsequently bolster Del Río's theory in two articles that encompassed moral and social preoccupations as well as developments in literature.[3] Disavowing the thesis that Romanticism was a purely literary movement in isolation from a broader context, Shaw felt the problem of its origin and definition to be closely connected with the collapse of one traditional world-view and its replacement by another, with concomitant changes in all categories of value. Romanticism, essentially revolutionary, involved a new vision of life: 'a view which orthodox opinion saw as subversive to those habitual preconceptions, values, and beliefs which were held to be essential to the safety and stability of society'.[4] Shaw then regarded Peers's conclusions as invalid, since they were based upon a restricted view of the Romantic movement itself. For the former, the limited success and modest achievements of Romanticism in Spain can be at least partly explained by 'the spirited defence of traditional Catholic values' which it provoked.[5] A hostile reaction to the movement, he claimed, soon found expression in the country and was well in force by the early 1840s. Shaw identified Alberto Lista and Jaime Balmes as the leaders of such a reaction, which advocated a return to 'the soundest principles of religious truth and morality'.[6] Shaw was here consciously enlarging upon Del Río's earlier claim that Catholic traditionalism was responsible for the failure of Romanticism to take root in Spain. Salvador García's study of Spanish literary criticism in the 1840s implicitly challenged the theory earlier outlined by Del Río and Shaw. García recognised that the allegedly immoral elements of the new school were overwhelmingly rejected by Romantic writers themselves.[7] In the light of this assertion, it is curious that he only slightly modified the idea of an Eclectic triumph previously mooted by Peers. I would share García's view (corroborated by a much more substantial body of evidence in the previous chapter of this study) that Spanish Romantics themselves rejected what they regarded as the unwelcome excesses of certain works, but would challenge his assertion that an Eclectic triumph nevertheless took place. While Del Río and, more specifically, Shaw were justified in pointing to a robust defence of traditional values during the period in question, I would suggest that this vigorous campaign was mounted by conservative Romantics who attacked rationalism, materialism and religious scepticism much in the same way as Böhl von Faber had done over twenty years before. As we shall see in this and in the two succeeding chapters, there took place in Spain a broad reaffirmation of the principles of historical Romanticism as outlined in the previous decade, accompanied by developments in critical method and perspective which can be viewed as the product of recent experience.

The central feature of Schlegelian Romanticism was the historicist approach to literary development, which itself involved the fundamental distinction between Classical and Romantic literature. This approach, which we have already seen reasserted by Alberto Lista, was likewise reiterated by Juan Donoso Cortés in 1838 in his series of articles entitled 'El clasicismo y el romanticismo'. Donoso described the two movements as not just opposing literary schools but as the expression of two differing civilisations which had evolved within different historical periods (I, 381). Employing this basic historico-cultural distinction, Donoso argued that literature must change along with other aspects of civilisation. Whereas the Greeks had established in their literature a 'cult of form', the mediaeval period had witnessed the creation of an emphatic spirituality, which reflected essential changes in religious belief and in social milieu (1, 388–90, 398–400). Sensual splendour had been replaced by contemplation and mystery. Donoso went on to draw attention, as A. W. Schlegel had done, to the markedly different attitude towards human love in the two periods, attaching great importance to the ideals of chivalry and courtly love. He also claimed that the development of individual character in drama stemmed from an apprehension of the various individual characteristics inherent in man, something which had not been possible in the Greek theatre. All these factors, declared Donoso, explained the differences between Classicism and Romanticism. In effect, he repeated the views he had earlier expressed in the *Discurso* at Cáceres in 1829 and in the more recent review of Pacheco's *Alfredo* in 1835. Similarly, Agustín Durán would reaffirm the historicist approach which he also had adopted in the 1820s. Analysing Tirso de Molina's *El condenado por desconfiado* in the *Revista de Madrid* in 1841, he remarked upon the way in which literary criticism had effectively transcended the prescriptions of Aristotle, Horace and Boileau. A more philosophical criticism would not only address itself to perceived rules of good taste, but would be founded on a far-reaching knowledge of the history of peoples, of their ways of life, and of the dominant set of ideas that informed the social structure of each age and inspired its various successes and failures.[8]

While Lista, Donoso and Durán were all restating the approach which they had advocated a decade earlier, a new generation of critics was now adopting the same perspective. In his *Emancipación literaria didáctica* of 1837, Antonio Ribot y Fontseré affirmed that it was possible to deduce the ethical character of any given country and period from an examination of its creative literature.[9] He consequently rejected the validity of Classical precepts, particularly in dramatic practice, claiming that drama was not subject to immutable laws but rather constituted a faithful means of communicating the essential spirit of every age and nation.[10] Like Ribot y Fontseré, Antonio Gil y Zárate would emphasise the application of historicism to the development of drama, writing in 1841 of the changing intellectual disposition of different countries through various historical periods. The scope of intellectual achievement, national custom, political and religious beliefs all contributed to national identity, and nowhere was such a constant process of change better reflected than in drama, the mirror of civilisation.[11] Writing in the *Revista de Madrid* in 1840, one of the magazine's most assiduous contributors, the writer and politician Pedro José Pidal, perceived two primary objectives in literary study: firstly, to appreciate the beauties of individual works; secondly, to study through these the physiognomy of a people and age and thus discover the philosophical premises and ideas that had been prevalent in them. Literature could thus be regarded as the emphatic expression of ideas, feelings and beliefs characteristic of the country and age in which it was produced, as an accurate reflection of the customs, habits and temperament of a people.[12] This opinion was echoed by Cayetano Cortés in Espronceda's magazine *El Pensamiento* in the following year.[13] A further twelve months later, in a series of articles dealing with the plays of Antonio Gil y Zárate and published in his own *Revista de España y del Extranjero*, Fermín Gonzalo Morón clearly reveals the influence of A. W. Schlegel upon his thought.[14] Gonzalo Morón had written in the previous year, in words reminiscent of the great German critic, of crucial aspects of the feudal age which had played no part in ancient society: the sense of honour and loyalty that dominated the creed of the mediaeval knight, deference towards the fairer sex, and the delicacy and inherently poetic qualities which typified knightly attitudes to women. These were the characteristic features of what Gonzalo Morón felt to have been Europe's truly poetic age.[15] In the later article he stressed the originality of the English and Spanish theatres of Shakespeare, Lope and Calderón, declaring that Spanish drama of the *Siglo de Oro* represented the sublime manifestation of national character. At the same time, A. W. Schlegel himself is praised as a pre-eminent critic.[16] Introducing in the same year a series of articles dealing with Golden-Age drama, Gonzalo Morón concisely expressed his adherence to the historicist approach, claiming that literary works effectively revealed the physiognomy of their respective countries. Literary criticism should be primarily concerned with this aspect of creative works, its major tasks being those of 'dando a conocer la vida íntima y moral de los pueblos' ('revealing the intimate moral existence of various peoples') and, related to this last, of highlighting the pleasure and enthusiasm bestowed by literary works that genuinely reflected national customs, traditions and beliefs.[17]

To insist further would only prove tedious. This historicist approach is virtually unanimous in articles of the period, clearly being regarded as the most valid critical perspective. While none of the writers cited above went so far as categorically to deny the merits of Classicism, it was usually viewed as no more than a product of its own age, and its precepts as no longer applicable. Nowhere does such an attitude emerge more forcefully than in the articles of the man widely acknowledged to be the most talented literary critic of the period after 1837: Enrique Gil y Carrasco (1815–46).[18] Enrique Gil had come to Madrid from his native Bierzo region of León in 1836, and had become well known in literary circles after his poem 'Una gota de rocío' had been read by Espronceda at the Ateneo in December of 1837. He later became literary reviewer of both *El Correo Nacional* and the *Semanario Pintoresco Español*. In reviewing the poetry of José Zorrilla, Enrique Gil subscribed to the notion of critical impartiality which, superficially at least, appears to have been *de rigueur* during this period. He disavowed any rigid division of works into categories and preferred instead an unbiased aesthetic judgement of whether a work was good or bad. Accordingly, neither would the inherent disorder of the moment of poetic inspiration be enough to shield poetry from the standards of judgement justly applied by logic, nor would cold and ignoble imitation ever touch the strings of the heart.[19] This might be considered a declaration of Eclecticism, yet Gil does not mention any of the rules of good taste, and the Classicist qualities he admires, 'la lógica del sentimiento' ('the logic of feeling') and 'la verdad de la inspiración' ('the truth of inspiration') (482), are not those typically associated with the school. His remarks are on the other hand consistent with those of A. W. Schlegel, who had felt that the poetic spirit ought to be limited to 'a becoming liberty'.[20] In the course of his critical articles as much as in his lyric poetry and his prose, Enrique Gil in fact reveals himself as a fully-fledged Romantic. In his earliest critical piece, for example, published in October of 1838, he follows the lead of A. W. Schlegel and Madame de Staël in his perception of the respective character of the northern and southern nations of Europe, differentiating between a contemplative people given to potent imaginative fantasy, i.e. Germany, and the more volatile and energetic temperament of Mediterraneans (404).[21] The image is repeated in Gil's critique, published in December of the same year, of García de Villalta's translation of *Macbeth*. The mists of Scotland, he comments, its terrain, its witches and spectres, and the remote and visionary temperament of its people in the age depicted in Shakespeare's play, all made it distant indeed both from the scorching sun, blue skies and sweet-scented landscapes of Mediterranean climes and from the uninhibited outlook and easy confidence of men of the South (421). Predictably, then, Gil adopts the historicist approach to literature. The sentiments expressed in his critique of Zorrilla's poetry are by now familiar ones: 'Cuando las creencias religiosas o sociales se alteran es imposible que la expresión de estas creencias no mude al mismo tiempo de forma; es imposible que las nuevas ideas no revistan formas nuevas también' ('When social and religious beliefs change it is impossible for their form of expression not to alter also; it is impossible for new ideas to fail to take on new forms') (481). Thus Enrique Gil remarks, in a later article,[22] upon the diverse forms of poetry found among various nations and peoples (486). He applies this method in his consideration of literary developments in Spain since the late eighteenth century. Pointing to the degeneracy of the Spanish stage then dominated by the inept and overly sentimental pieces of Comella, Zabala and others, he viewed the *comedia nueva* established by Moratín as a welcome imposition of order and discipline.[23] Yet the *comedia nueva* should have given way to a new era; Moratín and the other *restauradores* ought to have realised that the principle of imitation was a sterile one, and that the Classical precepts tended to stifle genius. The necessary literary revolution in fact arose from a growing awareness of the unsuitability of the ideas put forward by the *restauradores*, proponents of a literature which, for Enrique Gil, had fallen short of reflecting society's moral state and had failed to interpret in its texture the religious and philosophical beliefs of modern nations (476). He felt this to be a natural consequence, for it was impossible for two societies so different in character as the Classical and the modern European to find identical expression in literary form. He went on to view the new school as a manifestation of new ideas, emotions and preoccupations, being prepared to countenance some of its excesses since the previous literary order, neo-Classicism, had become bankrupt of ideas. There are significant parallels here with both Durán's *Discurso* and, more notably, with Alcalá Galiano's prologue to *El moro expósito*.[24] In fact, in his review of the Duque de Rivas's *Romances históricos* (1841), Enrique Gil devotes considerable attention to the earlier narrative poem.[25] In this lengthy article he reiterates his objections to the actions of the *restauradores*: as literature was undoubtedly the mirror of society, those who, motivated by blind obedience to rules and weakly imitative in spirit, had attempted to bring to Spain foreign models inspired by ideas and feelings incompatible with those of Spaniards, had acted erroneously (511). Enrique Gil goes on to praise enthusiastically Alcalá Galiano's prologue, describing the aesthetic framework there expounded as eminently reasonable and acceptable, as a wise degree of literary freedom stemming from an awareness both of the progressive course of ideas and of the special needs of the age. Furthermore, he shares the spirit of nationalism inherent in that prologue, and is at one with Alcalá Galiano on the issue of the course to be followed by talented writers in the current 'regenerative' literary phase (512). Exactly what he meant to take place will become clear later.

Enrique Gil also referred to the critical work of Larra, praising the latter's assessment of the drama of Dumas, and, specifically, *Fígaro*'s view of *Antony*. Gil likewise felt that the play contained no spiritual consolation nor moral instruction but only a damaging attack upon society and contemporary values (453–5).[26] He would himself later censure literary extravagance in a passage expressly linked to French Romantic drama and more measured than many of the more febrile attacks made during the same period. Spain, he felt, had experienced in an attenuated form the effects of that literary revolution which had overtaken France. Such violent changes and vicissitudes had not arisen spontaneously in Spain; instead, an ill-fated weakness for imitation had led some writers to indulge in 'extremos y exageraciones que debieran excusarse, y que no hallaban consonancia ni respuesta en el corazón de nuestro pueblo' ('exaggerations and extremes which ought to have been avoided, and which could find no sympathetic accord or response in the hearts of our people') (477). Consequently, while able to praise *Don Alvaro* as one of the best dramas of the new school, Enrique Gil qualified his approval by remarking that its philosophy, an extension of that informing Hugo's *Notre-Dame de Paris*, was the product of a comfortless and sceptical vision lacking any constructive social purpose (479). Beneath the adventurous dramatic effects of *Don Alvaro* lay the kind of pessimistic outlook which had made many French Romantic works, in the eyes of Spanish critics, a disturbing phenomenon in that they seemed to embody a profound lack of spiritual direction and even to exemplify social distintegration. Enrique Gil viewed this destructive philosophy as an unfortunate consequence of the imitation of French writers, regarding it as something intrinsically alien to the essential character of Spain. He had adopted a similar position when assessing, in much broader terms, recent radical changes in Europe, insisting that they had not affected 'el fondo homogéneo vigoroso y compacto de la nación española' ('the homogeneous, vigorous and compact bedrock of the Spanish nation') (443). Enrique Gil's terms of reference are different – socio-political rather than literary – but the vocabulary used is strikingly similar and the essential premise is the same. Accordingly, in his review of Espronceda's play *Amor venga sus agravios* (1838), Gil applauded the dramatic success of the denouement, which involved a poisoning and a suicide, but disapproved of the philosophy underlying the work (401–5). However, writing in November of 1838 in his review of Hartzenbusch's *Doña Mencía*, which again ended with suicide after a father had mistakenly married his daughter, he felt able to refer approvingly to the constructive framework of ideas informing the play, and observed that whenever the public could find meaningful instruction in the contemplation of failings or misdemeanours then the theatre was continuing to fulfil an important moral purpose (410). Enrique Gil was therefore willing not only to countenance, but actively to encourage, daring dramatic effects provided that they were positively directed and morally instructive. This we perceive also in his two articles on *Macbeth* already cited, where he writes with special enthusiasm of the character of Lady Macbeth (422–3). His position is thus close to that adopted by Larra just two years previously.

Enrique Gil was deeply affected by Shakespeare's presentation of the Middle Ages as a dynamic and sublime age. This idea of the mediaeval period as a particularly poetic one had constituted a major element of the lectures of both Schlegel brothers, and a cult of mediaevalism had been a prevalent part of the Spanish literary scene since the 1820s, but the works of Shakespeare did not prove popular in the country at this time. Enrique Gil attributed this lack of success to differences in cultural background and literary expression. It disappointed him, however, as did a situation he viewed as sadly ironical: Germany was alive with passionate enthusiasm for Calderón while Spain had spurned its greatest dramatist (422). There was no diminution, on the other hand, in the popularity of Walter Scott, whose work had helped to create an unprecedented degree of imaginative sympathy for the past and had led writers and their readers alike to sentimentalise and dramatise past events. In the wake of those wilder Romantic productions that had involved the deliberate falsification of history in the cause of dramatic effect, critics advocated the faithful depiction of historical episodes and periods. An anonymous reviewer of Patricio de la Escosura's historical play *Bárbara Blomberg* (1837) commented that if episodes from mediaeval chronicles were to be dramatisied then playwrights ought to be duly concerned with fidelity to historical truth. Artistic licence might allow them to embellish their subject, but in no way to alter it beyond recognition.[27] Alberto Lista, writing in 1840, outlined conditions for historical fiction which explicitly stressed the concept of an imaginative and empathetic leap increasingly seen as a corollary of Romantic historicism: 'Es necesario colocar al lector en medio de la sociedad que se pinta: es necesario que la vea, que la oiga, que la ame o la tema, como ella fue con todas sus virtudes y defectos' ('It is essential to place the reader at the heart of that society which is being depicted: it is essential that he see it, that he hear it, that he love or fear it, just as it really was with all of its virtues and defects').[28] Lista felt that historical fiction should capture the spirit of a particular age, and regarded Scott's novels as exemplary. Those qualities which he outlined would later earn Enrique Gil's *El señor de Bembibre* (1844) extensive praise.

Interest in national history was at its height, and not only in creative productions. As Antonio Gil y Zárate observed in 1841, imaginative evocation of many aspects of the Middle Ages – its traditions, ways of life, heroic events and historical monuments – held untold attractions for the popular mind.[29] His comments were fully justified; magazines and periodicals regularly carried illustrations of the best examples of Spanish architecture, both religious and secular, usually accompanied by an account of famous events connected with each building's history. At the same time, the amount of space devoted to the consideration of episodes from Spanish history, of folkloric and religious traditions and of the history of Spanish literature furnishes striking evidence of popular interest in the past. More specifically, the Catalan critic Pablo Piferrer was one of the driving forces behind the *Recuerdos y bellezas de España*, a mammoth project involving the publication, in instalments, of studies on the history, traditions and other beauties of the various regions of Spain. Piferrer's colleague Parcerisa declared that inspiration for the work came from the *Romancero* and from

Chateaubriand's Les Aventures du dernier Abencérrage.[30] Looking ahead, it was a project which would in its turn inspire Gustavo Adolfo Bécquer's *Historia de los templos de España*. Meanwhile, scholarly historical study would be equally indelibly impressed with the Romantic vogue for mediaevalism: Manuel Moreno Alonso's assessment of historiographical work in nineteenth-century Spain has conclusively shown this to be the case.[31]

Many of the historical themes now the object of enthusiastic interest had been successfully brought to the Spanish stage in the Golden Age. Three centuries later, the rehabilitation both of early Spanish literature and of the drama of the *Siglo de Oro* represented, for Spanish critics, the most important element of the lectures of the Schlegel brothers. The vindication of the Golden-Age dramatists, especially Calderón, had played an essential part in the development of a historical Romanticism in Spain during the reign of Ferdinand VII, while the national drama had continued to be defended along patriotic lines by a variety of critics during the years of controversy between 1834 and 1837. Now that the impact of French Romantic dramas on the stage had subsided, Golden-Age plays were regaining popularity.[32] In the critical articles of this later period, two fundamental attitudes involving Golden-Age drama can clearly be seen to emerge: firstly, the continued identification of the drama of the *Siglo de Oro* with the Spanish society of its period and the perception of such drama as the embodiment of national character, which involved the highest praise for dramatists like Calderón, Tirso and Moreto; secondly, the manifestation of widespread support for the idea of dramatic regeneration based upon the adaptation of Golden-Age drama to meet contemporary needs, again expressed in a strongly nationalist fashion. Indicative of the first trend are Enrique Gil's prefatory comments in his review of Bretón de los Herreros's *No ganamos para sustos* (1839), a comedy of manners written in a style typical of its author.[33] Enrique Gil commended the depiction of Spanish society in the work of the Golden-Age dramatists, and felt such a faithful representation to be instructive, since 'El medio de enseñar y moralizar un pueblo es el de mostrarle palpitante y vivo su verdadero carácter' ('The best means of providing a people with moral instruction is to present them with a living, breathing portrait of their true character') (443). He would later welcome the appearance of a collection of Tirso's plays published by Hartzenbusch and Durán in 1839, seeing it as a brilliant and gracious example of Spanish literary genius (462).[34] In 1839, Agustín Durán himself reiterated his view of the drama of the *Siglo de Oro* previously expressed in the *Discurso* of 1828. In the seventeenth century, he stated, Spain's national poetry had exchanged its essential narrative structure for that of poetic drama. Accessible to the people, it was an embodiment of collective beliefs and practices which expressed the indelible character of the nation.[35] Durán would, in a subsequent article of two years later, point to Tirso de Molina's play *El condenado por desconfiado* as a fine example of this type of drama, one that successfully revealed the essential physiognomy of the age in which it was written.[36] Meanwhile, Salvador Bermúdez de Castro would also praise the same aspect of Spanish Golden-Age drama, which he called 'el mágico espejo de la verdadera poesía' ('the magical mirror of true poetry').[37]

In the same year of 1841, the former *afrancesado* Javier de Burgos (1778–1849) joined the debate. Like Lista, Burgos had been forced to emigrate before the end of the Peninsular War. He had later worked with Lista on the journal *El Imparcial* in 1822, and had eventually been given official posts under Ferdinand VII. In a series of lectures published in the magazine *El Panorama*, Burgos regarded Calderón's drama as a broad and authentic representation of the character of a great nation within a given historical period, fully deserving of the respect and veneration it had been accorded by critics everywhere, particularly by the most pre-eminent of German theorists.[38] For Burgos, the drama of the *Siglo de Oro* possessed a majestic national character not only on account of its faithful reproduction of and deference to customs and beliefs; its patriotic flavour memorably evoked the incomparable military and religious glory of the 700-year Reconquest.[39] Ardent literary nationalism was reinforced, continued Burgos, by a vigorous and emblematic employment of the magical phrase '*Dios y el Rey*' ('God and King').[40] This vision of Golden-Age drama is akin to that adumbrated by A. W. Schlegel and first promoted in Spain by Böhl von Faber, while Burgos's idealistic evocation of the war against the infidel leads back to material earlier examined in the first chapter of this study. The spirit of Böhl is further evident in later comments made by Fermín Gonzalo Morón. Writing in the *Revista de España y del Extranjero* in 1842, Gonzalo Morón felt that Golden-Age drama and early literature sublimely expressed the poetic grandeur of Spain's historical character. He went on to declare that, in exchanging its traditional literary forms for those of French neo-Classicism in the previous century, Spain had shamefully abjured the glories of nationhood.[41] Finally, in his 1842 essay 'De la originalidad', Jaime Balmes, in terms immediately reminiscent of A. W. Schlegel, enthusiastically described the achievement of the *Siglo de Oro* as a literary equivalent of the Empire of Charles V, upon which the sun never set (VIII, 233).

Clearly, the perception in this period of the drama of the *Siglo de Oro* is very much that of the Schlegels and of Böhl von Faber. The efforts of the latter were acknowledged by his former opponent Alcalá Galiano, who wrote of Böhl in the *Revista de Madrid* in 1838 as a man of imposing erudition, and confessed that his own views had radically changed since the time of the polemic.[42] Böhl, who died in 1836, would certainly have approved of the direction now being taken by literary criticism. Writing in 1838, Enrique Gil even advised Hartzenbusch (414) and Bretón de los Herreros (581) to look to the example set by Calderón for inspiration. Nevertheless, whatever the outstanding merits of the Golden-Age dramatists, it was felt that nineteenth-century theatre required a new type of play which could satisfy contemporary needs. Whilst Lope and others had written dramas that had possessed the distinctive character of their age, modern dramatists could not now produce identical works. As Gil y Zárate pointed out in 1841, in a judgement itself stemming from the application of the historicist approach to literature, society had radically changed since the times of Lope and Calderón. Literary tastes were now different, and intellectual needs had become more rigorous and demanding. Spanish drama had therefore altered, both in its form and in its essence.[43] In his prologue to *El moro expósito*, Alcalá Galiano had stressed the need for a new literary genre in Spain which would adequately reflect modern progress and intellectual development, and mooted the idea of reworking the drama of the *Siglo de Oro* to meet such a requirement. Larra had subsequently made an impassioned plea for a literature which could genuinely be seen as the product of the contemporary age. In a particularly nationalistic fashion, numerous critics began again to put forward, from about 1838, the idea of dramatic regeneration through the adaptation of Golden-Age drama to modern requirements. Such a play would constitute an authentic 'drama nacional'. In 1839, Enrique Gil confidently asserted that 'la escuela dramática verdadera y filosófica de nuestro país consiste en no imitar servilmente a nuestros artistas de los siglos

XVI y XVII, sino en continuarlos y acomodarlos al estado de las ideas, necesidades y adelantos que son propios de Ía edad presente' ('our nation's true and philosophical dramatic school consists not of the servile imitation of our sixteenth- and seventeenth-century writers, but of a process of continuity, of their adaptation to the ideas, needs and advances of the present age') (443). Writing in 1841, Bermúdez de Castro similarly viewed the way forward for the Spanish stage; by making the traditional Spanish *comedia* compatible with the demands of the nineteenth century, it would be possible to 'regenerate' in an organic fashion the national theatre, linking the broad trunk of past tradition with the new offshoots springing up in the future.[44] Bermúdez felt that the tide of imitation, especially of French Romantic drama, was firmly on the ebb, and confidently forecast a regenerative impulse along nationalistic lines, with a glorious return to the spirit of Lope and Calderón.[45] In the following year, Balmes also lent his support to such a proposition, advising writers that, in order to restore national literature, they must prove themselves above all else to be Spaniards (VIII, 239). He directly linked the brilliance of Golden-Age literature with the splendour of the Spanish empire, and bemoaned the later servile imitation of French neo-Classical drama (VIII, 233–5). Balmes praised Spanish literature of the Golden Age for its ability to portray its contemporary society and, while recognising the immense differences between seventeenth-century Spain and the present period, nevertheless believed that the influence of the *Siglo de Oro* was, quite properly, still clearly felt (VIII, 240). Meanwhile, in the *Revista de Teatros*, the issue was again set out by an unnamed reviewer who felt that the envisaged regeneration was already taking place, and who pointed to recent works by Zorrilla, the Duque de Rivas, and Tomás Rodríguez Rubí as examples.[46] Replying to the article by Bermúdez de Castro cited above, Hartzenbusch declared that the modification Bermúdez had called for was already in practice. He saw recent plays by Zorrilla and the Duque de Rivas as directly inspired by the national dramatic tradition in characterisation, style and plot.[47] However, it was not these *comedias*, but the new historical dramas which gained greatest critical approval. These latter plays were the ones usually regarded as examples of the 'drama nacional' which had been so eagerly envisaged. Durán's 1837 review of Roca de Togores's *Doña María de Molina* was an accolade for what he considered to be the authentic modern school of drama: a play that imitated Spanish seventeenth-century drama without copying it slavishly, and adapted it to contemporary times.[48] Similarly, Bermúdez de Castro praised Gil y Zárate's *Un monarca y su privado* (1841) for its combination of Golden-Age elements with those of modern Romantic drama.[49] In the following year, Fermín Gonzalo Morón wrote that the same play imaginatively transported its audience to the last chivalric period of national history, and brought intimately to mind the noble ladies and gallant gentlemen of Lope and Calderón.[50] Gil y Zárate, who strove to promote the concept of a new national drama in his 'Teatro antiguo y teatro moderno', produced, between 1839 and 1843, nine historical plays evidently intended to demonstrate this idea in practice. Most of them had a mediaeval setting, and the majority related themes from Spanish history.[51] José Zorrilla also dealt principally with national historical themes, often choosing episodes and characters previously brought to the stage by Golden-Age dramatists.[52] This kind of play would be prevalent in the Spanish theatre throughout the following decade. By 1841, Agustín Durán could regard the situation with some satisfaction:

apenas ha penetrado en nuestra escena el asqueroso, repugnante y atroz monstruo, hijo del desenfreno revolucionario que se pasea por toda Europa y que no falta tampoco en nuestras ciudades. Algunos de nuestros ilustres y jóvenes ingenios fueron deslumbrados por el Romanticismo malo, pero después que estudiaron la poesía nacional, le abandonaron, y siguiendo el camino trazado por la buena crítica, produjeron obras que honran la presente generación.[53]

(That loathsome, repugnant and fearful monster, spawned by the revolutionary licentiousness that stalks Europe and is abroad in our own cities, has only rarely appeared on our stage. Certain young talents were at first dazzled by this unpleasant Romanticism, but, after studying our national poetry, they soon abandoned it and, following the course prescribed by sound criticism, produced works which do some honour to their age.)

Durán's comments are verified to an impressive degree by the corpus of evidence adduced in the present study. French Romantic drama, perceived as the embodiment of a despairing outlook stemming from an unwelcome revolutionary view of the world, had failed to take hold in Spain: here Durán's view coincides markedly with that of Gil y Carrasco. Writers were now looking to the national past for inspiration, as Spanish critics like Durán himself, Gil y Carrasco and Bermúdez de Castro had indeed widely recommended. The tone of revulsion for the disturbing philosophy of some literary works is still perceptible, but Durán's note of assured optimism contrasts with the anxious note often struck by critics in 1835 or 1836. In the same article, Durán again stressed the impact of literary criticism on creative literature, being adamant that the successful plays of the day represented the kind of adaptation of Golden-Age drama advocated by critics. He drew attention to works like *Doña María de Molina*, *Los amantes de Teruel*, *Rosmunda* and numerous other works by young Spanish writers that preserved Spain's national physiognomy and in which could be seen the influence of the popular verse tradition, modified by the intimate workings of a more modern civilisation.[54] Likewise, Mesonero Romanos named Gil y Zárate's *Rosmunda* and Zorrilla's *El zapatero y el rey* as prime examples of plays which represented a return to the school of Rojas and Calderón.[55] Such plays remained faithful to the spirit of the *Siglo de Oro* in their tone of language, in their employment of themes of love, honour and duty, often in conflict, and in their sense of intrigue and theatrical effect. However, the humour exemplified by the character of the *gracioso* was sacrificed as unsuited to contemporary drama, and the social and political relevance of themes was more powerfully stressed. As a result of this last factor, these plays often appeared particularly topical, presenting contemporary audiences with lessons to be learned from events of the past. A good example of this trend was *Doña María de Molina* (1837), a modification of Tirso's *La prudencia en la mujer*. Writing in 1838, Muñoz Maldonado insisted upon the topical relevance of the rôle of María de Molina, linking her achievement with that of María Cristina de Borbón in the 1830s.[56] The impact of Romantic elements in both staging and in the choice of *dramatis personae* is also clear. Zorrilla successfully adapted a Golden-Age theme and dressed it in wholly Romantic guise, while at the same time addressing himself to the contemporary religious debate, in his *Don Juan Tenorio* (1844). The only kind of eclecticism in such a development was the often skilful combination of Romantic and Golden-Age elements in a single dramatic production. But more importantly, the creation of this historical drama represented the natural culmination of existing trends in theory and practice. The cultural nationalism inherent in the ideas expressed in the reign of Ferdinand VII, the new sentimental aesthetic that typified the Romantic school, the increasing perception of literature as inextricably linked to its contemporary society, all contributed to the development of this 'drama nacional'. Classical precepts and Classicist practices were excluded, as were the wilder aspects of those Romantic dramas inspired by France. Instead, it was essentially a cohesive blend of various trends present in the earlier historical Romanticism which constituted the dramas of the 1840s. This trend effectively began with Hartzenbusch's *Los amantes de Teruel* in January of 1837. In assessing this play, Fermín Gonzalo Morón commented on the wealth of inspiration to be found in Spain's history and traditions, and stated that 'no concebimos ciertamente más noble y gloriosa carrera para nuestros vates, que excitar en nuestros pechos los elevados y pundonorosos sentimientos de nuestros mayores' ('we can think of no more worthy and glorious course to be followed by our bards than that of arousing in our hearts the elevated and noble feelings of our forebears').[57]

A further element of the earlier historical Romanticism derived from the Schlegels had been the vindication of the qualities of the *Romancero* and the view of the *romance* as Spain's national poetic metre. Interest in the *romance* now remained strong, with Durán's collections gaining enormous critical acclaim. In addition, many young poets were adopting it as a metrical form, especially in narrative poetry with a mediaeval setting, a literary vogue which had steadily increased in popularity. In those collections of verse published in the years 1840 and 1841, widely regarded as the apogee of Spanish Romantic poetry, the *romance* form figured prominently. The sentiments expressed by Bermúdez de Castro in his 1841 review of Durán's *Tesoro*, published that same year, are reminiscent of Herder and the Schlegels. In the simple originality and vigorous grace of the *romances*, commented Bermúdez, could be found priceless evidence regarding the character of Spanish society in a period often distorted or ignored by historians.[58] His words remind us especially of Friedrich Schlegel's commentary on the Poem of the Cid. Meanwhile, in the prologue to his *Romances históricos*, again of 1841, the Duque de Rivas reiterated the view of the Spanish ballad found in the lectures of the Schlegel brothers. He described the old ballads as 'nuestra verdadera poesía castiza' ('our true-blooded and characteristic national poetry'), an original and robust poetic form struggling to find expression in what was an incipient and semi-barbarous tongue.[59] As the true national metre of Spain, it was especially suited, he insisted, to the soaring fantasy of Romanticism. It seemed to him surprising that the form had not attained pre-eminence in a period when poets were consistently looking to the feudal age and to mediaeval history for inspiration.[60] The Duque de

Rivas here seems either unaware of the popularity of the *romance* as a verse form or intent upon stressing the originality of his own collection. What is certain is that the success of the *Romances históricos* and of the verse narratives of Zorrilla, who also regularly wrote in the *romance* metre, together with the appearance of further collections of old ballads, maintained enthusiastic interest in what continued to be viewed as the national poetic form. In this way, another element of the earlier historical Romanticism was reaffirmed.

Zorrilla's work responded to an increasingly potent popular nationalism, and he soon came to be regarded as 'el poeta nacional'. Nicomedes-Pastor Díaz (1811–63), eminent poet, journalist and politician, had accompanied Zorrilla from Larra's graveside confident of the abilities of the younger man; that same evening, Díaz introduced Zorrilla to Donoso Cortés and Pacheco, and the youthful poet was offered work on their newspaper *El Porvenir*. In his prologue to Zorrilla's first volume of poetry, published in 1837, Díaz had expressed the opinion that the poems captured a mediaeval grandeur lost to the present age, effectively contrasting 'lo que hay de mezquino, glacial y ridículo en la época actual, con lo que tienen de magnífico, solemne y sublime los recuerdos de los tiempos caballerescos y religiosos' ('the cold, ignoble and ridiculous qualities of the present era, with the magnificence, solemnity and sublimity inherent in our recollections of the age of religion and chivalry').[61] Zorrilla's dramatic appearance on the day of Larra's funeral in February of 1837 would undoubtedly have brought to the surface instinctive Romantic sentiment. However, his work responded to several existing trends and played an important part in strengthening them. Zorrilla chose almost all his themes from Spanish history and tradition; he employed the *romance*, the national poetic metre, in much of his verse; he imitated the Golden-Age *comedia* and wrote historical plays which could be seen as the adaptation of the drama of the *Siglo de Oro* to contemporary needs; his work exemplified the Romantic cult of mediaevalism. Zorrilla himself was both aware and justifiably proud of his status as 'el poeta nacional'; when called onto the stage at the end of the first performance of *Cada cual con su razón* (1839), he insisted that, whether good or bad, his play was undeniably *Spanish*. As a patriotic writer, he had spurned any thought of imitating French models and had instead followed the national dramatic tradition.[62] Reviewing his poetry in 1839, Enrique Gil described Zorrilla's motivation and aims as those of awakening and rejuvenating poetic nationality, shaking off the dust from Spanish traditions, and restoring to the nation that elevated and chivalresque spirit, sadly lost with past glories but the seed of which remained dormant in the hearts of the people (484). Similarly, Bermúdez de Castro referred in his review of Zorrilla's *Cantos del trovador* (1841), to the almost limitless poetic possibilities afforded by Spanish history and tradition.[63] The interest shown by Zorrilla and other writers in Spain's historical past represented far more than a mere literary vogue. It was a preoccupation intimately related to a broader conceptual framework characteristic of the Romantic mind: in Alice Chandler's well-chosen words, the mediaeval revival constituted 'a way of reorganising man into a closely knit and organic social structure that could engage his emotions and loyalties with a wealth of traditions and customs'.[64] The pertinence of these remarks is perhaps further accentuated when we consider what is possibly the best example of the positive critical reaction to Zorrilla's work, a judgement itself loaded with features of historical Romanticism. It belongs to Pablo Piferrer's 1842 review of the second part of *El zapatero y el rey*, a play based on the death of Pedro I at the hands of his half-brother Enrique. Piferrer here praised both Zorrilla's knowledge of much earlier Spanish dramatists and his recreation of a chivalresque and Calderonian dramatic colouring, which had enraptured all of those capable of appreciating the genuine poetry of their country's glorious past. By reviving the flame of poetic enthusiasm with the fire of nationality which had burned so bright in the Golden-Age *comedia*, wrote Piferrer, Zorrilla then 'resucitó esa bizarría y generosidad españolas que fueron las dotes características de nuestros antepasados' ('reawakened the gallantry and nobility which were the characteristic gifts of our ancestors').[65] Piferrer's appraisal, representative of critical reaction to the work of Zorrilla, reveals preoccupations typical of Spanish literary criticism during the period under discussion. The nostalgic references to past glory and to national character and tradition lead once more back to Böhl.

In the same year of 1842 Antonio Gil y Zárate (1793–1861) published the first volumes of his *Manual de literatura*, the most extensive work of its kind to appear during the Romantic period, and one characterised by Schlegelian judgements and perspectives. The opening volume of the *Manual* contained a chapter which enumerated the salient differences between Classicism and Romanticism.[66] Essential changes in aesthetics necessarily accompanied a broader process of transformation which made the respective worlds of ancients and moderns irreconcilably different. Gil y Zárate emphasised that both the old and new aesthetic were valid, but each within its own period. There followed an evocation of Greek society and literature, characterised in the author's view by fatalism, materialism, the supremacy of citizenship over individuality and, in literature, perfection in simplicity. All of these determined Greece's literary precepts, which were not themselves applicable to other societies and periods (I, 142). Modern societies were more complex and diverse; with the replacement of pagan religion by Christianity, materialism was replaced by an inherent spirituality which rejected the beauties of the flesh in favour of beauty of the soul (I, 143). There are notable affinities here with the lectures of the Schlegel brothers, affinities accentuated by Gil y Zárate's evocation of the mediaeval period, an age exemplified in his view by the spiritual values of chivalry, love and honour (I, 149). The author's subsequent definition of Romanticism reinforces the same link with the German Romantic theorists: 'es romántica la [literatura] que nació en la edad media como producto de la nueva civilización que brotó y se arraigó en Europa después de la caída del imperio romano' ('"Romantic" describes the literature born in the Middle Ages as a product of the new civilisation which had sprouted and taken root in Europe after the fall of the Roman empire') (I, 152–3). Employing the arguments outlined above, Gil y Zárate declared in a subsequent section of the *Manual* that the dramatic unities could not be regarded as applicable to modern drama since contemporary writers and the spirit of the age required a broader approach.[67] The second part of the *Manual de literatura*, a historical résumé of Spanish literature, appeared in 1844. In these two volumes, Gil y Zárate continued to follow the premises of Romantic historicism. His appraisal of national character in the opening chapter is reminiscent of Böhl von Faber and Agustín Durán; the author comments: 'El espíritu cristiano y monárquico, el galanteador y pundonoroso, estaban, pues, fuertemente impresos en el carácter español, y debía reflejarse en la literatura' ('The spirit of Christianity and monarchy, of gallantry and honour, was deeply impressed upon the character of the Spaniard, and was necessarily reflected in his literature').[68] This was then the only kind of literature that could accurately reflect Spanish society by representing an embodiment of its essential ideas and principles, and which could thus be regarded as genuinely original and spontaneous in its inspiration.[69]

Beginning his consideration of Golden-Age drama, Gil y Zárate included an extensive quotation from Agustín Durán on Lope de Vega's rejection of Classical precepts.[70] He went on to view Calderón as Spain's greatest dramatist and a man of enduring genius. Furthermore, he insisted that Calderón had done more than just depict the social customs of his age; he had reproduced in his work the spiritual character, the intimate beliefs, the feelings of love and friendship and the language of his own times, all with astonishing accuracy (415). Dealing then with the renewed acclaim enjoyed by the works of Calderón in the nineteenth century, Gil y Zárate drew attention to the enthusiastic reception accorded them in Germany and, in view of the efforts made by German critics to popularise Calderón, felt it appropriate to cite A. W. Schlegel's 'eloquent encomium' of the Spanish dramatist (420).[71] This is subsequently contrasted with Sismondi's less favourable appraisal; for Gil y Zárate, Schlegel had considered Calderón from an elevated poetic sphere and had accordingly placed him at the pinnacle of Romantic achievement, whereas Sismondi had viewed him from the 'prosaic' perspective typical of French neo-Classical drama (425). Sismondi's judgement, he felt, had further been coloured by typically Protestant prejudice against the Roman Catholic religion. Gil y Zárate, equally wary of 'exageraciones' and 'rigorismo', would not fully share either critical judgement, yet he emphasised that literary taste is relative; apparent defects in Calderón's *comedias* disappeared when the reader was capable of an empathetic approach: 'necesitamos transportarnos en idea a la época en que se escribieron' ('we must imaginatively transport ourselves to the age in which they were written') (425–6). The ideas mooted in the *Manual de literatura* were not new, but they do reveal the author's firm adherence to Romantic historicism. The references to A. W. Schlegel strengthen the contention that throughout the work, Gil y Zárate relied upon the basic premises of the Vienna lectures, directly or, as is more likely, indirectly. Meanwhile, this extensive exposition of aesthetics reflects, to an impressive degree, the prevailing nature of Spanish literary criticism.

In summary, trends both in literary criticism and ideas and also in creative work during the years 1837–44 point to a renewed affirmation of the earlier historical Romanticism. The trends that emerge from this later literary criticism provide a clear perception of the development of literary ideas during the period, while the direction taken by Spanish literature in the 1840s reinforces the same assessment. Two of the most wholly Romantic works to appear in Spain, Zorrilla's *Don Juan Tenorio* and Enrique Gil's *El señor de Bembibre*, appeared as late as 1844. We therefore conclude that the only way genuinely to comprehend the character and significance of Romanticism in Spain is to recognise the intimate links between the historical Romanticism inspired by the Schlegels, outlined by Böhl and fully developed during the 1820s, and those Romantic ideas expressed by critics more than a decade later.

6

The religious spirit in literary ideas and the influence of Chateaubriand

The Schlegel brothers assigned to the Christian religion a fundamental rôle in the development of European literature. The religious spirit of the Middle Ages was regarded as the essential difference between literature in the Classical tradition and those new forms of literary expression which they designated 'Romantic'. While the Classical literatures had been a product of the pagan religion of Greece and Rome, and had responded to the senses in their depiction of the physiological aspects of men, Romantic literature was felt to embody the spiritual aspirations which beliefs based upon contemplation and mystery had engendered. The increased preoccupation with individual character displayed in modern literature and the lack of importance attributed by modern writers to questions of external form were both viewed as natural consequences of such a change. Chateaubriand's *Le Génie du christianisme* (1802) had already highlighted, in a masterly and inspired presentation, the poetical qualities inherent in the Christian religion. With the influence later enjoyed by the dramatic lectures of A. W. Schlegel all over Europe came a broad perception of Romantic literature as essentially mediaeval and Christian in character.

As we have seen, the association of Romanticism with Christian belief characterised the promotion of Romantic ideas in Spain during the reign of Ferdinand VII: in Böhl von Faber's emphatic defence of the Christian and monarchical character of Spanish literature and in his vituperation of French Enlightenment philosophy; in Ramón López Soler's view of Christianity as the most important distinguishing factor between the Classical and Romantic literatures; in Agustín Durán's stress upon the changes in religious belief and social custom which had contributed to the character of mediaeval literature, and in his assessment of Spanish literature as the embodiment of an essentially Christian morality and outlook;

and in the distinction likewise made by Juan Donoso Cortés between the Classical world and mediaeval literature and society. A similar stress on religious values was to be a salient feature of literary criticism after 1837. Salvador García, in a brief outline, has referred to the markedly moralistic tone of critical articles during the period, perceiving an attack upon materialism and religious scepticism. He felt that Romantic freedoms were voluntarily limited and restricted in Spain by an intense religious spirit.[1] D. L. Shaw detected, on the other hand, an increasingly potent anti-Romantic reaction, in which several influential writers counselled a return to the soundest moral principles. Whilst acknowledging, in this important article, the direction taken by literary ideas in earlier years, Shaw contended that the situation had since changed, pointing to *Don Alvaro*, *El trovador*, and *El diablo mundo* as works which appeared to exemplify disruptive attitudes and to undermine the established moral order. He found, in the work of several literary commentators in the late 1830s and early 1840s, a 'grave concern for what seemed to them the growing ideological confusion and religious scepticism' which the Romantic movement had engendered, identifying Jaime Balmes as the leader of a philosophico-religious counter-movement which was emerging at this time and naming both Alberto Lista and Donoso Cortés as further protagonists.[2] Shaw then confidently stated that 'by the early 1840s a reaction against romanticism was already well under way'.[3] As I have already shown in this study, however, Balmes, Lista and Donoso all employed the historicist approach to developments in European literature, stressing the need for creative works which could respond constructively to contemporary needs. All three writers distinguished between those elements of the contemporary Romantic movement which they viewed as desirable and those aspects of the new school which they regarded as subversive and anti-social. Whilst Shaw shrewdly highlights a very spirited and consistent defence of traditional values in the critical writing of this period, I feel that he is less accurate in his interpretation of its direction. I prefer to see, in the fervent religious spirit of critical articles during these years, a renewed association of Romanticism with Christianity and a fresh attack upon the materialism and irreligion inherent in the philosophical spirit of eighteenth-century France, and would suggest that this trend denotes a further continuity of outlook between critics of the 1820s and later writers.

A clear indication of the kind of religious spirit that was to characterise Spanish literary criticism in this later Romantic period is to be found in the pages of Jacinto de Salas y Quiroga's magazine *No me olvides* in 1837. In the very first issue Salas y Quiroga made a strident defence of what he felt Romanticism represented.[4] After condemning the 'ridícula fantasmagoría' of horrors which the more extreme Romantic works had brought to the stage, he painted a very different picture of the potential mission which the movement could fulfil. In *No me olvides*, plays like Hugo's *Marie Tudor* and García Gutiérrez's *El paje* were condemned for their immorality, and, in a particularly vehement review article, Salas y Quiroga attacked what he saw as subversive tendencies in Gil y Zárate's *Carlos II el hechizado*. Here, however, he also specified his view of poetic mission:

En los escandalosos tiempos que alcanzamos, cuando los lazos sociales se van de día en día aflojando más, cuando la tendencia del siglo nos arrastra a la anarquía del pensamiento, anarquía que precede siempre a la ruina de los imperios, cuando el germen de la incredulidad y el escepticismo está haciendo estragos, es preciso que el escritor público se revista de toda su dignidad para oponerse al torrente que lo va todo arrasando y que lejos de adular las pasiones populares se alce tremendo como sacerdote de paz que es a predicar una religión de fraternidad.[5]

(In the scandalous times in which we now stand, when social ties are slackening day by day, when the tendency of our age is dragging us towards intellectual anarchy, an anarchy which always precedes the downfall of empires, when the germs of scepticism and unbelief are ravaging us, it is essential that he who writes for the public, invested with his full dignity, oppose this torrent which is carrying all away with it, that, far from pandering to the passions of the masses he stand erect and awesome as the high priest of peace that he truly is and preach his fraternal religion.)

We at once note the religious implications of the writer's rôle and the vision of literature as an integrationist means of establishing constructive social ties and thus stimulating collective moral improvement. This is an issue with which I shall deal in some detail in the following chapter of the present study. Crucial in the above passage also is Salas's allusion to the conceptual pattern of Giambattista Vico (1668–1744). According to the cyclical theory of history expounded in the third and definitive version of Vico's *Scienza nuova* (1744), a chaotic period of degeneracy constituted the final stage in the *corso* or historical development of a given civilisation, from its origins and subsequent efflorescence into its eventual decline. After an inevitable calamitous fall into barbarism, a fresh period of renewal could begin. Vico's work, popularised in Germany by Herder, was attracting renewed attention in Europe thanks to Jules Michelet's French translation of 1827. The Italian thinker's increasingly pervasive influence was given impetus in Spain by a series of articles entitled 'Filosofía de la historia. Juan Bautista Vico', the work of Juan Donoso Cortés and published in *El Correo Nacional* in 1838.[6] Donoso assimilated Vico's system in expatiating upon a philosophy of history in which societies are born, grow, weaken and die, in obedience to 'ciertas leyes inalterables que presiden a su infancia, a su progreso, a su decadencia y a su muerte' ('certain unalterable laws which govern their infancy, their development, their decline and their death') (1, 540). Although Donoso claimed that his subject was entirely new to Spain, Salas, writing a year earlier, seems already aware of the Italian thinker's conceptual framework; perceiving in Spanish society disturbing indications of an imminent descent into degeneracy, he advocates a strengthening of spiritual values. Vico's cyclical theory (in effect a theory of spirals, since each *corso* reflected and incorporated progress made in the previous historical sequence) would have held considerable appeal for those Spanish writers who regarded their age as an apocalyptic period characterised by the collapse of established values, since it afforded an optimistic perspective based upon a regenerative future. Vico's theories allowed traditionalists to view the rationalist philosophies of the eighteenth century, the French Revolution and subsequent violent political changes on a broad front as indications that European civilisation had suffered a relapse into barbarism. This would explain the apocalyptic vision of 'el siglo positivo' ('the positivist age'), the widespread revulsion engendered by materialism, and the emphatic call for a regenerate society founded upon spirituality. Vico's cyclical process involved mankind's inexorable movement between three ages designated 'divine', 'heroic' and 'human'; it was then felt to be time for the historical cycle to begin afresh with a new 'divine age' fortified by the lessons of previous generations.

Salas himself would further consider the unsettling tendency towards religious scepticism in contemporary society in an article entitled 'Religión católica'. He here attributes its cause to the increased preoccupation with material wealth and power; Roman Catholicism had slowly but inexorably lost ground as nations had sought means of accumulating progressively greater wealth and power.[7] This implicit dichotomy between spiritual and material things will assume greater importance later in the present study. What concerns us here is that, in the pages of *No me olvides*, Salas y Quiroga decried the materialism and irreligion of contemporary society and counselled writers to employ in their works the kind of religious spirit which might bring peace and harmony (a key term which recurs in articles of the period) to a world racked by conflict of all kinds. While he condemned what he felt to be the immorality of some Romantic works, it would nevertheless be Romanticism which Salas regarded as the means of fulfilling his desired moral and social mission.

The powerful voice of Enrique Gil y Carrasco was later added to that of Salas y Quiroga. Gil dealt extensively with similar issues in his review of the poetry of Espronceda, published in the *Semanario Pintoresco Español* in July 1840. He felt that nineteenth-century society had inherited a climate of destructive tendencies from the age of the Enlightenment, in which material interests had been allowed to predominate. A reawakening of spirituality, however, had begun to take place; the hearts of men desired feelings and beliefs which reason alone was unable to provide (490–1). The essential antagonism between 'razón' ('reason') and 'alma' ('soul') is both representative and significant. Enrique Gil admits the difficulties involved in the attempt to re-establish traditional values during a period of social and political transition. He thus accounts for the doubt and spiritual anguish which he feels had become a feature of the age, and which were reflected in the creative arts. He concluded that if literature was to be, in accordance with its historical 'mission', the reflection and expression of its age then contemporary writing must needs represent the anguish and fear, the hope and disappointment that ceaselessly racked society (491). Turning to Espronceda's poem 'A Jarifa', Enrique Gil described it as a forthright example of 'esa poesía escéptica, tenebrosa, falta de fe, desnuda de esperanza y rica de desengaño y de dolores, que más bien desgarra el corazón que lo conmueve' ('that sceptical, dark poetry lacking in faith, stripped of hope yet rich in disillusionment and pain, which, rather than stirring the heart, rends it asunder') (495). Despite regarding pessimism as inevitable in a period of philosophical uncertainty, Gil remained adamant that the abandonment of hope could only prove destructive, for it led to an anarchic state of morality. Literature should provide consolation instead of disenchantment, since doubt and despair could fulfil no constructive purpose. Enrique Gil voiced no such reservations about Espronceda's *El estudiante de Salamanca* (1840), referring instead to the adventurous features of the dramatic section and to the poem's 'tragic conclusion' (496). Gil elsewhere expressed admiration for what he considered daring characterisation and plot, as in his commendation of Shakespeare's Lady Macbeth. His criterion appeared to be that daring effects should actively contribute to the writer's presentation of the philosophy underlying his work, and not constitute gratuitous or capricious self-indulgence. What is more surprising is that Gil did not detect in Espronceda's poem the same disruptive attitudes which led him seriously to qualify his approval of Rivas's *Don Alvaro*. The absence of any protest here can probably be best explained by his close friendship with Espronceda. Enrique Gil, along with José García de Villalta, was made responsible for the preparation of the edition of Espronceda's collected poems published in 1839. At the poet's funeral in 1842, Gil would read aloud his poem 'A Espronceda'; the *Eco del Comercio* reported that the voice of Espronceda's 'intimate friend' so trembled with emotion that he could barely articulate.[8]

Antonio Gil y Zárate, in a speech delivered on his admission to the Spanish Academy in 1839 and published in the *Revista de Madrid*, furnishes further evidence of a specific trend in literary criticism.[9] Pointing first to the fundamental rôle played by Christianity in the development of European literature, Gil y Zárate emphasised the replacement of a predominant materialism by an essential spirituality of content, in remarks reminiscent of the lectures of the Schlegel brothers.[10] He regarded attempts to resurrect Classical drama in the modern age as unworkable since the character of civilisation had changed, but felt that the immorality of some contemporary Romantic dramas had in their turn provoked a 'reacción provechosa' ('beneficial reaction').[11] This is exactly the kind of comment which could be misinterpreted without a broader knowledge of critical trends during this period. The type of reaction to which the author refers is not anti-Romantic in the wider sense, but the rejection of subversive tendencies and a return to the concept of spirituality inherent in Romantic historicism. Writing in *El Pensamiento* two years later, Cayetano Cortés perceived the state of religious belief in a given society as the most reliable indicator of the character of its literature. Religious faith is therefore defined as an elevated and superior set of principles which engendered the whole moral, artistic and intellectual life of society.[12] He viewed the relative poverty of ideas in nineteenth-century Spain as directly attributable to the legacy of religious scepticism inherited from the previous age, and insisted that in an irreligious society there could only exist the kind of narrow and inadequate thinking which characterised material self-interest.[13] Cayetano Cortés, like several other Spanish critics of the period, stresses then a dichotomy between material realities and a higher sphere of spiritual activity. A similar viewpoint found expression in Salvador Bermúdez de Castro's preface to his *Ensayos poéticos*, one of the most important volumes of verse to appear in the *annus mirabilis* of 1840. Bermúdez (1817–83) described his poems as an intimate record of personal experience, and felt their character to have been largely determined by the spirit of the age, one of social and political upheaval, of ideological doubt and uncertainty. Bermúdez writes in strident terms of 'una sociedad que se cuartea para caer' ('a society which is breaking up and about to collapse'), in which a series of brilliant theories had momentarily commanded young men's imaginative allegiance before being cast contemptuously aside into the 'insatiable abyss of delirium'.[14] Presenting his reader with an apocalyptic vision Bermúdez, like Enrique Gil, felt that the melancholy and often despairing tones of modern poetry were the product of surrounding social, political and metaphysical turmoil. The poet necessarily responded to all-pervading confusion, for where could he turn in this dark labyrinth where every path petered out after a few faltering steps? Of what could he write but his own melancholia and doubt, which were representative and emblematic of contemporary society?[15] Society is viewed as, quite literally, directionless, and the poet as a being desperately in need of guiding principles. Nevertheless, Bermúdez expounded with equal clarity what he felt to be the constructive moral purpose to be followed by poetry at the present time; poetry today, he insisted, ought to sing of recollections of the past and of a faith sadly lost.[16] The change in tone between Bermúdez's own compositions of 1835 and 1836, years of an impressionable adolescence, and those which he had penned at a later date reflects his own commitment to this ideal. More significantly, Bermúdez's words anticipate with some accuracy the critical reaction to Zorrilla's collection *Cantos del trovador* of the following year, which would be felt to provide essential spiritual reassurance. The poet Gabriel García Tassara regarded

Zorrilla's collection as a superior bastion against an 'atheist literature', against menacing anarchic writing contemptuous of religious
ideals and of virtuous feelings, and concluded that through an
imaginative evocation of the past 'se deja de ser escéptico y materia-
lista' ('one ceases to feel sceptical and materialistic').[17]

The moral intention underlying thematic concern with past
history and tradition, at which I hinted in the previous chapter, now
acquires greater clarity. From all of the material cited above, we can
glean evidence of a common approach on the part of Spanish writers
to the broader issues involved in the conflict between faith and
reason. Literature, and specifically Romantic literature, is regarded
as spiritual in character and therefore capable of stimulating collective moral improvement in a world suffering from the breakdown
of traditional beliefs. As in the articles of Böhl, the philosophical
framework which formed an essential part of the age of the
Enlightenment is consistently blamed for the lack of social stability
and for moral degeneracy, even for intellectual aridity. Those disturbing tendencies which found expression in the work of some
Romantic writers are viewed as the inevitable consequence of the
earlier collapse of traditional values.

The theoretical framework used by critics in an attempt to
counter the rampant materialism and religious scepticism of their
age had its origins in the work of Chateaubriand. The French
nobleman's treatment of religion had exerted a potent influence
upon Romantic writers, and the emotional thrust of *Le Génie du
christianisme* involved its association of the spirituality of Catholicism
with the melancholy of the Romantic temperament. In Chateaubriand's response to Nature, we can detect the pervasive influence of
Rousseau. While both writers presented their readers with a
Romantic religion of the heart, Chateaubriand did not link the
beauties of Nature with vague notions of a natural religion, incipi-
ently oecumenical and independent of any institutionalised Church,
as Rousseau had done. Instead, natural beauty assumed emotional
significance as incontrovertible evidence of the existence of the true
Creator, and appeared as just one instance of the supremely poetical
qualities of Catholicism. For Chateaubriand, the Catholic doctrine
of mystery, the nature of miracle, liturgical ceremony and its accom-
panying music, the Gothic cathedral, Christian monuments and
ruins, and popular religious custom, were all integral elements in the
sublime poetry of belief. As A. W. Raitt has observed: 'The stress in

Le Génie du christianisme is laid on the beauty and consolations of religion, with reasoning relegated to a subordinate position and logic replaced by the most personal and emotional kind of rhetoric ... The philosophic disputes of the eighteenth century are dismissed as arid technicalities, of interest only to "les savants", and instead "le coeur" is extolled as the sole arbiter.'[18] The work was intended primarily as a response to the ideas of the *Encyclopédie*, which Chateaubriand regarded as a new Tower of Babel constructed from science and reason. The author strove to combat the charges of obscurantism and moral criminality that had been levelled against the Church, and to prove on the contrary that 'de toutes les religions qui ont jamais existé, la religion chrétienne est la plus poétique, la plus humaine, la plus favorable à la liberté, aux arts et aux lettres'.[19]

Chateaubriand's work had provided inspiration for earlier Spanish critics, and would continue to do so after 1837. Spanish translations of *Le Génie du christianisme* had been published in Madrid (1806 and 1818), Valencia (1832) and Barcelona (1842). Spanish editions of Chateaubriand's Complete Works were later published in Valencia (30 vols., 1843–50) and in Madrid (19 vols., 1847–50). There is considerable evidence to suggest that *Le Génie du christianisme* was well known to Spanish writers. Most immediately redolent of such inspiration is a piece by Balmes entitled 'Apuntes sobre Chateaubriand', which formed part of a series of fragments under the heading 'Apuntes de teoría literaria', certainly written by 1838.[20] Balmes felt that *Le Génie du christianisme* had appeared at a crucial time in France, where religious faith had been in decline for much of the eighteenth century. His assessment of events in that country is reminiscent of the account given by Chateaubriand himself, and displays the same kind of invective levelled against the *philosophes* by Böhl.[21] Balmes describes, in an effusive passage, the exile of Chateaubriand and the nature of his religious inspiration. He views Chateaubriand's return to France in messianic terms, regarding him as a prophet rekindling the flame of faith. Finding everywhere the gory imprint of atheism but hearing all around the sound of celestial music, the French nobleman had passionately sung the beauties of religion, had revealed its intimate relationship with the natural world and, through divine powers of utterance, had revealed to men the mysteries of this golden chain linking Heaven and earth (VIII, 477–8). Balmes here displays the same 'peremptory emotional certitude' felt by A. W. Raitt to be a consistent stylistic feature of

Chateaubriand's work.[22] The youthful Balmes was emotionally inflamed by the figure of Chateaubriand, and expresses a lyrical evocation of what he sees as the French writer's spiritual mission. The passage cited is part of a much longer section later included with only minor changes in Balmes's major work *El protestantismo comparado con el catolicismo* (1842–4).[23] Meanwhile, his assimilation of the principal features of *Le Génie du christianisme* is again evident in the conclusion of the earlier piece, where he reiterates Chateaubriand's association of religious feeling, and specifically man's awareness of his mortality, with Romantic melancholy; Balmes professes that 'esa tristeza, ese dolor, es grande, es poético en grado eminente' ('this sadness, this pain, is elevated, is poetical in the highest degree') (VIII, 479). I feel this entire piece to be important in its indication of the influences under which the young Balmes was writing. The man who was to become a distinguished neo-Catholic philosopher displays a fundamental attitude which immediately leads us to link him, in the Spanish context, with Böhl and López Soler. Both earlier critics had written in similar vein of events occurring in France during the last years of the eighteenth century. Like several other Spanish writers of the period, Balmes felt that the early part of the nineteenth century had witnessed a gradual rebirth, in poetic composition, of religious feeling and spirituality. In another fragment of the 'Apuntes de teoría literaria' he affirmed that poetry, an intimate imaginative record of society, had, in the early years of the nineteenth century, begun to acquire a religious tone which had since become accentuated and which would continue to flourish.[24] In his later essay 'De la originalidad', published in 1842, Balmes would adopt the historicist view of literature. Concentrating upon how unsuited to the present times was a literary school whose inspiration was derived from pagan mythology, he regarded the Christian religion as a distinguishing factor between the respective literatures of the Classical and modern worlds and praised Chateaubriand, who had shown how futile was the imitation of the spirit of Classical authors by modern writers (VIII, 238).

Between 1844 and 1846, Balmes was editor of a weekly magazine called *El Pensamiento de la Nación*.[25] Not surprisingly, it was characterised by its robust defence of Catholicism and its condemnation of irreligion. The first issue contained an important proclamation of Roman Catholic doctrine, more than ever necessary in order to 'reorganizar esta nación desquiciada' ('reorganise this unhinged society').[26] In the fifth issue, Balmes himself contributed a lengthy article entitled 'La Religión en España', in which he considered the ideological developments of the preceding decade. While irreligious ideas had been rampant, their capacity for harm, he claimed, had been effectively restricted in a society which instinctively rejected them. Spain had suffered less than had the majority of countries from the revolutionary spirit then dominant in a Europe now ashamed of having listened to eighteenth-century philosophers.[27] The French *philosophes* characteristically bear the brunt of the attack, yet Balmes chooses to emphasise the inherently religious character of the Spanish people, an essential part of the ideas outlined by Böhl and Durán.

When we turn to the work of Juan Donoso Cortés, we find that Chateaubriand's influence is evident in his 'El clasicismo y el romanticismo' of 1838. Donoso here reiterates the premise that, while Classicism was characterised by its preoccupation with external form, Romanticism was spiritual in its inspiration. First established in the new cultural ambiance of the Middle Ages, Romantic literature came to exemplify a 'culto del espíritu' derived from the overwhelming changes wrought by the Christian faith, so that modern-day literature, like its contemporary society, was especially concerned with things of the spirit. In his assessment, Donoso distinguishes between the two differing Romantic currents. He protests against excess as strongly as so many other critics, but remains committed to his view of Romantic spirituality, which he felt had elevated the minds of men (1, 407). This section of Donoso's essay may appear contradictory, since the above assertion is immediately preceded by a condemnation of the excesses of contemporary theatre. Donoso explicitly directs his attack upon 'los dramaturgos de nuestros días' ('our modern-day dramatists'), presumably a reference to the wilder dramatic productions; their extravagances are therefore contrasted with the spirituality which he views as a general characteristic of modern literature. Donoso's comments furthermore invite direct comparison, in terms of imagery, with those later voiced by Cayetano Cortés.[28] Donoso then writes of the superiority of Romantic idealism, inspired by Christian faith, to the abstractions of 'absurd rhymesters who call themselves Classicists' (1, 407). He employs the full force of Chateaubriand's emphatic vision to associate Schlegelian Romanticism with the Christian religion. Christianity was eminently poetic, and it was the

Romantic literature of the Middle Ages which lent it expression. Apart from certain immoral aberrations, contemporary Romanticism retained its original spiritual character.

In October of 1838, just two months after the first appearance of 'El clasicismo y el romanticismo', Donoso published a further series of three articles in *El Correo Nacional* under the heading 'Consideraciones sobre el cristianismo' (1, 573–82). In these articles, he expressed the familiar view of Christian belief in conflict with the philosophical rationalism of the eighteenth century, and detected a renewal of faith which he perceived as evidence of the defeat of rationalism and irreligion. Donoso saw Christianity as a bastion in a chaotic world dominated by 'la despiadada guerra que la razón humana mueve en el presente siglo a todo lo que es augusto y estable' ('the merciless war waged in the present age by human reason against all that is august and stable') (1, 573). In the midst of tumult and confusion, the people turned instinctively to the Church for protection and salvation. Reflecting the spirit of Chateaubriand, Donoso was at this time determinedly combating rationalism and irreligion. It was a campaign which in no way constituted a crusade against the alleged immoralities of Romanticism; Donoso continued to support the principles of Romantic historicism, and levelled his attacks against the *philosophes* and their adherents.

El Pensamiento de la Nación of Balmes, mentioned earlier, was not the first magazine of its kind. Between October and December of 1842, Madrid had seen the publication of *El Arpa del Creyente*, edited by Francisco Navarro Villoslada, who was later to write a series of historical novels much in the style of Enrique Gil y Carrasco. The second issue of this periodical contained an article by José Vincente Carabantes entitled 'Literatura religiosa'. Prominent in the article was a consideration of the effect of *Le Génie du christianisme* upon post-revolutionary France. The work had appeared, commented Carabantes, in the aftermath of the chaos that was the French Revolution; society was divided, and the Revolution had not yet concluded its terrible task. Chateaubriand's work, however, was received with eager enthusiasm.[29] Carabantes went on to compare that scenario with the one presently being experienced in Spain. A succession of political disasters had brought untold suffering and bloodshed, the corrosive spirit of the age had in many cases destroyed the possibility of spiritual consolation, and 'una literatura delirante importada de tierra extraña ha manchado su vista con los más espantosos cuadros de impureza y liviandad' ('a literature of delirium imported from foreign lands has stained the sight of our own with the most horrendous scenes of impurity and lewdness'). This last is an obvious reference to the elements of French Romantic drama widely felt to exemplify moral depravity and social rebellion. In such a climate, protested Carabantes, in phraseology wholly comparable with that earlier employed by Salas y Quiroga, Spain yearned for a consoling voice capable of pouring balm upon its wounds, still open to the inclemency of the age.[30] We encounter then another clarion call for a kind of literature which might aid a revival of faith and bring spiritual recovery. Worthy of mention also is the characteristically religious vocabulary which Carabantes, in common with other critics, chooses to employ; the term 'siglo' used to describe the secular world is a good example. Writing in *El Laberinto* in 1844, Antonio Ferrer del Río, biographer of many Spanish Romantic writers, made a further lyrical presentation of the impact of *Le Génie du christianisme*. Oppressed by scepticism and fearful of atheism, the minds of men had falteringly sought a guiding light, a protective haven, and had found both in the work of Chateaubriand.[31] Like Bermúdez de Castro, Ferrer del Río writes emblematically of a lack of direction and the necessity of a spiritual guide.

The influence exerted by Chateaubriand must now be clear. The French writer is often mentioned by name, and his efforts in the Christian cause widely praised. I feel that it would not be an exaggeration to view the religious spirit revealed in the critical articles of this period as an indication of the impact made by the principal concepts of *Le Génie du christianisme* in the minds of Spanish writers. For example, the tone of numerous passages in the critical articles of Enrique Gil y Carrasco is highly suggestive. Although Enrique Gil did not write specifically on the work of Chateaubriand, he nevertheless refers to the French writer on four different occasions. In perhaps the most significant of these references, he describes Chateaubriand as 'Cisne del cristianismo' (577); the employment of an image, the swan, which Enrique Gil in his lyric poetry more than once applied to himself, suggests that Chateaubriand's work possessed intimate meaning for him. Enrique Gil displays a familiarity not only with *Le Génie du christianisme* but also with Chateaubriand's work on the Congress of Verona and with the *Essai sur la littérature anglaise* (415, 420, 423–4).

In 1837, in his preface to the first edition of José Zorrilla's poetry, Nicomedes-Pastor Díaz referred to a mission which he felt that the younger poet was to fulfil. Díaz's view of Zorrilla's achievement brings reminiscences of the kind of literary mission which other writers had perceived in the efforts of Chateaubriand; Zorrilla is described as the first Spanish poet of his day to have sought in traditional sources and religious beliefs 'los gérmenes de grandeza y sociabilidad que abrigan' ('the seeds of grandeur and sociability which reside in them'); he had realised that the future was to be built on the bedrock of the past (I, 112). Díaz then highlights the regenerative power of cultural tradition and outlines his argument by employing a typically organicist image in 'germen', factors which serve to establish a link with the German Romantic theorists, and especially with Herder.[32]

Trends in creative writing dovetail with this salient feature of literary criticism. One work immediately reminiscent of the spirit of Chateaubriand is Enrique Gil's *Anochecer en San Antonio de la Florida*, published in two parts in *El Correo Nacional* in November of 1838 (253–60). In this largely autobiographical piece, a young writer called Ricardo, contemplating suicide after a series of personal tragedies, enters the chapel of San Antonio de la Florida in Madrid during an evening walk. Among the angels in the frescoes by Goya which adorn the ceiling of the chapel, Ricardo appears to recognise his dead love, Angélica. She brings him words of consolation which restore his faith and awaken in him spiritual resignation. The entire piece is written in a compelling elegiac style, while Enrique Gil successfully combines 'tristeza cristiana' and Romantic melancholy. D. G. Samuels has drawn attention to the apparent influence of Chateaubriand upon Enrique Gil in this piece.[33] Lyric poetry, as the most subjective of literary genres and consequently the most probable vehicle for the expression of a writer's pessimism, would be the kind of writing most likely to reflect the kind of disruptive attitudes which might fuel critical outrage. Admittedly, the overriding tone of the poetry of Enrique Gil, like that of Díaz, Bermúdez, Campoamor and a number of other contemporary writers, is one of profound melancholy. However, the often despairing vision of the world in these poems is tempered by religious faith and resignation. Those poems which represented a protest against the divine order, such as Espronceda's *El diablo mundo*, constituted a very small minority. In this respect, I would wholly concur with the comments of Juan

Ayuso Rivera, who saw few indications of untempered despair in the Spanish Romantic lyric. Fundamentally, he commented, virtually all Spanish Romantic writers were Roman Catholic believers. Their faith led them to put forward a religious solution to the philosophical doubts and quandaries which their verse contained. Unlike their French or English counterparts, on few occasions did they allow themselves to lapse into despair.[34] Meanwhile, the historical narrative poems of Rivas and Zorrilla contain no hint of metaphysical crisis. The work of the latter was, on the contrary, felt to serve a boldly constructive purpose. Antonio Ferrer del Río, in his biographical essay on Zorrilla, wrote lyrically of faith, God and immortality as the 'gérmenes fructíferos y vivificadores que atesora la mente de Zorrilla' ('fruitful and life-giving seeds which are stored like a treasure in the mind of Zorrilla'); once more the presence of organicist imagery should not be ignored. Ferrer del Río goes on to describe elements of Zorrilla's poetry as pure and fertile sources which had wrought salutary effects, as broad and rich seams of virtue.[35] This evocation of Zorrilla's work as writing which had brought comfort to those broken in spirit through worldly tribulation provides an immediate link with other contemporary critics. Switching our attention to a different genre, the type of drama being widely promoted during the same period was equally unlikely to have engendered religious scepticism and ideological confusion. Works like Zorrilla's *Don Juan Tenorio* would appear calculated rather to encourage and stimulate religious faith and confidence in redemption. Finally, the historical novel, which remained highly popular in the 1840s, was characterised by a concentration upon Spanish themes and reflected what were felt to be traditional Spanish values. After the demise in Spain of French Romantic drama, attacked by both Classicist and conservative Romantic critics, Spanish literature continued to follow the direction suggested by the ideas of the Schlegels and of Chateaubriand. The influence of *Le Génie du christianisme* would extend into further decades, exemplified by some of Bécquer's remarks in the *Historia de los templos de España*. Bécquer began the important introductory section of his volume on Toledo with the observation 'La tradición religiosa es el eje de diamante sobre el que gira nuestro pasado' ('Religious tradition is the diamantine axis on which our historical past revolves'). If this appears representative of earlier positive critical reaction to the work of Zorrilla, Bécquer's evocative description of the church of San Juan de los Reyes yields an apprehension of the pervasive influence of Chateaubriand; the deep silence of its marvellous cloister, wrote Bécquer, made this shrine of art and tradition 'un copioso manantial de recuerdos, de enseñanza y de poesía' ('a plentiful spring of memories, of instruction and of poetry').[36]

The religious spirit in literary ideas undoubtedly possessed political, as well as intellectual and emotional, implications. The compelling attraction of *Le Génie du christianisme*, and the passionate evaluation of the work as a restorative in an irreligious society, had much to do with a perceived attack on religion which appeared to be creating, in Spain, a scenario comparable to that encountered by Chateaubriand in post-revolutionary France. I refer to Juan Alvarez Mendizábal's legislation of 1836 and 1837. In 1836 all monastic property was converted into national assets, while in 1837 Mendizábal proposed the sale of the landed endowment of the secular church and the abolition of tithes.[37] Mendizábal came to power in 1836 boasting that he was neither an aristocrat nor a politician but a businessman, something which would have proved anathema to idealistic young writers who abjured materialism and all its works. The shadow of the financier who expropriated church property to pay off the national debt – and thus restore the borrowing power of a bankrupt government – would have loomed large over literary men who were insisting upon the transcendent value of religious ideals and advocating a literature which celebrated and revitalised religious tradition. Balmes's reference to the majestic ancient churches shattered by the hammer-blows of barbarism (VIII, 477–8) acquires considerable immediacy written as it was in Spain in 1838: Mendizábal's measures would lead, in Madrid alone, to the disappearance of forty-four churches and monasteries, nine of them sold as building sites.[38]

In this chapter we have seen a recognition of the chaotic character of the age, involving a protest against the rationalist theories perceived as its cause, and a call for a literature which could promote a revival of religious faith. It constitutes very much the defence of traditional Catholic values highlighted by Shaw. However, it should not be seen as indicative of an anti-Romantic reaction, but rather as an attack upon the rationalist doctrines of the *Encyclopédie* and the whole philosophical spirit of eighteenth-century France. Authentic Romanticism is meanwhile regarded as essentially spiritual and is closely associated with the Christian religion. The influence of Chateaubriand played a fundamental rôle in developing this perception. While it is, on numerous occasions, difficult to assert categorically the direct influence of the French writer, it is equally hard not to suspect that the ideas of *Le Génie du christianisme* created a powerful impression upon Spanish writers. Most importantly of all, the same men who display this kind of religious spirit in their critical articles appear elsewhere as consistent supporters of the principles of Schlegelian Romanticism. There are strong links with the character of critical articles of the 1820s, while the fierce attack upon rationalism and religious scepticism leads us back to Böhl. As in the previous decade, Romantic thought in Spain remained traditionalist in character, in accordance with what Spanish writers had always felt Romanticism to represent: a spiritual literature which was the product of Christian belief and which was directly opposed to rationalism and materialism.

7

The perception of literature's role in society

Herder had stressed that the essence of history lay in the cultural evolution of nations and peoples, emphasising the developmental character of historical change and the organic manner in which it occurred. In the early nineteenth century, after Madame de Staël's pioneering study *De la littérature considérée dans ses rapports avec les institutions sociales* (1800) and the lectures of the Schlegel brothers, the emphasis in literary criticism shifted more and more away from the judgement of excellence according to immutable criteria, and towards an understanding of the particular factors – social, historical and religious – which underlay and influenced creative writing in different countries and in different periods. A major Romantic idea was that artistic taste was neither universal nor eternal, but had varied in ways intimately related to contemporaneous changes in social order. For the Romantic artist, a literary work was necessarily influenced and conditioned by the 'spirit of the age'.

Böhl von Faber, writing in the wake of the Napoleonic invasion, had viewed a return to the Christian and monarchical spirit inherent in Spain's characteristic literary forms as a means of combating the rationalist doctrines of the Enlightenment, which he regarded as a threat to social stability. In his emphasis upon 'piedad cristiana' and 'sana doctrina', Böhl was in effect subscribing to the traditional idea of literature as moral guide. Ramón López Soler, writing in 1823–4, shared Böhl's view of literature as the manifestation of intellectual progress. Appalled by the prejudicial effects upon society of the French Revolution, he looked to the promotion of religious ideals and healthy morals by his own generation as a potential solution to social strife. The return to constitutional government after the death of Ferdinand VII, however, was accompanied by a concomitant change of emphasis in the work of some literary critics, away from unqualified nostalgia for past certainties towards a more rigorous preoccupation with literature as the reflection of its contemporary society. Alcalá Galiano, in his prologue to Rivas's *El moro expósito*, viewed Romanticism as a specifically contemporary movement and stressed that Spain should possess its own original and spontaneous literature. This would not only reflect the Spanish *Volksgeist* but respond also to the character and aspirations of nineteenth-century society. Larra had insisted that the analytical and positivist spirit of the age was not necessarily detrimental to literary creativity. Instead, he felt it was essential that the aspirations of a radically new social order find meaningful expression in creative writing. Yet if Larra viewed the purpose of literature within society as the communication of relevant and significant moral truths, the nihilism of works like Dumas's *Antony* convinced him that moral freedoms or 'libertad moral' should not be unlimited. Certain of the French Romantic dramas had shown that the theatre could corrupt.

D. L. Shaw has pointed to the widespread revulsion awakened by the negative vision of works like *Antony*, highlighting critical awareness of the deeper issues underlying what was perceived as a profoundly disturbing literary phenomenon. Shaw drew attention to the reactions of both Donoso Cortés and Larra to works which seemed to embody a crisis of belief.[1] The reaction provoked by what were consistently seen as anti-social tendencies in drama, the influence of a critic of the stature of Larra, and the experience of life in a period of rapid political change all contributed to a fresh perception of literature's role in society in critical articles published in the years from 1837. While critics continued to apply the Schlegelian distinction between Classicism and Romanticism, they viewed the character of contemporary literature, especially of lyric poetry and drama, as a product of the philosophical, social and political factors which had influenced the current generation. This trend is exemplified by the forthright comments made by Alberto Lista in his series of three articles entitled 'Estado actual de la literatura europea' (I, 31–7). If the title suggests a broad perspective, it is France which receives the greater part of the author's attention. The tone of these articles is firmly established in Lista's opening comment that contemporary literature was an inevitable consequence of eighteenth-century 'filosofismo'; materialism had stifled literary genius, since genius could not exist without enthusiasm nor enthusiasm without religious beliefs and convictions (I, 31). Again it is the *philosophes* who bear the brunt of his sharp attack: the pejorative term 'filosofismo' is revealing. For Lista, as for the majority of Spanish critics, it was not Romanticism but philosophical rationalism which had created a despairing literature lacking in vital convictions. The stifling of poetic inspiration by a doctrine excessively dependent upon materialism did not in his view constitute the whole of the damage caused by eighteenth-century philosophy. Lista subsequently pointed to disruption of a much more far-reaching kind, alleging that the *philosophes* had, under the pretence of reform, determinedly set out to destroy existing values and beliefs. Their *disolvente* ideas (and Lista here uses this term, used to describe the 'corrosive' effect of ideas which undermined established beliefs) had been the cause of fruitless carnage, since the supposed reformers had failed to implant a fresh scale of values to replace that which they had destroyed (1, 31). Referring to Madame de Staël's complaint concerning the lack of creative inspiration in the early years of the century, Lista insisted that the prevailing climate of crisis and upheaval, social, political and philosophical, had been responsible for this. Like other Spanish critics, he establishes the idea of irreconcilable conflict between, on the one hand, the essentially spiritual nature of creative imagination, and, on the other, materialist philosophy, charged with the crime of 'demoliendo poco a poco todas las ilusiones, todas las ideas, todos los sentimientos del corazón humano' ('demolishing little by little all the aspirations, all the ideas, all the feelings of the human heart') (1, 32). Jaime Balmes had written in a similarly scathing manner of men who believed themselves to be progressive and up-to-date solely because they had swallowed whole the works of the eighteenth century, of men who saw in society nothing more than material self-interest (VIII, 460). Lista's position is meanwhile close to that adopted by Böhl von Faber in the latter's own rejection of the materialism and irreligion of the *philosophes*. Böhl had likewise emphasised the spirituality of literary creation and appreciation, regarding it as incompatible with a rationalist philosophy. Lista had now witnessed the arrival, particularly on the stage, of exactly the kind of *disolvente* works which Böhl had striven to combat. He attributed their appearance not only to philosophical concerns but also to the corrupting power of ambition and to disregard for existing literary models. He sums up the unfortunate result, commenting that nothing was sure and certain any more; everything was problematic. What outraged Lista was that the most monstrous depravity, in literature as in morality and in politics, now found some degree of approbation and inspired some form of jealous imitation (1, 33); the disruptive tendencies found in certain contemporary works he regarded as the regrettable but inevitable consequence of the baneful influence of the age. Nevertheless, Lista departed from this pessimistic tone in concluding the last of the three articles, asserting that a period of recuperation had finally begun; Spanish society was witnessing a slow but sure recovery of 'las ideas morales que antes la sostenían, y las creencias que se solicitó en vano destruir para siempre' ('the moral ideas which used to support it, and the beliefs which some had sought in vain to destroy for ever') (1, 37).

A crucial element in these articles is Lista's claim that philosophical rationalism was the true cause of the depravity which characterised much of contemporary literature, or, to use his favoured term, 'la literatura actual'. Elsewhere in Lista's work, this last phrase is consistently used to describe the kind of Romanticism typified by the dramas of Hugo and Dumas. 'De lo que hoy se llama romanticismo', published in 1839, was a piece almost exclusively devoted to what Lista regarded as the aberrations of these two dramatists.[2] He alleged their calculated besmirching of monarchy and religion was part of an attempt to destroy every guiding social and moral principle. The furious Lista went on to accuse the French writers of wishing to recreate that demented state of affairs which had caused the catastrophic events of the French Revolution (11, 39). an anonymous reviewer writing in *El Pensamiento* in 1841 would voice a similar opinion in declaring that Dumas's morality placed him among the disruptive grouping spawned by the French Revolution, garbed in eighteenth-century scepticism.[3] Lista himself claimed that the plays of Hugo and Dumas were incompatible with the values of a Christian and monarchical society, values which he felt authentic Romanticism to represent; hence Lista's distinction between 'el romanticismo', based largely upon Schlegelian theory, and 'lo que hoy se llama romanticismo', certain works fashionably called 'Romantic'. His condemnation of the latter is often misconstrued as an anti-Romantic declaration.

A further illustration that philosophical rationalism, and not Romanticism, was regarded as responsible for all kinds of contemporary uncertainty, is provided by Fernando de la Vera's article 'Verdadera poesía'. This was published in Salas y Quiroga's *No me olvides* in 1837. Vera insisted that it was not Romanticism that had dragged contemporary society into a mire and had seriously weakened social cohesion; the causes of this nefarious situation ought to be sought elsewhere, in philosophy rather than in literature.[4] In blaming a particular climate of ideas, rather than the character of literature, for the degeneracy which existed in many spheres of society, Vera was echoing an opinion earlier expressed by Larra.[5] This was not to deny the necessarily intimate relationship between literature and society. Cayetano Cortés, writing in *El Pensamiento* in 1841, stressed this latter point; it was inconceivable, he declared, that a society in turmoil should produce a literature of a solid, stable and peaceful character indicative of ideological continuity.[6] For Cayetano Cortés as for Lista, the violent and traumatic nature of much contemporary literature must be seen as a legacy of the prevailing spirit of the age. Like Lista, Cayetano Cortés was not entirely pessimistic. He felt that, despite the climate of materialism, sensibility continued to reside in a select minority; in his words, certain individuals enjoyed an accentuated spirituality, the poetic spark was struck most powerfully in a small number of sensitive souls, and idealism appealed to a few privileged intellects.[7] The comment embodies the Romantic idea of a sensitive élite, able to overcome the philistine limitations of contemporary society through their gift of sensibility. The dichotomy between crude materialism and poetic spirituality thus recurs in the articles of both Lista and Cayetano Cortés.

A further attack upon contemporary values came in a speech made by Javier de Burgos and published in the *Revista de Teatros* in 1841. Burgos subscribed to the idea of literature as the expression of its society, adducing the examples of ancient Greece and the France of Louis XIV, and drew conclusions even more disconcerting than those affirmed by Lista from the example of the present age: with the existing social order undermined and traditional beliefs called into question, wrote Burgos, society was a chaos that had no imaginative expression.[8] Thus, he argued, the dramatic school of Hugo and Dumas was indicative only of the abrupt political changes that had affected France, and so could provide no coherent philosophy, but only violent confusion. If Burgos had opted for a more reasoned analysis, he would have realised, along with other Spanish critics, that the confused and often despairing vision underlying many contemporary works was itself a product of the uncertainties of the age, and represented, in this sense, the expression in literature of preoccupations typical of the period.

Fermín Gonzalo Morón, writing in 1842, linked the violent excesses of French Romantic drama with the complexion of French society during the same period, an age whose characteristic features had been corruption and vice. 'Enciclopedismo' and the Revolution, continued Gonzalo Morón, had bred anarchy and depravity.[9] There followed a long tirade against the immorality and licentiousness of the drama of Hugo and Dumas.[10] Since Spain was inevitably affected to a degree by French taste, 'se ha hecho sentir algo aunque por corto tiempo en nuestra literatura el depravado gusto y maléfica tendencia de la francesa' ('the depraved taste and pernicious tendencies of French literature have, although only for a short time, made themselves felt in our own').[11] Once more the excesses of contemporary French drama are seen as a consequence of the immorality and irreligion provoked by philosophical rationalism, and not as a product of Romantic aesthetics.[12]

References to the chaotic circumstances of the age, enunciated in passionate terms by several critics, reflect an erratic state of political affairs. After the *sargentada* of 1836 the persecution of political opponents was again rife, while the rising had itself encouraged revolutionary threats to the established social order. The Carlist war ended only in 1839, long after Mendizábal's attempt to resolve it by financial means had failed. At the same time Spain had known no stable government since 1835; a succession of short-lived administrations, usually lasting no more than a few months and terminated by the intervention of the military or the Crown, left no room for complacency. While short on specifics, the denunciations made by writers like Lista and Burgos reveal an understandable lack of confidence. Critical response was not, however, one of unmitigated pessimism. Affirmation of the intimate relationship between literature and its contemporary society led to much more than the impassioned disavowal of rationalist philosophy and condemnation of contemporary French drama which I have already detailed. An important feature of critical writing was the formulation of a concept of 'regeneración', dependent upon the power of the creative imagination and involving the promotion of a spiritual literature which would assuage feelings of doubt and despair and stimulate social recovery. The earliest consistent promotion of the idea came from Jacinto de Salas y Quiroga. It formed a prominent part of the prospectus of Salas y Quiroga's magazine *No me olvides*, which first appeared in May of 1837 and which succeeded *El Artista* as the defender of the Romantic cause. In this 'Prospecto', Salas y Quiroga employs the phrase 'regeneración social', and vividly outlines his interpretation of the term: an idealistic new generation, dynamic and constructive in attacking retrenchment and fanaticism of all kinds and acting for the common good, creating the sublime spectacle of 'el germen de la ventura social dominando el universo corrompido' ('the seed of social happiness dominating a corrupt universe').[13] Salas y Quiroga's reference to political fanaticism implies both Carlists and radicals, while Mendizábal was frequently a target for such accusations. Important also is the inclusion of both pen and sword as arms brandished by these modern-day knights. Salas further outlines the activities undertaken by the young generation: to end mean-spirited rivalry, to cultivate a healthy spirit of fraternity, to extinguish hatred arising from misunderstanding, to choke off every form of evil and to reveal to men the goodness which existed throughout Creation.[14] His vision of social regeneration is therefore based upon the concept of shared ideals within society, ideals which it was the writer's task to inspire and promote. As such, it is an integrationist approach which owed much to the impact in Spanish of German Romantic idealism. In the editorial written for the first issue of *No me olvides*, Salas is more specific about the rôle to be played by literature in his regenerative vision. Writers are called upon to fulfil a crucial mission at a time of social and political uncertainty, when corruption and perversity appear to exert universal dominance. Salas y Quiroga therefore abjures the traditional idea of literature as simply a form of recreation for the imagination; rather, he insists, 'la misión del poeta es más noble, más augusta' ('the poet's mission is more noble, more august').[15] It was for this reason that young writers of the day had recognised the futility and irrelevance of the trappings of neo-Classicism, a literature which could not respond to the needs of Spanish society in the nineteenth century.[16] It was instead historical Romanticism which the author felt could fulfil his envisaged mission, closely bound up with a revival of faith; he writes, in organicist terms, 'es el romanticismo un manantial de consuelo y pureza, el germen de las virtudes sociales, el paño de lágrimas que vierte el inocente, el perdón de las culpas, el lazo que debe unir a todos los seres' ('Romanticism is a spring of purity and consolation, the seed of social virtue, able to dry the tears of the innocent, to absolve guilt, to bind all men together').[17] Salas y Quiroga's phraseology immediately suggests a linkage both with the idealistic premises of Spanish Krausism and with the concept of 'spiritual doctors' favoured by Azorín, Ganivet, and other intellectuals of the Generation of 1898.[18] When Salas makes reference to the rôle of writers as 'predicadores de la santa doctrina' ('preachers of sacred doctrine') the suggestion is reinforced, as we are reminded both of the messianic fervour with which Julián Sanz del Río and Francisco Giner de los Ríos would later disseminate the gospel of Krausism, and of the superior status of *vates* accorded to writers, especially poets, by Rubén Darío and the Spanish Modernists. Sanz del Río had arrived in Madrid in 1836, and thus could have been familiar with ideas put forward in *No me olvides* and other contemporary periodicals. More specifically, the following passage from Sanz del Río's Castilian version of Krause's *Urbild der Menschheit* bears some comparison with Salas y Quiroga's perspective: 'Nacidas de una fuente común y alimentadas por una *vida superior*, están llamadas las bellas artes a realizar una efectiva armonía artística-social' ('Springing from a common source and nurtured by a *superior existence*, it is the calling of the Arts to achieve the realisation of an effective social and artistic harmony').[19] We might likewise reflect on Rubén Darío's much later reference to a young generation that had discovered its gospel; the Nicaraguan poet described his fellow *modernistas* as 'nuevos apóstoles que dicen la doctrina saludable de la regeneración' ('new apostles who speak the salutary doctrine of regeneration'), disinterested men in pursuit of spiritual virtue.[20] Several fruitful comparisons can be made between *No me olvides* and the *modernista* periodical *Helios* (1903–4). Perhaps of even greater importance, meanwhile, is the use made by Salas of 'germen', already employed in a similar context in the magazine's prospectus. Herder's extension of the plant metaphor to the collective values of a nation or era, which led M. H. Abrams to describe the German thinker as 'the founding father of historical organology' was to be a major component in the Romantic conceptual pattern.[21] Meanwhile, a more recent essay by Geoffrey Hartman provides us with valuable insights into the significance of organic metaphors and similes in the first half of the nineteenth century. As Hartman stressed, the sequence of revolutions and restorations in that period seemed to argue that history possessed a definite structure which, equally, allowed some scope to the individual. Many then subscribed to the Saint-Simonian theory that history alternated between 'organic' (religious, strongly uplifting) and 'critical' (sceptical, full of reasoning and unbelief) ages.[22] I have already suggested that Salas subscribed to the kind of historical sequence elaborated by Vico, and looked to a regenerative future. Hartman's concise analysis then seems particularly relevant when he writes: 'the crucial question was whether to be of one's time or whether to hasten the turn into the coming (organic-religious) phase. To be of one's time might mean standing against the historical "stream of tendency".'[23]

Salas y Quiroga, urging the adoption of a regenerative, spiritually uplifting impulse in Spanish literature, was swift to condemn those writers who had, in his opinion, failed to employ their talents in a constructive manner. In the third issue of *No me olvides*, he aggressively condemned all writers who depicted criminality without representing it as odious, who revelled in scenes of immorality, who delighted in corrupting the human heart, who did not dedicate all of their energies to improving the condition of men, who did not battle against heterodoxy, who did not preach the true word; such men he regarded as debased, as deserving of public execration.[24] The vocabulary commonly used to denigrate disruptive works, upon which I commented in chapter 4, recurs here. Present also, however, is a different framework of imagery which once more reveals the potent religious implications underlying Salas's vision of the writer's rôle. Salas consistently judged dramatic works by these criteria. He would condemn García Gutiérrez's *El paje*, Castro y Orozco's *Fray Luis de León*, Gil y Zárate's *Carlos II el hechizado*, and *El rey monje*, another play by García Gutiérrez, all for their immorality or for their falsification of history.[25] In his review of *El rey monje*, Salas y Quiroga made reference to the idea of drama as the faithful reflection of its society, and disputed the view that, in an age of transition, drama could possess no particular characteristics: contemporary theatre represented immorality and social destruction.[26] Salas y Quiroga's view of society, and especially that of the most shocking Romantic dramas, corresponds closely with the perceptions made by Lista and Burgos. However, he strives to promote a solution to contemporary problems, and appears optimistic that a regenerative impulse has begun; here too we find a parallel in the less emotive concluding words of Lista quoted above.

The idea of promoting this kind of regeneration had preoccupied

Salas y Quiroga for some years. The edition of his poetry published in 1834 was dedicated to 'the Spanish people in the hour of their literary and political regeneration'. Subsequently, *No me olvides* would provide an impressive platform for just such a campaign; Pablo Cabañas has stressed the importance of *No me olvides* in the history of the Spanish Romantic movement, despite the magazine's short life.[27] Later still, the protagonist of Salas y Quiroga's novel *El Dios del siglo*, published in 1848, pursues an identical goal, desiring 'la regeneración social de España'. R. F. Brown comments in a brief study: 'He, or his creator – for there must be a large element of autobiography in this representation of the ideal Romantic possessed of a social conscience and mission – was no whit less passionately involved than *Fígaro* in the crusade to promote regeneration.'[28] The setting of the novel in Madrid in the summer of 1836 reinforces the idea that the character of Félix is a self-projection of the author. The position of Salas y Quiroga and his colleagues on *No me olvides* has been briefly assessed by María Cruz Seoane, who points to the defence of a salutary nationalistic Romanticism but fails to draw attention to the editor's preoccupation with literature's rôle in society.[29] Another important point missed is the link between Salas y Quiroga's position and the determination of Böhl von Faber to counteract prevailing radical ideology and restore to prominence a spiritual literature unaffected by rationalist philosophy.[30]

Salas y Quiroga's idea of regeneration was echoed in the same year of 1837 by Nicomedes-Pastor Díaz in two articles entitled 'Del movimiento literario en España en 1837', and published in the *Museo Artístico y Literario* (I, 101–6). Díaz begins by noting the apparent paradox in the appearance of a new and idealistic generation of writers at a time of social and political instability. At the same time as conflicting political and material interests did battle, the forces of intellectual enquiry, order and beauty were putting on the forms they had traditionally worn in 'todas las sociedades nacientes' ('all nascent societies'): those of poetry, song, passionate inspiration and the irresistible power of harmony (I, 102). In Díaz's words, as in those of Salas y Quiroga, we can detect the underlying influence of the concept of historical sequences or cycles, perhaps again attributable to Vico's *Scienza nuova*; in Vico's system, when a society is young, vigorous and disciplined, it is 'poetical'.[31] Díaz's perspective is more optimistic than that of Salas, in that he vouchsafes signs of an incipient recovery belonging to a society entering a period of regeneration rather than ones foreshadowing a descent into barbarism. What is more, Díaz seeks to separate literary creation from the prevailing climate of material self-interest. He goes on to lament the accusations made against the young generation of his day, observing that its idealistic prescriptions had met with ridicule in a materialistic and positivistic age (1, 102). Díaz later insists that his articles have been inspired by an apprehension of the contrasting situation prevailing in the socio-political and literary spheres respectively (1, 103). With regard to the latter, he feels encouraged by the enthusiasm for literature displayed by the young generation, typified by full theatres, a diversity of literary magazines and the many recitals and other activities of the moment. He finds all this reassuring since he believes that literature, as the intimate expression of vital feelings and beliefs, has a special rôle to play in contemporary society, a social purpose (1, 103). In the prologue to his volume of poetry, published in 1840, Díaz would again insist that 'la poesía debe tener un fin social, y una misión fecunda, moral y civilizadora' ('poetry must have a social purpose, a fertile moralistic and civilising mission').[32] Díaz views literary creation as a balm provided by divine Providence, to heal wounds in society and to stimulate moral recovery at a time of crisis, concluding that Spain perhaps now found itself in just such a period. Allowing this perspective, then, at no other time should poetry, a natural medium of communication and instruction, enjoy greater influence upon the social order (1, 103). Díaz appears to share Larra's view that literature should communicate moral truths, but the approach of the two men to the problems besetting society is very different. Whereas Larra had proclaimed the necessity of a literature that would embody the aspirations of a new and progressive society, Díaz falls back upon the idea of literature as moral guide. He then reiterates his argument in strident and emotive terms, proclaiming the moral duty and social mission of writers to be that of directing towards society at large a voice of consolation (1, 105). The vocabulary used again typifies an organicist vision of society, visualised as a sick patient waiting to be cured of its afflictions, while, in both tone and content, the passage invites comparison not only with the declarations of Salas y Quiroga considered above but also with several pieces examined in the previous chapter.

Díaz would in fact extend the dichotomy between idealism and self-interest into an assessment of political events. He regularly accused radical liberals of being motivated by selfish ambition, and more than once contrasted the destructive tendencies inherent in the radical *progresista* programme with what he regarded as the more valuable attitudes of the majority. In one passage which reveals notable similarities with parts of 'Del movimiento literario', Díaz proclaimed that generous-minded and intelligent young men were almost without exception *moderados* who supported the eternal principles of order and justice; their eager desire, moreover, was to found upon these twin bases the concept of government and social organisation held religiously dear in their hearts.[33] The piece dates from December 1839. Two years later in the newspaper *El Conservador*, which he had helped to found, Díaz wrote in similar terms of a fresh generation of politicians who were making an energetic and serious-minded protest against the 'rancid revolutionary ideas', anti-monarchical spite and fanatical atheism espoused by 'decrepit Jacobins' (II, 36). Díaz's own idealistic programme is therefore carried into the conceptual framework of *moderado* politics. He envisaged the fulfilment of this plan of national reconstruction, made possible by the peace of Vergara (1839), under the Queen Regent María Cristina and moderate government. Díaz's offer of unconditional loyalty to the Queen Regent was a display of support likewise made by several other writers featuring in this study: Donoso, for example, accompanied María Cristina to Paris when she was forced to flee Spain in 1840, and shared with her the experience of enforced exile. Like Donoso, Díaz violently opposed Espartero – he was briefly imprisoned during the hegemony of the general – and, in condemning what he regarded as radical persecution of María Cristina, blamed the instigation of anti-monarchist feeling by the liberals of the Cadiz parliament and the 1812 Constitution, whom he labelled 'anacronismos vivos del siglo' ('the walking anachronisms of our age'). These he regarded as a threat to national recovery, since they were declared enemies not only of monarchy and religion but also of all those institutions that lent strength, binding and cohesion to the body politic and to society as a whole (II, 35). Díaz, then, reverts to the kind of imagery first seen in his assessment of developments in Spanish literature, now employing it in a political cause to vituperate radical liberalism.

The sentiments so forcibly expressed in 'Del movimiento literario en España en 1837' were reasserted in Díaz's prologue to the first volume of poetry published by Zorrilla, written in October of 1837. Díaz evokes the events at Larra's funeral in February of the same year which had brought Zorrilla sudden prominence. He is saddened by the fact that many will treat his reflections with the kind of sardonic irony reserved for what was not logical and positivistic (1, 108). Díaz views Zorrilla as the youthful poet who encapsulates the idealistic spirit which he had earlier found so encouraging among young writers, as the authentic literary representative of a new generation, of the generation's ideas, opinions, feelings and beliefs (1, 109). Going on to consider the poetry of Zorrilla against the background of the contemporary age, Díaz declares that modern poetry could not reflect the certainties of the past since the foundations of society itself had crumbled. Poetic composition, stifled by an uncomprehending society, had sought refuge in the most intimate reaches of men's hearts, where, 'a despecho de la filosofía y del egoísmo, un corazón palpita y un espíritu inmortal vive' ('in defiance of philosophy and egoism, a heart beats and an immortal spirit lives') (1, 109–10). It is interesting to compare Díaz's assertion with similar comments made by Eugenio de Ochoa in the first issue of *El Artista* two years earlier. Ochoa had insisted that man could not banish poetry from his secular world; when poetry had seemingly disappeared from the face of the earth, it had been forced to seek asylum in the depths of certain noble and sensitive hearts, just as, in turbulent times of old, religion had sought asylum in caves and lonely monasteries.[34]

While Díaz stresses the incompatibility of the spiritual qualities of poetic inspiration with the destructive tendencies of the age, he recognises that the poet cannot live and write in isolation from the social context but is instead necessarily influenced by external reality; when society is beset by a period of turmoil, poetic composition inevitably reflects this. Consequently, the character of the present age has produced 'poesía de vértigo, de vacilación y de duda; poesía de delirio, o de duelo; poesía sin unidad, sin sistema, sin fin moral ni objeto humanitario' ('a giddy poetry of vacillation and doubt; a delirious poetry of mourning; a poetry without unity and system, without moral purpose and humanitarian aims') (1, 110). Díaz's description of this kind of poetry largely coincides with the depiction of contemporary society made by Javier de Burgos. While Burgos failed to detect the significance of the link between social disintegration and disruptive attitudes in literature, Díaz would reiterate just such an association, declaring his own verse to be bred by sorrows peculiar to the age; his poems, he wrote, belonged neither to the future nor to society at large, neither to religion nor to any universal or humanitarian aim.[35] Díaz's judgement of contemporary literature is consistent with those made by Lista and Salas y Quiroga, and would soon be echoed by Enrique Gil y Carrasco and Salvador Bermúdez de Castro.[36] He felt, on the other hand, that Zorrilla had seen beyond the superficial indications of a genteel and prosperous society and had recognised the moral debasement underlying them. Similarly, he continued, Zorrilla had quickly perceived that the kind of poetry seemingly demanded by this age of social disorganisation and religious scepticism was sterile, a passing vogue, as were egoism and scepticism themselves (I, III). Zorrilla had nonetheless sought and found, in the glorious traditions of Spain's national past, not only poetic inspiration but also exemplary models far superior to the trivialities of his own age; the mediaeval period seemed to offer 'una sociedad homogénca y compacta de religión y de virtud' ('a homogeneous and compact society of religion and virtue'), rich in feeling and grandeur (I, III–12). Zorrilla would thus provide moral lessons for the contemporary age in his celebration of Spanish history and especially of the poetic qualities of religion, which was the keystone of society (I, II2).

For Nicomedes-Pastor Díaz, then, a literature embodying spiritual values could effectively combat materialism and religious scepticism and lend impetus to social regeneration, while Zorrilla's poetry exemplified the kind of writing which he desired. In a critique of the poetry of Gertrudis Gómez de Avellaneda, published in January of 1842, Díaz reiterated this view; the publication of a volume of poetry was a heroic act in a prosaic society living in a positivistic and brutally commercialised age, while poetic composition represented the only protest left to the virtuous heart against religious scepticism and selfish ambition (I, 124–9). His comments illustrate a fundamental change of approach in the use of the term 'positivo': for Larra, it represented exciting new possibilities only now beginning to emerge after an intellectual marasmus; for later critics, it exemplified all that was rotten in a society dominated by material values. In his article 'Literatura', Larra had warned that the analytical and positivistic tendencies of the age should not on any account be seen as heralding the death of literature (II, 133). On the other hand, Díaz reveals a wholly different approach, lamenting the prevailing attitude towards verse composition 'en medio de esta fútil y prosaica sociedad, en medio del siglo positivo y financiero' ('in the midst of this futile and prosaic society, amid this positivistic age of finance') (ⅼ, 124). Díaz's political career strongly reflected his desire to stimulate collective moral improvement through the dissemination of desirable attitudes and values common to all spheres of society. His later lectures at the Ateneo in 1848–9 on the dangers posed by socialism would highlight religious belief and Christian values as the only ultimate solution to social strife, and his Liberal Union party would likewise aspire to a commendable, if implausible, ideal of 'armonismo'.[37]

The same issue of literature's rôle in contemporary Spanish society was considered by Enrique Gil y Carrasco in one of his earliest articles, a review of Hartzenbusch's *Doña Mencía* (1838). Here Enrique Gil affirmed that drama was the most complete literary expression of the present age, the literary genre destined to exercise greatest influence in contemporary society (407). He went on to assert that the changing character of society resulted in the predominance of different literary genres in different historical periods, each giving expression to the spirit of its respective age: the ode in the infancy of nations; the epic in their adolescence; and drama as the faithful expression of their maturity (408). There appears to me to be little doubt that these comments were inspired by a remarkably similar passage found in Hugo's preface to *Cromwell* of 1827. Here Hugo had ascribed to the history of poetry three different ages, each corresponding to a particular stage in the development of society: 'l'ode, l'épopée, le drame. Les temps primitifs sont lyriques, les temps antiques sont épiques, les temps modernes sont dramatiques.' Like Hugo eleven years earlier, Enrique Gil subscribes to the organic view of different stages of progressive civilisation.[38] He then turns his attention to the part played by drama within contemporary society. Pointing to the importance of moral instruction, he declares that parliamentary debate, the press, schools, and even the Church, are unable adequately to fulfil such a rôle; material interests, partisanship, an exaggerated preoccupation with the mechanics of learning, and a prevailing climate of religious scepticism and retrenchment, are all to blame. Consequently, he described the theatre as the only remaining medium of direct communication with the masses (408). Unfortunately, the responsibilities attendant upon this privileged position had not until now been prudently exercised: Enrique Gil expresses his regret that there had recently been too many lamentable excesses in the theatre. However, he strongly asserts what he feels to be the only course to follow, and his words invite immediate comparison with the ideas expounded by Salas y Quiroga and Díaz a year earlier. The duty of all writers, he stated, was to point out to men of letters the magic weapons which they could and should brandish if they were to exercise the moral supremacy that was their calling:

El sentimiento es lo único que hay de común entre los hombres: las teorías que a él no se refieren, y los intereses, jamás podrán ofrecer en medio de su choque y perpetua movilidad un sólido cimiento a la reconciliación y fraternidad universal; así que a apoderarse de este lazo común y anudarlo estrechamente, deben enderezarse todos los esfuerzos del genio. (408)

(Feeling is the only thing common to all men: theories which choose to ignore it, and self-interest, in a permanent state of collision and instability, will never be able to provide a solid foundation for universal reconciliation and fraternity; all the efforts of genius should be directed towards seizing and tightening this common tie.)

Enrique Gil, like Salas and Díaz, fixes upon the idea of a moral crusade to be championed by a select group of sensitive intellectuals, attributing to literature those special qualities needed to establish harmony where there was previously chaos. The vocabulary used helps us to reinforce the comparison, since Gil employs the same metaphor of strengthening social ties earlier chosen by Salas y Quiroga to denote the broader reorganising powers of literature.[39] Meanwhile, Gil follows Salas y Quiroga and Díaz in linking this vision of literature as an effective moral guide with religious faith. He makes it clear that 'sentimiento' is to be understood as spiritual feeling, and concludes that it is the only quality capable of transforming the egoism of the age (409).

In a subsequent article published in June of 1839, Enrique Gil would observe that his own generation had been born into a period of transition, one of instability lacking in guiding principles (453–4). The passage is suggestive of Alfred de Musset's *La Confession d'un enfant du siècle* of 1836, with which Enrique Gil, as an avid reader of French literature, was probably acquainted. As A. W. Raitt reminds us, Gérard de Nerval had likewise been 'indelibly marked by the scepticism of the *philosophes*', describing himself in his *Voyage en Orient* as 'fils d'un siècle déshérité d'illusions'.[40] Enrique Gil, aware of the surrounding climate of destruction and of the deficiencies of contemporary society, is in no doubt about the best means of improvement: this could only be achieved by the widespread dissemination of 'la buena fe y la verdad' ('good faith and truth') (454). Gil therefore argues that the presentation of depravity in plays like *Antony* could serve no constructive purpose. His plan for moral improvement continues to be based upon the communication of religious truths, and it is the duty of the theatre to fulfil this need. A year later, in his critique of the poetry of Espronceda, Enrique Gil shares the optimism earlier expressed by Salas y Quiroga, Balmes, Díaz and Donoso Cortés regarding the growing degree of spirituality which has steadily begun to combat the legacy of materialism inherited from the previous generation. Philosophers of the Enlightenment, he claimed, had mistakenly believed the attainment of happiness to lie in the progressive development of material interests and concerns. His own century, on the other hand, beginning to profess a new spirituality, had thrown back at these 'llamados filósofos' ('so-called philosophers') the hollowness of their universal panacea and had brought them to book for destroying the old order instead of attempting to reform it. The Enlightenment had been unable to deliver the happy future which it had promised, and had succeeded only in snatching away the tranquillity and contentment of the present age (490). While accepting Espronceda's poem 'A Jarifa', published in 1840, as the expression of a spiritual anguish caused by the character of the age, Enrique Gil felt it was not the kind of literature now needed by society; consolation and hope, not sarcasm, doubt and despair, were essential (496).

Clearly, Jacinto de Salas y Quiroga, Nicomedes-Pastor Díaz and Enrique Gil y Carrasco shared a common perception of the rôle that ought to be played by creative literature in contemporary Spanish society. All three outlined the idea of a mission that literature could fulfil by stimulating recovery in a chaotic spiritual environment. While describing in febrile terms the collapse of previous scales of value, and deploring the prevailing materialistic spirit of their age, all three detected a sense of idealism and spirituality among writers. This led them to regard with some optimism the prospects for Spanish literature in succeeding years. As a final example, Leopoldo Augusto Cueto's review of *Ciencias y desengaños*, a novel by Ramón de Navarrete, in the *Revista de Madrid* in 1843, displays the same perception of literature's rôle in society. There were still noble feelings and virtuous actions to be found, insisted Cueto; novelists should seek them out, and with them triumphantly combat perversity and immorality.[41] Like Salas y Quiroga, Díaz and Enrique Gil, Cueto views literature as potentially an effective moral guide.

This common perception of literature's rôle in society constitutes, in the literary criticism of the period, another readily identifiable trend, one which leads us to form several conclusions. Firstly, the ideas about literature and society enunciated by these critics effectively placed them beyond the reach of the charges of superficiality often levelled against Spanish Romanticism in general: E. L. King, for example, declared: 'The Spanish Romantics did not really, in a profound way, go through the spiritual experience behind the Romantic attitudes.'[42] I would instead contend that the considerable textual evidence assessed in both this and the previous chapter proves otherwise. Acutely aware that they were living in a period of disintegration and crisis, many writers strove to promote ideas which they felt could lead Spanish society in a positive and constructive direction. Secondly, the divergence of their ideas from those of Larra deserves emphatic stress. The only common denominator between the vision of *Fígaro* and the attitude of these later critics is the recognition of literature's social significance. Larra had championed an investigative and progressive literature which would dynamically reflect the aspirations of contemporary society. Men like Salas y Quiroga, Díaz, Enrique Gil, Donoso Cortés and Lista felt that the experience of the preceding decades had been not progressive but retrograde and destructive. They desired a literature capable of reasserting the values that the previous age had sought to destroy. Whereas Larra had proclaimed the necessity of a literature which could celebrate the spirit of the age, later Spanish critics determinedly promoted the idea of a literature which could effectively combat the prevailing character of their contemporary society. *Fígaro*'s new approach to the relationship between literature and society had proved influential, but his major premise had now been turned upon its head. The attitude displayed by these young Catholic and conservative critics establishes instead another link with Böhl. In the critical articles of this later Romantic period we encounter the same condemnation of rationalism and materialism, the same accusations levelled against the *philosophes*. Böhl had drawn attention to the ideological threat presented by rationalism and irreligion; Spanish critics now bitterly lamented the effects of those doctrines upon contemporary society and counselled social regeneration on the basis of the recovery of traditional values. They therefore adopted the same concept of literature as moral guide so unhesitatingly asserted by Böhl more than twenty years previously.

Ultimately, the attitudes considered in this chapter are inseparable from those examined in the previous one, and in this respect the two have inevitably overlapped. When we assess the Spanish critics' view of the age in which they lived, it is possible to perceive a common outlook shared by a large number of influential critics. All considered contemporary society to be irreligious, insensitive to the things of the spirit as well as the heart, dominated by ambition and money-grabbing self-interest. Some of these writers, notably Díaz, did display a tendency towards deliberate rhetorical and emotional effect in their critical articles. This emotionalism could be seen as an unburdening of intolerable tension, as an escape into self-indulgent attitudinising or into a self-induced sense of high-minded suffering in a world where the majority, particularly those in positions of authority, are repeatedly seen as philistine and uncaring. However, the consistency with which this view of society is expressed, and the genuine passion underlying its presentation, both lead me to accept the sincerity of these writers' convictions. Unfortunately, such an emotional response meant that the intellectual implications of the concept of 'regeneración' were not more fully explored. What is nevertheless clear is that the awareness of social and metaphysical crisis provoked among literary critics a positive integrationist response characteristic of Romantic idealism.

The ideas expressed by these Spanish critics are representative of the Romantic conviction that literature inevitably responded to the values, the collective way of looking at life, the complex process of thought and response in a given country at a given historical period. The view of the importance of shared beliefs, of 'armonía' and 'fraternidad' within society, typified by religious ideals, valuable attitudes and desirable emotions, is again representative of the period. Romantics everywhere stressed not only the relevance of their writing but also its philosophical and religious significance. In France, Chateaubriand, and especially Musset in *La Confession d'un enfant du siècle*, presented their readers with a view of contemporary society compatible with that expressed by Spanish critics. Meanwhile, the Romantic concept of 'poetic mission' clearly appears, albeit in a slightly unfamiliar guise. The writer is seen as an especially gifted and sensitive individual. However, he is not regarded as a figure somehow excluded from a conventional social existence and burdened by his own sensibility; instead, he occupies a privileged position through his ability to fulfil a constructive mission. The poet suffers more acutely than others from the surrounding climate of uncertainty, yet possesses the power to lead society into a period of regeneration.[43] The links with Spanish Krausism and with the positions later adopted by Spanish Modernists and by intellectuals of the Generation of 1898 begin to grow clearer. It is illuminating, for example, to compare the tone and content of some of the texts considered here with those features of Azorín's description of the motivation and aims of the Spanish intellectuals of his own generation: 'el desinterés, la idealidad, la ambición y la lucha por algo que no es lo material y bajo, por algo elevado, por algo que en arte o en política representa pura objetividad, deseo de cambio, de mejoría, de perfeccionamiento, de altruismo' ('disinterested idealism, an ambitious crusade not for what is crude and material but for something elevated, for something that in art as in politics signifies unblemished impartiality, a desire for change, for improvement, for perfectibility, for altruism').[44]

After the most controversial years in the development of Spanish Romanticism, the dominant accent in literary criticism had changed. The agitated tone of outrage and wholesale condemnation of literary excess had given way to idealistic fervour. What remained constant was a determination to exclude works which were felt to exemplify disruption of any kind. As in 1835 and 1836, there was a calculated attempt to suppress 'negative' tendencies – whether revolutionary attitudes to society or, more intimately, 'desasosiego metafísico' or spiritual malaise. Those felt to write in a destructive manner risked being marginalised, as both Enrique Gil's reservations about the work of one of his closest friends and Salas y Quiroga's trenchant reviews in *No me olvides* amply demonstrate. In creative literature, there is abundant evidence to show that trends in literary criticism did not constitute empty theorising. I have already pointed to Salas y Quiroga's expression of the attitude displayed in his critical articles in his own *costumbrista* novel. Both Nicomedes-Pastor Díaz and Enrique Gil published novels which can justifiably be viewed as the practical application of their theory of 'regeneration': the first part of Díaz's *De Villahermosa a la China* was written in 1844–5, while Enrique Gil's *El señor de Bembibre* was published in 1844. Gil's *Anochecer en San Antonio de la Florida* (1838) provides a further example of the expression of this common preoccupation in creative terms.[45] Once again, however, it was Zorrilla, who exemplified in his creative output several salient trends in literary criticism, who produced works most easily identifiable with this theory. His celebration of the glories of the national past, of the beauties of religious belief and tradition, and especially the spiritual qualities and moral teaching inherent in so much of his drama and verse, lent meaningful expression to the ideals of contemporary critics. We immediately think of the *Cantos del trovador* (1841) and of *Don Juan Tenorio* (1844) in such a context. Díaz's description of Zorrilla as the authentic representative of his literary generation certainly rings true.

Two additional considerations need to be borne in mind here. Firstly, the revival of the Spanish dramatic tradition and its adaptation to contemporary needs was consistently regarded as a means of literary regeneration. It would be logical, in the light of developments examined in the present chapter, to view such a dramatic production as a literary vehicle well equipped to serve the kind of wider purpose envisaged by critics. Some Spanish critics themselves made exactly this association.[46] To adopt Frank Kermode's terms, the underlying 'essence' of the Spanish national drama would remain unchanged; its 'disposition', meanwhile, would alter as it was reworked and made to serve the specific needs of a wholly different century.[47] Secondly, it should be noted that several of the novels of Fernán Caballero, which display an unashamedly moral didacticism and celebrate the kind of values regarded as eminently desirable by critics of the period, were actually written at this time if not published until later.

Finally, the whole of the material examined in these last three chapters – material concerned with the exposition of literary ideas in the years from 1837 and seriously analysed here for the first time – furnishes conclusions which challenge existing perceptions of the literary thought of the period. In my view, there was not a movement towards a spirit of eclecticism during these years, nor did the critical writing of the period constitute a reaction against Romanticism. The evidence adduced in this study instead points to the survival and further cohesive development of a Schlegelian Romantic historicism, profoundly Christian in inspiration and orientation, characterised by an intense idealism and a belief in the potency of national traditions.

8

Romantic traditionalism in the work of Fernán Caballero

Cecilia Böhl, under her chosen pseudonym of Fernán Caballero, captured the attention of the Spanish literary world in the most striking fashion. The year of 1849 witnessed the publication of four novels and several shorter pieces by this author of seemingly extraordinary fecundity.[1] What critics and readers alike did not realise was that Cecilia Böhl had been writing steadily since the 1820s; her novel *La familia de Alvareda*, for example, had been completed by 1828.[2] Nevertheless, her appearance upon the Spanish literary scene was a late one – she was fifty-two years old at the time of the serialisation of *La gaviota*. Cecilia had already published her short story *Una madre* in *El Artista* in 1835 under the initials 'C. B.', and *Sola* had been published in German in 1840, but she remained unknown until 1849. Her work is often hailed as having paved the way for the emergence in Spain of the realist novel, but more important in the context of the present study is the way in which Fernán Caballero's *costumbrismo* links with the Romantic conceptual pattern prominent in literary criticism.

Javier Herrero's lucid study established several important affinities between the outlook of Cecilia Böhl and the attitudes earlier expressed by her father Johann Nikolaus, ably linking Fernán Caballero, and specifically *La familia de Alvareda*, with the prevailing current of historical Romanticism.[3] I believe it possible, enlarging upon Herrero's thesis, to adduce further specific evidence linking Fernán Caballero with attitudes and sentiments which had consistently appeared in Spanish literary criticism from 1814. Characteristic aesthetic and ideological perspectives constitute, in my view, a forceful link between Fernán Caballero and the spirit of Spanish literary criticism in the 1830s and 1840s. The work of Fernán Caballero therefore represents the culmination of identifiable trends emerging from literary theory and criticism in Spain during a period of some thirty-five years.

A substantial part of Fernán Caballero's production can be seen to possess the salient features of *costumbrismo*. In the Spanish context, this is generally understood to have involved the creation of colourful and humorous sketches depicting the manners and customs of a particular age and region, usually containing characters who appear as representative types. The origins of *costumbrismo* are frequently associated with the rise of a popular press, and it is tempting to view the success of the *Escenas matritenses* of Mesonero Romanos in this light. The *costumbrista* pieces of Fernán Caballero, however, were more than witty fictional reconstructions of popular custom and social behaviour. A further view, linked with Romantic thought, was highlighted by Herrero. He asserted that the *costumbrista* vogue represented two important contemporary themes: the expression, on a profound level, of a sense of nationhood; and, intimately related to this, an underlying spiritual disquiet produced both by the experience of the Napoleonic invasion and by the process of social transformation which had followed it.[4] The author herself tells us that much of her writing celebrates with nostalgia a way of life rapidly disappearing from nineteenth-century Andalusia under the pressures of social change. In linking the character of Fernán Caballero's *costumbrismo* with Romantic thought, I wish to concentrate initially upon two further issues. The first of these is the influence upon the author of the ideas of her father Johann Nikolaus Böhl. The second is her interest in the concept of *Volksgeist*, ultimately stemming from Herder and propounded by the Schlegel brothers.

Herrero considered the influence of Johann Nikolaus Böhl upon his daughter to have been decisive in her intellectual formation, and regarded Cecilia's literary production as the recognisable fruit of her fidelity to his personal ideals. In Herrero's view, Cecilia Böhl faithfully adhered to the set of values which formed the basis of her education and, in strictly literary terms, subscribed to the conservative Romanticism expounded by her father. Herrero pinpointed the fundamental affinities arising from the adoption of this conservative Romanticism: the establishment of a recurring dichotomy between Christian spirituality and the materialistic nature of contemporary society; the vindication of Spain's essentially spiritual cultural tradition, felt to be at war with the corrosive influence of positivism; the conviction that a return to what was authentically Spanish, as reflected in popular tradition and folklore, could ensure victory in the struggle against the effects of Enlightenment rationalist philosophy.[5] Although the scope of Herrero's study made it impractical for him to adduce a corpus of specific evidence to support this assertion, such evidence can readily be gleaned from Fernán Caballero's literary output. The author's respect and admiration for the endeavours undertaken by her father emerge from her letters. Writing in 1859 to Antoine de Latour, the private secretary of the Duc de Montpensier and a passionate admirer of Spanish literature, she vociferously repudiated the charge of poor literary taste attributed retrospectively to Johann Nikolaus Böhl by the young Juan Valera, and on a subsequent occasion warmly praised her father's achievements.[6] Cecilia had negotiated, albeit unsuccessfully, with a German bookseller in an attempt to secure the publication of the second volume of her father's *Teatro español anterior a Lope de Vega* (1832).[7] In addition, in a letter to Juan Eugenio Hartzenbusch referring to the première of his play *El mal apóstol y el buen ladrón*, Cecilia commented in terms reminiscent of the articles of her father on this 'beautiful work of piety and faith', inspired by Spain's national dramatic tradition and likely to prove unpalatable to 'Neovolterianos'.[8] Similarly in her creative writing, Fernán Caballero appears to espouse, on numerous occasions, opinions and attitudes redolent of the influence of her father. One such passage occurs in the *relación* entitled *No transige la conciencia*, published in 1850. In a typical digression, Fernán Caballero refers to the Greek models adopted in France in the wake of the Revolution; the subsequent Restoration, she continued, had brought with it monarchical ideas and religious sentiments, feelings of chivalry, loyalty and faith, all of which would inspire literary Romanticism and a preference for Gothic art.[9] Romanticism here clearly benefits from its identification with those desirable attitudes which are seen to have replaced 'el despotismo de la democracia' ('the despotism of democracy') (II, 255). Her employment of this last emotive phrase serves to associate her, in the Spanish context, with Juan Donoso Cortés. The passage taken as a whole, meanwhile, constitutes a powerful rejoinder to those who would label Fernán Caballero as wholly anti-Romantic.

In *La familia de Alvareda*, the first of her novels to be written,[10] Fernán Caballero had echoed her father's idealistic assessment of the character of mediaeval Spain. She here points to the noble qualities of Ferdinand III, admired as hero, venerated as saint and loved as king, and therefore personifying 'el ideal del pueblo español' ('the ideal of the Spanish people') (I, 145). These qualities – heroic, monarchical and Christian – neatly encapsulate the broader Romantic response to the Middle Ages as adumbrated by A. W. Schlegel. Further affinities with the ultimately inseparable aesthetic and ideological currents strongly supported by Johann Nikolaus Böhl will emerge throughout my subsequent assessment of Fernán Caballero's work. Prominent among them is the enthusiastic promotion of popular literature and tradition. I earlier pointed to the influence of Herder in the powerful sense of *Volksgeist* that characterised the endeavours of Böhl. It should be emphasised that this influence, largely through the nature of her education, reached Cecilia also. Like her father, she strove to capture the authentic essence of Spain through the study of 'lo popular'; but whereas Johann Nikolaus Böhl had concentrated upon mediaeval Spanish literature, Cecilia directed her attention to the popular traditions of her native Andalusia, describing herself on several occasions as 'recolectora' or 'recopiladora' ('collector') of these. During her second marriage, as Marquesa de Arco-Hermoso, the author had taken advantage of regular visits to her husband's country estate at Dos Hermanas for the purpose of gathering traditional tales, poems and popular refrains at first hand from villagers. Illustrative of this practice were the 'anecdotes' written up by Fernán Caballero and shown to Washington Irving at the time of his visit to her in 1828.[11] At this early date, the future author was already noted for her interest in 'lo popular'. Both José F. Montesinos and José Luis Varela have thus linked Fernán Caballero with Herder and the Schlegels. Montesinos considered her to be a proponent of the Romantic theory established by Herder, founded on the spirit of nationhood.[12] Varela, meanwhile, felt that the author's rôle as collector of folk literature effectively placed her beneath the auspices of the 'populist' ideas of the Romanticism expounded by Herder and the Schlegels, and shrewdly pointed to her typically conservative adherence to folkloric traditions which found themselves under serious threat from the pressures of change.[13] By reinforcing the above assertions with textual evidence not brought together hitherto on this scale, it is possible firmly to establish Fernán Caballero's debt to the German concept of *Volksgeist* as exemplified by Herder and, in the Spanish writer's own generation, by Ferdinand Wolf.

In her prologue to the 1853 edition of *La gaviota*, Fernán Caballero viewed her task not as one of writing a novel but as one of presenting an authentic and accurate portrayal of Spanish society, 'del modo de opinar de sus habitantes, de su índole, aficiones y costumbres' ('of its inhabitants' modes of thought, of their disposition, attachments and customs') (v, 431). The same features had constituted, for men like Johann Nikolaus Böhl and Agustín Durán, the most precious qualities of the ancient Spanish ballads. Fernán Caballero evidently wished the fruits of her labours to supply an authentic vision of rural Andalusia in the early part of the nineteenth century, in much the same way that the *romances* and early Spanish drama furnished unique evidence of the character and values of mediaeval Spanish society. Prefacing her *Cuentos y poesías populares andaluces* (1859), the author stressed the significance of popular song, not only in maintaining the noble and patriotic qualities of nationalism but also in clarifying historical events and making known to future generations the spirit of the age in which they were composed (v, 63). Here Fernán Caballero actively promotes the view of popular literature expressed by Herder and the Schlegel brothers and later enthusiastically adopted by Böhl and Durán. The point is reinforced when, in a letter written to Hartzenbusch during that same year, she writes of popular poetry as genuinely Romantic; natural and spontaneous, with a simple vigour, independent of literary precepts and cultivated artistry.[14] Exactly the same point is made by Clemencia, in Fernán Caballero's novel of the same name, in her discussion on literature with Sir George Percy and the Viscount Carlos de Brian; a clear example of the way in which a sympathetic character acts as the author's spokesman. Further testimony is to be found in *Una en otra*, published in 1849, where Paul Valery expresses sentiments which surely reflect the author's own position: popular beliefs and traditions, he affirms, bear the unmistakable imprint of true poetry and spontaneity, so that the country people of Andalusia have retained in these qualities the essential elements of the mediaeval Spanish character (III, 239). Fernán Caballero stalwartly defended what she viewed as the national character and values in the face of growing incursions made by foreign models and conventions. This spirit of cultural nationalism itself links with the ideas of Herder and with the position of Johann Nikolaus Böhl. Meanwhile, in *Cosa cumplida ... sólo en la otra vida* (1852), Fernán Caballero's spokeswoman, the Marquesa de Alora, expounds the importance and merit of popular narrative and song. She laments the fact that its true worth remained unrecognised in Spain, whilst in countries that placed greater value upon their literary culture examples of it were enthusiastically gathered, published and treasured (IV, 39–40). Here she is thinking of the interest shown in Spanish popular literature by German writers, while appreciation of popular culture is necessarily closed to the 'presumptuous men of the Enlightenment' and to 'inflexible Classicists'; thus in *Clemencia*, the unprepossessing Sir George Percy finds tiresome the 'exploits of bandits' celebrated in *romances de ciegos*.[15] As in the case of Herder, Fernán Caballero's concept of *Volksgeist* is inseparable from broader ideological considerations. What remains to be stressed at this point is the author's belief in the value of popular culture as the authentic expression of national character. Since she defended the vision of the Spanish character as inherently dignified, noble and religious, Fernán Caballero introduces into her work innumerable anecdotes, traditions, popular beliefs and superstitions in order both to assert this view more forcefully and to provide Spaniards with an authentic record of a way of life rapidly disappearing in the face of the encroachments made by contemporary change. The framework of ideas underlying Fernán Caballero's *costumbrismo* is therefore intimately related to the conceptual pattern formulated by German Romantic theorists and defended by Johann Nikolaus Böhl. In addition, the author herself explicitly links Romanticism with monarchy and religion, as her father had done. Fernán Caballero's *costumbrismo* in this way approximates to some of the major currents of Spain's dominant Romantic historicism.

The task of collecting wide-ranging examples of popular cultural expression and incorporating them into her literary production represented only a part of Fernán Caballero's endeavours. She approached writing with very clear ideas concerning the rôle which the novel should play in contemporary society and the values which it should strive to inculcate. Her clearest statement of intent is found in the prologue to the Mellado edition (1858) of *Lágrimas*, where she describes her aim as the rehabilitation of all those things which had been nonchalantly trodden underfoot by the nineteenth century. In this broad sweep she wished to propagate the following: all forms of Christian religious belief and practice; traditional Spanish customs, national character and values; social cohesion and family life; and a spirit of self-control, especially regarding those 'absurd passions which are affected rather than genuinely felt'.[16] In similar vein, she had published, in 1853, an open letter constituting a reply to criticisms made of her work by Vicente Barrantes, in which she proclaimed her instinctive desire: 'espiritualizar el sentir que las novelas modernas han materializado tan escandalosamente' ('to spiritualise Feeling, which modern novels have so scandalously reduced to materialistic terms').[17] Here she voiced her support for the work of Juan Donoso Cortés, now Marqués de Valdegamas. The unashamed didacticism which manifested itself throughout her creative production would necessarily attract either enthusiastic praise or vehement condemnation from critics of different persuasions. Her reference to the corrupting influence of modern novels and to extravagant and insincere passions might be construed as indications of her opposition to Romanticism. We have already seen, however, that Fernán Caballero's interpretation of Romanticism was very much that earlier expressed by her father. Her position on this issue remained consistent, and was in no way anti-Romantic. It involved the distinction between 'romántico', signifying positive qualities of a given sort, and 'romancesco' or 'romanesco', embodying various forms of extravagance; it is ironic, even paradoxical, that the word 'romancesco', employed by Johann Nikolaus Böhl to designate and to champion Romantic ideas, should later be used by his daughter to vilify what she viewed as the corruption of literary taste. Referring to the plot of *La familia de Alvareda*, Fernán Caballero felt that its literary possibilities could have been further exploited had she chosen to employ the dramatic emphasis typical of Classicism, the rich colours of Romanticism or else 'la estética romancesca' (1, 143). This separation, not only of Romanticism from Classicism but also of 'romántico' from 'romancesco', would emerge more clearly in Fernán Caballero's correspondence. Writing to Hartzenbusch in 1859, she thanks him for his contribution to a *Corona poética* whose publication she herself had organised to celebrate the restoration of the historic chapel of Valme, commenting that never before had he produced such a perfect model of Romantic poetry 'in the true sense of the word'.[18] Yet while 'lo romántico' is evidently desirable, 'lo romancesco' is treated very differently. In a letter to the literary critic Manuel Cañete, Fernán Caballero referred to her low-key treatment of the theme of adultery in *No transige la conciencia*, claiming that she had sacrificed, for the sake of morality, this rather pathetic 'romancesco'

feature.[19] Given the author's attitude, it is clear that, in *Cosa cumplida
... sólo en la otra vida*, the Marquesa de Alora is to be regarded as her
spokeswoman. This work includes a discussion of literature, in
which the Marquesa elaborates upon a distinction between 'poético'
and *romancesco*. The former involves the depiction of characters
who enjoy moral superiority over the misanthropic and rebellious
creations of the latter (IV, 26–7). The *romanesco* style, observes the
Marquesa, prescribes for misfortune only despair, madness and
death; for happiness it provides dizzy rapture and a lot of noise (IV,
27). Similarly, in *La gaviota*, the author comments unfavourably on
the nature of María's relationship with Pepe Vera, a savage love
affair which seemed more appropriate to tigers than to human
beings, disgustedly exclaiming that such were the feelings attributed
by modern literature to elegant ladies and dignified gentlemen (I,
117). Her condemnation of excess is founded on principles similar to
those which led Spanish critics to reject what they regarded as the
exaggerated passions of French Romantic drama in the 1830s. One
notes that, in *Lágrimas*, the pretentious and less than engaging
Tiburcio, a laughing-stock in the novel with his self-consciously
sombre air, is nicknamed Antony, no doubt after Dumas *père*'s
dramatic hero (II, 170). When, therefore, in *La gaviota* there is a
lengthy discussion about the best possible type of novel, those
described as 'lugubrious' are hurriedly rejected. Two kinds of novel
eventually gain approval: the historical novel and 'la novela de
costumbres'. The former is seen as the preserve of erudite men, to be
left in the hands of those writers with sufficient knowledge of a
period to be able convincingly to recreate it in fiction. The 'novela
de costumbres', on the other hand, when written with accuracy and
based upon attentive observation, could greatly benefit our study of
history and our intimate knowledge of places and ages (I, 85). These
comments provide a succinct exposition of the concept of historicism
in literary theory. In keeping with her support for the historicist
position, on several occasions Fernán Caballero draws attention to
the incongruities and artificiality of Classicism. Describing the
mutual attraction felt by María and Pepe Vera in *La gaviota*, she
makes passing reference to the typically Classical imagery of Cupid
and his arrows, adding dismissively that she did not possess sufficient
temerity to seek membership of 'aquella escuela severa e intolerante'
('that severe and intolerant school') (I, 78). In the same novel,
General Santamaría is angered by gallicisms, the use of which he

regards as affectation. Speaking to the Countess, he compares their usage in Spanish with the appearance of Classical gods wearing powdered wigs on the eighteenth-century French stage (I, 130). This charge of incongruity, of the type frequently made against French neo-Classicism by Romantic critics, is a typical example of Fernán Caballero's strident *casticismo*.

Several of the points noted so far indicate an affinity between Fernán Caballero's position and the characteristic attitudes discovered in earlier literary criticism. An examination of the principal ideological trends in the author's work will lead us to conclude that there existed a marked continuity of outlook not only between Johann Nikolaus Böhl and his eldest daughter but also between the same Fernán Caballero and Romantic critics of the 1830s and 1840s. In Fernán Caballero's work, for example, the reader is at once struck by an aggressive cultural nationalism, a prominent feature both of the articles of Böhl and of later literary criticism. The ferocity of Fernán Caballero's *casticismo* more than equalled that of Larra, and English and French values and attitudes rarely escape her disdainful scrutiny. In a passage from her 1853 prologue to *La gaviota*, in terms reminiscent of Mesonero Romanos, she lamented that it was usually foreign writers who attempted to depict the physiognomy of Spain; in the majority of cases 'sobra el talento, pero falta la condición esencial para sacar la semejanza, conocer el original' ('there is abundant talent but a lack of the one essential condition necessary to produce a convincing portrayal, that is to be acquainted with the original') (v, 432). Like Mesonero, Fernán Caballero protests against the distorted image of her country, of the 'España de pandereta', circulated throughout Europe. Illustrative of this protest is, in *La gaviota*, Fernán Caballero's creation of the French aristocrat the Baron de Moude, who is writing a book entitled *Viaje científico, filosófico, fisiológico, artístico y geológico por España. (a) Iberia, con observaciones críticas sobre su gobierno, sus cocineros, su literatura, sus caminos y canales, su agricultura, sus boleros y su sistema tributario* (I, 68). On the other hand, in *Una en otra*, Paul Valery has evidently transcended this presumptuous superficiality and has arrived at a true appreciation of the merit and significance of popular culture, the essence of the Spanish soul. If the kind of unrealistic depiction against which she protests was widely regarded as a 'romantic' one, Fernán Caballero's own emphatic stress upon popular tradition and national cultural identity more accurately reflected serious preoccupations characteristic of the Romantic movement. While the majority of foreign travellers had signally failed in their attempt to convey to their readers an authentic portrayal of Spain and its inhabitants, it is Fernán Caballero's intention, in her *costumbrista* pieces, to remedy this situation and to depict with veracity the people and customs of her native region. However, to no less an extent in her letters and novels, the author is determined to stress what she feels to be the inherent characteristics of Spanish literature and of the Spanish people. In a letter to Antoine de Latour, she claimed that there was no national literature generally more chaste than that of Spain.[20] Fernán Caballero's novels abound with references to the essentially religious, noble and morally upright qualities of the Spanish people: simple faith, spontaneous generosity and inherent goodness were their hallmarks. All this further links Fernán Caballero with the attitudes expounded by her father. Meanwhile, she had found a staunch supporter in Manuel Cañete, whom she admired both for his conservative political stance and for his literary ideas. Cañete himself referred approvingly, in his *Poesías* of 1859, to the work of Fernán Caballero, which he felt to contain the purest Christian morality, and concluded that the author's popularity among both cultivated and untrained readers could be attributed to her creation of an 'espejo fiel donde se refleja la vida íntima de nuestro pueblo con toda su poesía' ('a mirror reflecting faithfully the intimate life of our people in all its poetry').[21] Describing to Cañete the ceremony marking the restoration of the chapel of Valme in 1859, Fernán Caballero declares that she encountered there all of the enduring, historically authentic elements of the Spanish nation: religion, monarchy, and the country folk.[22] Cañete's positive vision of Romantic ideas as a means of regenerating Spanish literature through the recovery of the national tradition would undoubtedly have been seconded by the daughter of Johann Nikolaus Böhl.[23]

Like Larra, Fernán Caballero reveals herself to be deeply preoccupied by the adoption in Spanish society of foreign, usually French, models of behaviour, terms of speech and artistic preferences. Her sense of *casticismo* leads her to condemn the ludicrous affectation which constituted the superficial 'buen tono'. She fixes her attention upon neologisms in the Spanish language, upon the deliberate cultivation of attitudes and poses, and upon the tendency to belittle traditional Spanish manners and conventions in favour of foreign ones. Good examples are the conversation at the *tertulia* in *La gaviota* (I, 94) and, in *Elia*, the changes made by Clara in accordance with French taste. The characters who display affected *bon ton* are, without exception, treated unsympathetically by the author. The clearest expression of Fernán Caballero's vehement *casticismo* occurs in *La gaviota*, where María captivates her initially disdainful audience with some inspired singing. When traditional Spanish songs are then announced, the frivolous Eloísa declares them inappropriate to a society of 'buen tono'; in her view, foreigners were perfectly correct to regard Spain as a backward country, unwilling to adapt itself to modern European ways (I, 97). The author deliberately lends this speech a burlesque character, representative of the stupidity of the opinions expressed, while her treatment of Eloísa displays her contempt for the pretentious and affected nature of 'buen tono': Eloísa is introduced as an impressionable girl who, recently returned from Madrid, expresses only contempt for anything characteristically Spanish (I, 72). She secretly marries a self-styled French prince named Abelardo who claims to have collaborated with Dumas (another indirectly pejorative reference to the dramatist). However, he is in reality a bigamist and abandons her after spending her money. As Fernán Caballero herself tells us, the girl believed that she had found the ideal man previously only glimpsed in her dreams; her parents, who had opposed the match, she saw as tyrants of the sort encountered in melodrama, reactionaries with obscurantist ideas (I, 130). In contrast, the author describes with warm enthusiasm María's performance at the *tertulia* and launches into a defence of the Spanish character. Throughout the novel, she writes sympathetically of María only when describing her talent as an artiste, chiefly as an interpreter of popular song. Likewise in *Lágrimas*, the author pointedly satirises the 'seudoextranjerado', who criticises all that he sees with the terrible phrase 'cosas de España' ('Spanish things'); this remark is reminiscent of Larra.[24] On the other hand, she also criticises the hollow patriotism of the 'seudoespañol', for whom everything is better in Spain than anywhere else (II, 129–30). A third unnatural type is the outmoded xenophobe, represented in *La gaviota* by General Santamaría. Characters like the General, however, are not treated entirely unsympathetically. While it may have been Fernán Caballero's intention to admit the value of meritorious foreign characters and traits, she too often herself displays an exaggerated mood of xenophobia. The only sympathetic foreign characters are those who reveal themselves to be enamoured of Spain and traditional Spanish culture, a point which itself illustrates the author's *casticismo*. This cultural nationalism is not only reminiscent of the tirades against French philosophy and letters so characteristic of Johann Nikolaus Böhl. The defence of traditional Spanish cultural values constituted an important feature of literary criticism in Spain throughout the Romantic period, and it was often accompanied by violent francophobia. Fernán Caballero admittedly represents an extreme example, but her attitude was not without precedent.

If Fernán Caballero's work is remembered for its preoccupation with one particular ideological trend, that is its wholehearted defence of Catholicism against what is consistently viewed as the poisonous doctrine of Enlightenment rationalist philosophy. In this context, a firm link can be established between the attitudes expressed by Fernán Caballero and the considerable body of material examined in chapter 6 of this study. Her purpose is made clear in a letter written to Hartzenbusch in 1850, where she insists that her energies, such as they are, will be directed against the impious enemies of Roman Catholicism, and concludes by describing her religion as the ideal of ideals, as the apogee of every sublime feeling of light and life.[25] In Fernán Caballero's creative work, this preoccupation manifests itself in the repeated commendation of traditional Catholic values, the equally consistent vituperation of the French Enlightenment, and strident condemnation of any attacks upon the Church. Typical of the author's method is the description, in *La familia de Alvareda*, of an evangelical mission in which two Capuchin monks preach to the country folk, awakening in some repentance and contrition and providing others with reassurance and consolation; she subsequently complains: 'En el siglo ilustrado, en que todos somos buenos, fervientes, firmes y felices, se han suprimido como superfluas' ('In our enlightened age, when we are all good, faithful, happy and assured, they have been abolished as superfluous') (I, 190). The savagery of Fernán Caballero's irony reveals the bitterness behind her scathing condemnation of the Enlightenment. Her most declamatory tone is reserved for her protests against the closure of monasteries and convents and against the contempt displayed by the *ilustrados* for the practices of popular devotion. In the second chapter of *La gaviota*, the exhausted Stein arrives at the abandoned convent inhabited by la tía María and her family. Fernán Caballero, in an extensive aside, contrasts the spirituality of past ages with the irreligion and materialism of contemporary society: the convent has been built in an earlier age of religious enthusiasm and faith, of elevated and beautiful virtues excluded from 'este siglo de ideas estrechas y mezquinas' ('this age of narrow and mean-minded ideas') (I, 9). The passage bears close comparison with Nicomedes-Pastor Díaz's comments regarding Zorrilla's thematic inspiration.[26] The convent has been stripped of its treasures and the building sold for 'a few pieces of paper'. The author would return to the same theme in *Clemencia*, and in the later work takes the opportunity to censure liberalism. After the death of her husband, Clemencia gives way to gloomy reverie since she is unable to return to her convent, now closed not only to those with a religious vocation but also to those left alone in the world and to those suffering from a broken heart, with all of whom Liberty had had no compunction in acting like the most capricious despot (II, 46). Meanwhile, in *Callar en vida y perdonar en muerte*, Fernán Caballero attacks, with bitter irony, the speculators who amass considerable fortunes from the demolition of religious houses and the sale of their assets (II, 247). She thus instils in her readers an acute awareness of the destructive legacy of Mendizábal.

No less marked is the author's hostility towards *ilustrados* who mock the simple practices of popular devotion found in Spain. A good example occurs in her description of the chapel of the Cristo del Socorro, in the first part of *La gaviota*. After describing the *ex-votos* placed there by the poor people of the locality, she refers contemptuously to self-important *ilustrados* who systematically deny the efficacy of prayer (I, 17). Similarly in *La familia de Alvareda*, when the church bell tolls for the death of Ventura, Fernán Caballero regards the sound as 'intempestiva en el siglo de las luces' ('an unseasonable one in the age of enlightenment'); the Enlightenment had sought to silence the importunate voice of the Church (I, 182). In her determination to expose the fallacies of Enlightenment philosophy, Fernán Caballero created, in *Elia*, a character who personifies her view of the *ilustrado*: Narciso Delgado (*Elia* was certainly written by 1845, since Fernán Caballero refers to it in a letter of that year; this letter, addressed to Doctor Julius, a German friend of her father's, was later published by Camille Pitollet).[27] This unattractive figure becomes the butt of the full force of Fernán Caballero's caustic treatment of his kind; his opinions are voiced only to be met with inevitable disapproval by more sympathetic characters. Thus Delgado's assertion that nuns are egotistical and malicious, and their supposed vocation rarely genuine, is countered by a eulogy of the values of convent life (III, 25). Subsequently, we are treated to an account of the changes made to her house by Clara with the connivance of Narciso Delgado, which provoke a violent reaction (III, 27–8). Inside the house, Delgado identifies the newly installed portrait of Voltaire with relish. The *asistenta*, however, describes the French thinker as an iniquitous man whose works are decried by the Church (III, 28); Fernán Caballero leaves us in no doubt with whom we are meant to sympathise. Delgado blackens his record further by his disdainful reaction to Elia's poem and his pedantic reference to Boileau (III, 32). Later he informs the Countess that in Paris, holy temple of liberalism and philosophy, sacred torches which burned for the future of mankind, he had encountered a detestable form of hypocrisy instigated by the Restoration and calculated to extinguish these symbols of enlightenment (III, 35). His diatribe has in fact been provoked by the attendance at church of people whom Delgado regards as less than devout. Interestingly, he cites as one of the reasons for large congregations the fact that German Romanticism had made the mystic aura of Gothic churches extremely fashionable. It comes as no surprise when his arguments are refuted by the *asistenta* by reference to Christian doctrine. During the same discussion, when Delgado refers to men like 'Voltaire, Diderot, Helvetius, Rousseau, d'Alembert ...', the *asistenta* is swift to label the *philosophes* followers of the devil (III, 37). Yet another transgression committed by the unfortunate Delgado is to vilify popular religious tradition; on this point too, he is severely reprimanded.

Fernán Caballero herself commends popular devotion, viewing it as evidence of the devoutly Christian character of the Spanish people and as an effective barrier against the tide of rationalism and irreligion. Nowhere is her attitude better expressed than in the following passage from *La familia de Alvareda*, where she addresses herself to the *philosophes*: 'Guardad allá vuestras máximas impías y disolventes, que en España no son los entendimientos bastante obtusos para que los engañéis, ni las almas bastante innobles para que las pervirtáis' ('Keep to yourselves your impious and corrosive maxims, for in Spain our minds are not dull enough to be deceived by you, nor our souls ignoble enough for you to pervert them') (I, 159). D. L. Shaw, who viewed Fernán Caballero's defence of traditional values as necessarily anti-Romantic, evidently misconstrued the above passage. Quoting the phrase 'máximas impías y disolventes', he felt it to be indicative of the author's awareness of the dangerous legacy of Romanticism.[28] Shaw contended that Romanticism did not retain the ardent religious spirit that had characterised its origins, and consequently saw the re-emergence of the Christian viewpoint in Balmes and Fernán Caballero as fiercely anti-Romantic. For Shaw, the popular success of Fernán Caballero's novels, coupled with the sympathetic attention which her work received from traditionalist critics, marked the culminating point in Spain's anti-Romantic reaction. When the phrase is seen in its proper context, however, Shaw's reference to 'the strictures of Lista, Balmes, Donoso and Fernán Caballero, and their united demand for the rejection in literature of "máximas impías y disolventes"' acquires very different implications. I reiterate that Enlightenment rationalist philosophy, and not Romanticism, was the target at which the censure of all these writers was directed.

Given her perception of the national character, Fernán Caballero felt that a Catholic reaction against these 'máximas impías y disolventes' must necessarily triumph. In a letter to Cañete dated 1863 she writes approvingly of a reaction in favour of 'sound religious principles', which she felt to be widespread, and arising in part from the excesses of its ideological opponents.[29] Subsequently, she refers to the irreligious tendency of the age, and commends the men of high intellect who have taken a firm stand in the name of religion. She does not in this letter mention names, but in her creative work Fernán Caballero had pointed to the efforts of Donoso Cortés and Balmes in the cause of Roman Catholicism. In *Cosa cumplida ... sólo en la otra vida*, the Marquesa tells the Count that he has a disconsolate air similar to that of 'our sublime marqués de Valdegamas', i.e. Donoso, a man specially chosen by God to interpret His work on earth (IV, 8). Later in the same work, she refers to Donoso and Balmes as torches of holy faith (IV, 32).

The religious spirit of Fernán Caballero's work provides a forceful link with comparable attitudes finding expression in literary criticism from 1837 (discussed in chapter 6), as well as with positions defended by Johann Nikolaus Böhl. If any further proof of Fernán Caballero's affinity with the spirit of Donoso and Balmes is required, it is found in her numerous references to Chateaubriand, Bonald and De Maistre, all Catholic traditionalists. Some examples are

Fernán Caballero's references, in *Clemencia*, to Chateaubriand and to Bonald (ii, 87; *Clemencia*, ed. Rodríguez-Luis, 323); her quotation from Chateaubriand in *Justa y Rufina* (ii, 316); her quotation, in *El ex-voto*, from *Le Génie du christianisme* and, in the same work, her reference to Chateaubriand as the great poet of Catholicism (iv, 272–3, 279). In addition, we note her choice of epigraphs: she quotes from De Maistre (ii, 305); from Bonald: 'On avait considéré la Religion comme un besoin de l'homme. Les temps sont venus de la considérér comme une nécessité de la société' (iii, 11); from Chateaubriand (iv, 267).

Another connection between the attitudes of Fernán Caballero and earlier critical ideas lies in a common perception of nineteenth-century society as insensitive and materialistic, dominated by ambition, self-interest and *positivismo*. In an undated letter to Latour, the author lamented the preponderance of 'la libertad' in contemporary society, so that all was upheaval and there was no tranquillity.[30] Writing to Cañete in 1857, she again settles upon a dichotomy between the desirable values of the past and the erroneous conceptions characteristic of the present, declaring herself in favour of 'traditional things' and expressing abomination for the nineteenth century.[31] In a later letter to Cañete, dated 1859, the author specifically cites ambition as the root cause of social strife, of 'trastornos materiales y morales' ('physical and moral upheaval').[32] These preoccupations with the prevailing character of contemporary society emerge again in Fernán Caballero's creative work. In *Clemencia*, the learned and respected Abbot, a character with whom the author obviously sympathises, warns Clemencia against the dangers of the present age. He exhorts her to flee from the sensuality and cynicism which have come to dominate the modern world, summed up in the arrogant and contemptuous clarion call 'Material self-interest conquers all'. Materialistic concerns, he insists, must be secondary to those of public morality (ii, 64). In an aside, Fernán Caballero herself refers to the hostile character of an age which displays scorn for the past, hatred for the present and trepidation at the prospect of its own future (ii, 66). In *Lágrimas*, the author vilifies the ambitious speculators who wish to turn the abandoned convent into a factory. What is spiritual and sacred passes them by, for they are 'hombres *positivos*'. Fernán Caballero defines positivism as a shameless banner proclaiming the triumph of materialism over spirituality; by following it, nineteenth-century Spain had disgracefully rejected the grandeur of a previous age of faith, emotional dynamism and chivalry (II, 208). I perceive here both the influence of Johann Nikolaus Böhl in his daughter's reference to the spiritual values of the Middle Ages and echoes of the acclaim elicited from literary critics by the work of Zorrilla. In *Lágrimas*, don Roque la Piedra (note the name) appears as the personification of unfeeling ambition and material self-interest, the symbol of 'el hombre positivo'. Into this caricature Fernán Caballero pours all her hostility towards what she regards as the pernicious materialism of her age.

The author would return to her theme of change and its unwelcome consequences in *Una en otra*. Visiting Seville after years of absence, Javier Barea finds the city irreparably altered. He writes to Paul Valery that the physiognomy of the nation as reflected in it is irrevocably disappearing, something which those of heightened imaginative capacities would undoubtedly perceive (III, 240). The complaint suggests how closely Fernán Caballero's position approximated to that of men like Donoso Cortés, Salas y Quiroga and Nicomedes-Pastor Díaz. There is the same tone of bitterness at the pre-eminence enjoyed by material values, the same contemptuous treatment of 'lo positivo', the same nostalgic desire for past certainties, the same note of high-minded suffering in a world dominated by a philistine creed. By fixing upon the concept of a spiritually-minded minority possessing an accentuated capacity for 'imaginación' and 'sentimiento', Fernán Caballero echoes the Romantic concept of an aristocracy of sensibility. In *Justa y Rufina* the author would point to a reaction against rationalism and materialism among the young generation, proclaiming an aristocracy of 'religion and virtue' and adamant that cynicism and corruption would soon encounter the same abject ridicule with which the cynical irreligion of the past century had already met (II, 308). We are struck by the similarities between Fernán Caballero's perception of a virtuous reaction against scepticism and immorality and the promotion of the idea of regeneration made by Romantic critics. While earlier critics had unanimously commended José Zorrilla's quest for inspiration and instruction in past events, and had welcomed his work as a potential corrective to the spurious rationalist and materialistic creed of the contemporary age, Fernán Caballero presents her readers with a similar antidote to 'positivismo'. Her nostalgic portrayal of the eminently desirable values of a society now threatened by extinction, and her emphatic faith in the continued validity of such values in a chaotic age, reveal the profound disquiet with which she viewed developments in nineteenth-century society. They likewise bear testimony to the reactionary nature of her proposed solution to a characteristically Romantic dilemma.

For the ideological and thematic bases of her work, Fernán Caballero was especially indebted to two foreign writers: Balzac and Walter Scott. The underlying principles which Balzac claimed for his novels were expressed in his prologue to *La Comédie humaine*: 'J'écris à la lueur de deux vérités éternelles: la religion, la monarchie', and, subsequently, 'Le christianisme, et surtout le catholicisme . . . est le plus grand élément d'ordre social.' As Montesinos has pointed out, these premises are equally applicable to the work of Fernán Caballero. He notes Clemencia's very exact reference to the above statements from Balzac's prologue.[33] Clemencia renders the words of 'the profound Balzac' as follows: 'Escribo a la luz de dos verdades eternas, la religión y la monarquía' ('I write in the light of two eternal truths, religion and monarchy'), and 'El cristianismo, pero sobre todo el catolicismo, siendo un sistema completo de represión de las tendencias depravadas del hombre, es el mayor elemento de orden social' ('Christianity, but above all Roman Catholicism, being a complete system for the repression of man's propensity for depravity, is the strongest contributory element of social order').[34] Fernán Caballero in fact refers to the French writer on numerous occasions in her novels. Balzac's own model had been Walter Scott, who he felt had dignified the novel as a *genre*. More importantly, Scott and Fernán Caballero shared several characteristic attitudes and preoccupations. In Spain, Scott had been fêted as the European novelist best able to recreate in literature the society of a past age. His antiquarian researches had enabled him to describe mediaeval Scotland with compelling authenticity. However, many of Scott's novels dealt with events in the same country around the time of the 1745 rebellion, and they incorporated in their texture eye-witness accounts gathered from the country folk by the author himself. It is not difficult to perceive the attractions which such a method would have held for Fernán Caballero, herself a tireless collector of popular traditions and anecdotes. She consistently pointed to the authenticity of many stories narrated in her novels, and *La familia de Alvareda* was just one literary reworking of real events.[35] Fernán Caballero also stressed the historical basis for Diego's identification of the murderer of his father twenty years after the event, and for the blind husband's jealous murder of his wife, both described in *Una en otra*. She wrote to Hartzenbusch on this very point.[36] As an epigraph for *Magdalena* Fernán Caballero chose to translate a passage from Scott's preface to *The Tapestried Chamber*, where the author affirmed that he had faithfully recorded from memory material with which he had been made personally acquainted (II, 375). Scott's words appear eminently applicable to Fernán Caballero's own method. If the two writers shared a dedicated interest in the history and traditions of their native region, backed by exhaustive personal enquiry, their respective labours also approximated in their desire to record for posterity the customs and values of a rapidly disappearing society. We have already noted this aspect of Fernán Caballero's work. Scott's Waverley Novels were chiefly devoted to the expression of the changes in human life which accompanied social change in his native Scotland.[37] Despite his committed Toryism, Scott's depiction of change was less partisan than that of Fernán Caballero. While regretting an irreversible transition from one kind of society to another, Scott accepted this situation more readily and sought to mediate between the old and the new.[38] Another factor which would have endeared Walter Scott to Fernán Caballero was the unashamedly didactic aim of his novels. Indeed, he referred, in the first chapter of *Waverley*, to 'the moral lessons, which I would willingly consider as the most important part of my plan'.[39] These several likenesses between the work of the two writers would have contributed to Eugenio de Ochoa's description of Fernán Caballero as the 'Walter Scott español'.[40] The differing degree of partisanship and demagogy with which the two writers undertook their respective tasks may be viewed as an eloquent illustration of the differing nature of Romanticism in their native countries.

Fernán Caballero's wide-ranging references to many nineteenth-century writers, including Balzac, Scott and Chateaubriand, suggest an impressive degree of acquaintance with contemporary literature. Her references, however, are not always trustworthy. One spectacular error is her attribution to 'the great Schlegel' of the famous concluding lines of Kant's *Kritik der praktischen Vernunft* of 1788 (in *No transige la conciencia*, II, 269). As far as I am aware, this error has not been noted by modern critics. Rendered in English, the passage from Kant reads 'There are two things that fill the mind and soul with ever new and ever increasing admiration and awe: the starry heavens above me and the moral law within me.'

The didacticism of Fernán Caballero's novels and her criticisms of the extravagantly 'romancesco' episodes of many contemporary French works have led some modern commentators to consider her an anti-Romantic writer. Yet, as Susan Kirkpatrick has pointed out in a recent article, Fernán Caballero's novels are really examples of the didactic tale grafted onto the melodramatic novel of passion.[41] A consideration of some of the 'romantic' scenes and episodes encountered in Fernán Caballero's work rapidly convinces us that she did not shrink from the melodramatic, the macabre or the gruesome, despite her criticisms of 'lo romancesco'. She employs such elements without hesitation when they can be adapted to her purpose, and only recoils from what appears to her to be gratuitously violent or extravagant. In *La familia de Alvareda*, the first of the author's full-length novels, such episodes abound. Ventura murders in cold blood the French soldier who has insulted his father; Perico exacts terrible revenge on Ventura for his adulterous relationship with Rita; the family rush from Ana's house at the approach of the men who are bearing a corpse in time to recognise the dead man as Ventura. During Perico's flight, we are treated to a typically Romantic scenario as, the moon obscured by black clouds, a lugubrious sound is heard. Perico cannot identify it until the moonlight reappears when he sees five human heads fixed on posts. These heads are the source of the noise, described as an admonition to the living by the dead (I, 184). The last phrase indicates to us Fernán Caballero's intention in including such a macabre episode; she adds a footnote to point out that the phenomenon had a perfectly natural explanation, thus defending herself against any possible charge of excess. Later in the same novel, Rita is forced by the heaving crowd in Seville to witness the execution of a criminal whom she recognises, at the last moment, to be her renegade husband. After being borne home in a state of shock, she encounters the body of Elvira lying in a coffin. Fernán Caballero shows that Rita's repentance for her past actions stems largely from the shock of these experiences. Thus the gruesome and macabre incidents themselves are not included simply to produce a violent effect upon the reader. Fernán Caballero was putting into practice the kind of approach suggested and admired by Enrique Gil y Carrasco.[42]

Many more examples can be adduced from the author's work. The reunion of Elia with her brigand father, of whose existence she knew nothing, is again illustrative of Fernán Caballero's method. She claimed historical authenticity both for this episode and for the turbulent events recounted in *La familia de Alvareda*. Her criteria for the inclusion of 'romantic' incidents would therefore appear to be historical authenticity and didactic purpose. She would include nothing either gratuitously shocking or evidently untrue. It was the singularly vehement expression of this didactic purpose which led several critics to attack her novels. Juan Valera, writing in 1856 of *La gaviota*, recognised the undoubted talent of the author, but thought it lamentable that she indulged in political harangue and religious sermons which were tiresome to the reader and which were not always apposite.[43] Valera felt that her novels would be improved by the suppression of this anxiety to 'moralise and cate-chise'. Similarly, Joaquín Francisco Pacheco, in his prologue to Fernán Caballero's *La estrella de Vandalia* (1855), had advised the author not to abandon the rôle of narrator for that of preacher.[44] Intensely aware of and upset by these criticisms, Fernán Caballero protested to Cañete in 1857 that it was George Sand, Sué and Soulié who ought to be attacked, for their 'socialist philosophising'.[45] The majority of writers and reviewers would in fact support her moralis-ing mission and seek to promote it. The Duque de Rivas, in his prologue to the 1856 edition of *La familia de Alvareda*, railed against the flood of badly translated foreign novels which 'desnaturaliza y corrompe, ora introduciendo hábitos y costumbres que nos desfigu-ran, ora vulgarizando máximas peligrosas y doctrinas socialistas, ora presentando escenas de pernicioso ejemplo' ('pervert and corrupt, sometimes by introducing customs and habits which change us beyond recognition, at other times by spreading dangerous ideas and socialist doctrine, or by depicting scenes which set a pernicious example'); he praised in Fernán Caballero's work the inculcation of 'sanas y consoladoras creencias' ('salutary and consolatory beliefs').[46] Iris M. Zavala, who furnishes considerable evidence on this point, names Antonio Cavanilles, Luis de Eguilaz and Cándido Nocedal as writers supporting what they viewed as the laudable efforts of Fernán Caballero. Zavala highlights a premise common to neo-Catholics, conservatives, moderates and traditionalists: the con-temporary novel could corrupt. As she explains, French taste and foreign models were consistently contrasted with the Spanish tradi-tion; Antonio de Trueba, Ochoa, Ramón de Campoamor and Fernán Caballero all defended the enduring values of *casticismo* and opposed the impious doctrine of socialism which was then emanating from France.[47] Prominent also among these Catholic traditionalists, although not named by Zavala, was Juan Donoso Cortés. Commenting on Fernán Caballero's *El exvoto*, he praised the work's religious inspiration, which he regarded as especially important in the present age. The author, he felt, had effected a heroic deed worthy of considerable applause.[48]

In assessing the position of Fernán Caballero within the present context, that of developments in Spanish literary theory and criticism in the first half of the nineteenth century, we are drawn to several conclusions. Firstly, the evidence leads us to a reaffirmation of Herrero's premise that the author was deeply influenced by the ideas of her father Johann Nikolaus Böhl. In both aesthetic and broader ideological terms, Fernán Caballero retains those same preoccupations which characterised Böhl's contribution to the literary polemic with José Joaquín de Mora. Secondly, I have attempted to show the many affinities between the work of Fernán Caballero and the ideas emerging in Spanish literary criticism from the mid-1830s. In literary terms, I would point to an aggressive cultural nationalism, inextricably linked to Herder's interrelated concepts of historicism and *Volksgeist*. Romantic critics defended the *romance* and the drama of the *Siglo de Oro* as characteristically Spanish forms, as the embodiment of the national character. Zorrilla's concentration upon the twin themes of nationalism and religion led him to poeticise religious and popular traditions and to write on Spanish historical themes. Likewise, Fernán Caballero wished to encapsulate the authentic Spanish essence, which she felt continued to reside in the people, in its customs and manners, in its popular and religious traditions. Like the Romantic critics, she viewed the intrusion of foreign models as unwelcome. *Casticismo* remained a consistent feature of Romantic criticism throughout the period. Another link lies in the rejection of both neo-Classicism and some extreme Romantic works. Like earlier critics Fernán Caballero did not reject Romanticism *per se*. As they had done, she viewed the movement in the light of the work of the German theorists, regarding it as essentially spiritual. Her distinction between 'romántico' and 'romancesco' is illustrative of her desire to separate the early historical Romanticism from the alleged immorality of some of the movement's later manifestations. It is a common ideology, however, which constitutes the strongest link between Fernán Caballero and Romantic critics. The religious spirit displayed in Romantic criticism, the vilification of the ideas of the *philosophes*, the perception of nineteenth-century society as materialistic and philistine, the consequent virtuous protest against the prevailing spirit of the age, and the detection of a growing reaction in favour of Christianity and traditional morals, all these features recur in the work of Fernán Caballero. Given such an affinity of outlook, it would be tempting to view Fernán Caballero's novels as exactly the kind of literature envisaged by Romantic critics as conducive to moral improvement and social harmony, as a didactic literature capable of stimulating wider regeneration in the Christian tradition. Since many of her works were written several years before publication, it would not be unreasonable to argue that she was directly influenced by the character of literary criticism in Spain in the 1830s and early 1840s. It is therefore not surprising that Fernán Caballero's work, which exemplified the literature of 'buenas ideas' demanded by critics, should, when published, have gained immediate approval and popularity. The acclaim which greeted her work was, it must be admitted, rather more enthusiastic than the quality of the novels themselves deserved. Subsequent criticism, from Menéndez y Pelayo to Montesinos, has censured their often stultifying tone of moral instruction. They were nevertheless considered important enough to command serious attention in many parts of Europe: an article in the *Edinburgh Review* in 1861 extravagantly praised Fernán Caballero as the greatest Spanish writer to appear in 200 years. The unnamed reviewer wrote: 'the appearance ... of an author like Fernán Caballero, a really original writer of fictions offering vivid delineations of the manners and characters of the living populations of the most poetic province of the Peninsula, is an event in the literary history of Spain, and we may even add, in that of Europe'. He concluded that 'no living writer has shed so bright a lustre on Spanish literature'.[49] Meanwhile, in Germany, three editions of *La gaviota* were published in Leipzig by Brockhaus in the 1860s. The celebrated German antiquarian Ferdinand Wolf wished to write a biography of the Spanish novelist. Since she shunned personal publicity, if not literary fame, Fernán Caballero did not wish to provide Wolf with details for a biography; however, Wolf did actually publish, in Vienna in 1859, an article entitled 'Beiträge zur spanischen Volkspoesie aus den Werken Fernán Caballeros'.[50] Within Spain, her work would exercise an undeniable influence upon men like Trueba, Alarcón and Pereda, and contribute to the direction taken by the Spanish novel in the 1850s and 1860s. The author's originality and influence in her own country appears beyond question. As an indication of Fernán Caballero's popularity, it is worthwhile to note that five editions of *La gaviota* had been published by 1868, three editions of *La familia de Alvareda* appeared between 1856 and 1861, and three editions of the author's complete works began to be published in Madrid between 1855 and 1865. At the same time, the fact that the premises underlying Fernán Caballero's work so strongly approximated to the character of earlier literary criticism bears testimony to the continuing pre-eminence enjoyed by Romantic historicism in Spanish literature and ideas.

9

Conclusions: The mid-century

This systematic study of Spanish literary theory and criticism in the first half of the nineteenth century enables us to reach several firm conclusions regarding the character of the Romantic movement in Spain. Romantic literary theory, lent initial impetus by the tenacious endeavours of Böhl von Faber, developed cohesively in the 1820s. This Romantic historicism continued to provide the framework of ideas for Spanish literary criticism during the crucial years 1834–7, when the advent of a new and radical Romantic approach briefly gained the support of writers. Larra promoted the essential features of the historicist vision even while disagreeing with the ideological associations it had acquired. His more stringent sense of determinism contributed to a change in the emphasis of later Romantic criticism, towards a growing social awareness. With the development of the idea of literature as a stimulant to social regeneration, critics widely canvassed its dynamic potential as a positive moral guide, with the power to inculcate desirable attitudes and valuable emotions and with the ability to provide contemporary society with lessons to be learned by the consideration of past events. A progression from firmly established bases then culminates in the work of Fernán Caballero, in a developing cycle begun by her father Johann Nikolaus Böhl. Spanish Romanticism was therefore longer-lived than most modern critics have suggested, and more consistent in its embodiment of a specific framework of ideas than they have been prepared to recognise.

It was the conceptual framework outlined above that continued to form the basis for critical appraisal of Spanish Romanticism in the years immediately before and after 1850. Both experienced critics who had lived through the events described and those who represented a new generation of scholars adopted the same overview. Gabino Tejado (1819–91), one of a group of younger critics emerg-

175

ing in the mid-1840s, is a case in point. Tejado's regular articles in *El Laberinto* in 1845 covered considerable ground. For example, he censured Philip V for having slavishly introduced into Spain the cultural models and standards of France, and bitterly condemned Voltaire for having, as he saw it, instigated the destructive ideas that eventually led into the Reign of Terror. Tejado regarded the eighteenth century as a 'monstruo gigantesco de filosofismo y de incredulidad' ('awesome monster of philosophising and unbelief'), a comment characteristic of this Catholic apologist and follower of Donoso Cortés.[1] The legacy of the Enlightenment was in his view a spirit of rational analysis carried to harmful extremes and a rampant religious scepticism, so that by the early part of the nineteenth century man had found his most treasured aspirations and illusions systematically destroyed. In his assessment of developments in European literature, Tejado saluted those German writers who had championed Calderón and regarded favourably the incipient Romanticism of Goethe and Schiller. Passing on to France, he viewed that country's Romantic revolution as comparable with its earlier political one; he detected in it the same giddy emotions, the same air of blasphemy, the same awful grandeur.[2] Romanticism, he felt, had thus revealed the dangers pertaining to any kind of extreme; while the best features of the movement deserved to be preserved, its exaggerations had to be rejected. As far as Spanish literature was concerned, the artificial conventions of pastoral and the world of Greek and Roman mythology were out of date, but the vogue for plays like *La Tour de Nesle*, *Lucrèce Borgia* and *Antony* was similarly past. The most successful recent plays, he argued, had been those historical dramas by Hartzenbusch, Zorrilla and Gil y Zárate, works which contained 'tradiciones populares evocadas con oportunidad' ('popular traditions opportunely evoked').[3] What is more, Tejado detected in such plays a forceful tendency to reconcile thematic and stylistic elements of Golden-Age drama with the changed demands of the contemporary age.[4] In judging Spanish literary critics of the preceding generation, Tejado shunned Hermosilla and had only lukewarm praise for Martínez de la Rosa, but accorded rather more favour to Lista, Gil y Zárate, and especially to Larra.[5]

One consistent feature of Tejado's articles, in *El Laberinto* and elsewhere, was his vision of the *romance* as archetypically Spanish, as emblematic of Spanish poetic nationhood. In writing of the Duque de Rivas, he welcomed both *El moro expósito* and the later *Romances históricos* as examples of a beneficial change in the nobleman's literary output, from a sterile *arte de imitación* resulting from his Classicist education to a profound apprehension of Spanish nationality. Romanticism had brought, insisted Tejado, this search for inspiration in pure national models free from foreign influence, doctrinal or otherwise. The *Romancero* and Golden-Age drama expressed, he argued, the feelings and even the moral philosophy of the nation and of individuals as seen in their pleasures, beliefs and inclinations.[6]

A more established man of letters, Antonio Alcalá Galiano, wrote in the *Revista Científica y Literaria* in 1847 of the development of critical theory in Spain. He described a process of change in the early years of the nineteenth century, as the Middle Ages came to be recognised as the fountainhead of modern European civilisation; creative literature sympathetically delineated mediaeval society, its religion and mores, instead of imitating the entirely different society of pagan Greece and Rome.[7] This new critical framework, given the name 'Romanticism', was, he stated, the work of eminent German writers.[8] In France, Alcalá Galiano argued, Romanticism came to mean something different, and in Spain the term had eventually been applied to a multitude of diverse things: the authentic Romanticism originating in Germany had been corrupted by French influence.[9] Spanish writers and critics would do best, he felt, to apply flexible criteria capable of adaptation to various nations and periods.[10] Alcalá Galiano therefore concludes this article in the same way in which he had ended his prologue to *El moro expósito* fourteen years earlier: by stressing that each people ought to do as the Greeks had done, that is to produce creative works that reflected their beliefs, history and customs.[11] This premise is a historicist one, yet the author carefully avoids linking it with Romanticism since he feels the term to have been misunderstood.

Less circumspect in his judgements was the young Manuel Cañete (1822–91). In his 1848 lectures at the Ateneo on recent Spanish drama, published in the *Revista Científica y Literaria*, Cañete boldly viewed Spanish Romanticism as 'our literature of regeneration', as a return to characteristically national forms of expression.[12] He voiced his approval of this recovery of the national tradition in literature by avowedly paraphrasing Herder. Cañete insisted that, in order to make a fair judgement of any topic, it was essential to go back to its origins; nothing was as dangerous as condemning poetic images and feelings belonging to one age or people by drawing on criteria and standards of taste belonging to another.[13] Cañete's prior assessment of Golden-Age drama further illustrates this argument and effectively links him with earlier critics. The Spanish dramatists, he commented, were well aware of the temperament of their people and appreciated the inherent spirit of their nation; they were therefore able faithfully and intimately to depict their contemporary society, and achieved a degree of success unparalleled since the time of the great Latin authors.[14] He went on to praise the work of Agustín Durán, ending with the observation that in works of art, entire peoples had placed their most intimate thoughts and their most precious intuition.[15] If this last phrase is in itself reminiscent of Herder, an article published by Cañete in the following year establishes the important role he attributed to the German theorist. Herder is regarded as a visionary thinker, as a bold antagonist of a spurious neo-Classicism, and as the fountainhead of the critical theories that underpinned Spanish Romanticism. It would be appropriate, felt Cañete, that, 'al hablar de los regeneradores literarios de su país, sin cuyo conocimiento ni aún podríamos explicar la revolución dramática del nuestro, le consagrásemos un recuerdo de gratitud por haber sido el primero que hizo conocer en Alemania los tesoros de las musas españolas' ('in discussing the literary regenerators of his nation, without any knowledge of whom we should still be unable to explain the revolution in the drama of our own, we offer to his memory a vote of thanks for having been the first man to proclaim in Germany the treasures of the Spanish muses').[16]

Cañete's affiliation to this concept of 'regeneración' which he felt to reside in Romantic theory is illustrated in his prologue to the collected works of the Duque de Rivas, published in 1854. Angel Saavedra's arrival in France, wrote Cañete, coincided with the triumph of a revolution in literary ideas which had originated in Germany and had spread throughout Europe. Its doctrine, established as effective formulae by Friedrich and August Wilhelm Schlegel, had made possible in Spain the liberation of literary genius and the emancipation of literary criticism.[17] Rivas, like other Spanish writers, had turned aside from the course of sterile imitation in order to follow the impulse of this 'corriente regeneradora' ('regenerative current').[18] Cañete regarded Agustín Durán as the most influential proponent of Schlegelian theory. Durán's *Discurso*, he felt, effectively summarised the fundamental basis of 'las teorías regeneradoras' ('the regenerative theories'), while he praised Durán himself in the strongest terms; more erudite than Larra, if less flamboyant, he was not only the true precursor of the Romantic school, but a man who had reached dizzy intellectual heights not to be attained even by *Fígaro* himself.[19] Cañete's more direct assessment of Spanish Romanticism made in the following year both reiterates his previous formulations and retains the same image of regeneration: 'consideramos el romanticismo, no sólo como satisfacción de una necesidad accidental, sino como aurora de una regeneración indispensable y fecunda; como el sol que, pasado el vértigo revolucionario con su cortejo de exageraciones y absurdos, había de hacer germinar en el suelo removido las semillas de una literatura enriquecida con elementos de duración perdurable' ('we consider Romanticism not just as the satisfaction of a circumstantial necessity, but as the dawning of a fertile and indispensable regeneration; as a sun which, the exaggerations and absurdities of its giddy revolutionary gyration soon past, was to bring about the germination of a seed in this disturbed soil, a literary seed enriched with durable and enduring ingredients').[20] Cañete here refers to the assimilation of Romantic historicism by Alberto Lista, commenting that it was the invisible power of 'las ideas regeneradoras' ('the regenerative ideas') which was to inspire him to abjure the stringent and elitist neo-Classicism professed by his predecessors and by many of his contemporaries.[21] It hardly needs to be stated how markedly Cañete's ideas coincide with the principal trends in Spanish literary criticism assessed in this study. His adoption of the concept of 'regeneración', something which had preoccupied critics of the previous two decades, appears to me of especial importance. His overview of the Romantic movement, meanwhile, is a representative one, as is his employment of organicist vocabulary to describe the new direction which Romantic ideas had made possible. Writing retrospectively, Cañete viewed Romanticism just as men like Agustín Durán, Enrique Gil y Carrasco and Jacinto de Salas y Quiroga had done.

In 1854 in the *Revista Española de Ambos Mundos*, Jerónimo Borao (1821–78), professor of Spanish literature at the university of Zaragoza, submitted the Classical–Romantic debate to further scrutiny in a long article entitled simply 'El romanticismo'.[22] Borao began by stressing that Romanticism was now a thing of the past and, owing to its aberrations, best forgotten (150). He ascribed to German origins the movement's embodiment of fundamental changes in literature and aesthetics (152), and key passages in Borao's article suggest an employment of Schlegelian categories. Borao indicated, for example, that A. W. Schlegel had formulated a modern theory of drama based upon man's dual nature; modern drama united the opposing spheres of activity of body and soul (199). Again in accordance with Schlegelian theory, Borao felt the essential features of Romanticism to be nationality, freedom and Christianity (156). Cultural change necessarily precluded the eternal imitation of rigorously set models, while national literatures had always existed independently of Classicism, which in modern Europe had signified only hollow erudite imitation (190–1). Armed with these principles Borao comments that, in the origins of each national literature, poetry had been the product of popular inspiration, not cultivated artistry or imitation, and had thus broadly represented popular taste and needs. Consequently, it had been free from subjection to literary precept and, in this as in many other ways, 'eminently Romantic' (193). Discussing developments in nineteenth-century Spain, Borao pointed to Alberto Lista's articles on Romanticism, drawing attention to Lista's assertion that modern drama must reflect Christian values and accord with national taste. This, in his view, amounted to a promotion of Romantic ideas (184). As well as applauding Lista's application of historicist principles, Borao joined with him in condemning certain elements considered immoral while at the same time positively highlighting Romantic theory; the purpose of Lista's judgements, he felt, had been to 'cerrar la brecha que el abuso, literariamente seductor, estaba abriendo en la dramática del siglo' ('seal the breach that was being opened in nineteenth-century dramatic practice by a seductive literary excess') (185). Borao recognises and approves Lista's distinction between genuine Romanticism and distortions of its essential character: when vituperating Romanticism as anti-monarchical, irreligious and immoral, Lista had been avowedly attacking, as the title of his article in fact stated, what was then fashionably known as 'Romantic' (185).[23]

A large section of Borao's article is dedicated to the rebuttal of specific charges levelled against Romanticism by Classicist critics. His defence of Romanticism extends to much of the output of Hugo and Dumas. While disapproving of what he considers immoral, he is not prepared to condemn out of hand all of the adventurous features of characterisation and staging employed by these dramatists and their Spanish followers; there was immorality in the theatre, Borao stated, not when an audience saw the depiction of vice, but when vice was seen either openly or implicitly to thrive and triumph (166). He stressed that dramatists had employed scenes of murder, adultery, rape, incest and various other daring effects in all periods, including Classical antiquity and the Spanish Golden Age. Borao was here echoing one of the premises put forward by Lista in 'De lo que hoy se llama romanticismo'. Lista had argued that, in its depiction of such scenes and characters, contemporary French drama more closely resembled Classical tragedy than authentic Romantic drama.[24] Borao uses this argument to rebut Classicist complaints against Romantic excess, and himself condemns only the rewarding of vice. He concludes his consideration of Romanticism by associating it with the spirit of freedom that had characterised nineteenth-century society, with emancipation from strictures and impositions of all kinds, including censorship of literature, the feudal system and absolutist régimes. His identification of Romanticism with contemporary aspirations towards freedom and enquiry consti-tutes a reiteration of the famous declarations of Larra in his article 'Literatura'. In fact he ends his article by declaring Romanticism to be the expression of a truly great age, the literature of modern times (207).

Borao, then, associated Romanticism with the simple vigour of popular poetry, with the theatre of Lope, Shakespeare and Cal-derón, and with contemporary social and political freedoms. This last aspect of his article may appear out of line with the traditionalist associations of Spanish Romanticism. However, all of those things regarded by Borao as outmoded symbols of oppression were simi-larly attacked by Romantic critics. His condemnation of the Carlists and of political censorship was not unusual. More significant is that at no point did Borao associate Romanticism with a nihilistic world-view or with religious scepticism. Indeed he emphasised the Chris-tian and spiritual nature of the movement, and commented that Chateaubriand had shown the Christian religion to be a most worthy and appropriate poetic subject (181). His reference to the contemporary relevance of Romanticism constitutes for me the indication of an organicist approach to social and cultural, as well as literary, change. Borao perhaps best sums up his position in his comment that the Classical–Romantic debate fittingly ended with 'el triunfo del romanticismo y la derrota de sus extravíos' ('the triumph of Romanticism and the defeat of its aberrations') (155).

Again in 1854, Juan Valera (1824–1905), close friend of Manuel Cañete and already an influential literary critic, published an extensive article entitled 'Del romanticismo en España y de Espronceda'.[25] Valera's interpretation of the direction taken by Spanish literature during the Romantic period is a familiar one: having left behind outmoded and anachronistic neo-Classical conventions (like Fernán Caballero, Valera specifically mentions Apollo in a powdered wig), in the cultivation of the *romance* and in the development of a national drama Spanish literature had returned to its authentic and original forms of expression, with impressive results (II, 8). This idea of lending Spanish literature renewed vigour by reviving national traditions had been an important feature of Romantic criticism, and, as previous critics had done, Valera viewed the *romance* as the truly national poetic metre, as the seed of an authentically Spanish poetry – again we note the organicist image. He goes on to lament the sterility of neo-Classicism, associated with 'la pobre rastrera filosofía francesa del siglo pasado' ('the wretched and abject French philosophy of last century') (II, 8).

Valera refers to the climate of change after 1833, to the new literary and political freedoms. Spanish literature again became influenced by France, but Romanticism was assimilated to the national tradition and became so authentically Spanish that the movement could have been born there: Spain itself, felt Valera, was inherently Romantic (II, 8). While he points to French influence upon early Spanish Romantic dramas, he recognises that the first Romantic impulse came from Germany, and draws attention to its mediaeval and Christian orientation (II, 9). The kind of Romanticism that reached Spain from France in the 1830s had acquired such different shades of meaning that the Schlegels, who had proclaimed it in Germany, could not possibly have recognised it (II, 9). Valera therefore repeats the characteristic distinction made by critics in the 1830s. While he favoured the break with neo-Classical formalism and the revival of national literary tradition which had formed an essential part of Spanish Romanticism, he regarded the more radical elements of the movement in a different light, as 'exageraciones revolucionarias, que pasaron con la revolución, y de las cuales, aun durante la revolución misma, se salvaron los hombres de buen gusto' ('revolutionary exaggerations which, like the revolution itself, were now past, and which men of good taste had avoided even during the course of the revolution') (II, 9). Valera nevertheless felt that the best features of the school had been preserved; he therefore shared common ground with both Cañete and Borao.

Valera described with undisguised approval the renewed interest in the *romance*, and consistently praised the work of Agustín Durán. For example, in a later article on mediaeval Spanish literature, he would eulogise Durán as the only contemporary Spanish critic worthy to be considered alongside August Wilhelm and Friedrich Schlegel, and as the author of the most illuminating modern studies of Golden-Age drama written by a Spaniard. Valera here mentions specifically both Durán's *Discurso* of 1828 and his later article on Tirso's *El condenado por desconfiado*.[26] Durán in his *Romancero*, Valera would argue, had given popular poetry its most sublime tribute anywhere in the world.[27]

The esteem in which Durán was held is illustrated by comments made in an obituary published in the *Museo Universal* shortly after his death in 1862. Durán's *Discurso*, it was claimed, deserved to figure alongside those contemporary studies by the eminent humanist don Alberto Lista and the dedicated enthusiast Schlegel. Durán, it continued, was one of the first to help to shake off the 'ideas facticias' ('factitious ideas') of the eighteenth century. He had shown Spaniards worthy and authentically national literary models.[28] When the *Discurso* was reprinted by the Spanish Academy in 1870, it was described as the true precursor of Romanticism, a work which had paved the way for a 'renacimiento de la forma y del gusto genuinamente españoles' ('renaissance of genuinely Spanish literary forms and taste').[29]

Tejado, Cañete, Valera and Borao all adhered to premises characteristic of earlier criticism, notably to the distinction between differing types of Romanticism made by Lista and others in the 1830s. References to 'exageraciones' and 'extravíos', extreme elements which they felt had contaminated some Romantic works, hint at a continuing refusal to countenance not just gratuitous attempts to shock but also any form of radical philosophical questioning. Despite Valera's refusal to be drawn on the subject of Espronceda's world-view, however, it was not possible simply to wish away what were considered Romantic 'extravíos'. Gil y Zárate could publicly retract criticisms of the religious orders and of the sacrament of confession made in his *Carlos II el hechizado*,[30] but the memorable thread of metaphysical anguish encountered in Espronceda's verse would find renewed expression in succeeding generations – alongside the 'populist' elements of Romantic historicism, for example, in the work of Rosalía de Castro – and come to be considered one of the most enduring legacies of Romanticism to the twentieth century. The arguments first rehearsed in the 1830s would also return to the Spanish literary scene; Valera's review of Rubén Darío's *Azul...* (1888), in which he committed himself in no uncertain terms on the issue of the author's pessimistic world-view, being an important instance.

Returning, in conclusion, to the first half of the century, it should, I hope, be clear that the promotion of Romantic ideas by Böhl and their consolidation in the *ominosa década* played a more important part in the development and direction of Spanish Romanticism than many modern critics have been prepared to concede. As I have indicated, I would dispute the view that the returning political exiles somehow brought Romanticism to Spain as part of their baggage, a view to which some critics still adhere. María Cruz Seoane, for example, uses this very image, rejected by Courtney Tarr over forty years earlier, in her declaration that the exiles were to influence definitively the years after 1833 in journalism as in politics.[31] The exiles would contribute little to the development of critical ideas, while works like the Duque de Rivas's *Don Alvaro* and the *Canciones* of Espronceda are not really representative of the totality of the creative work of the period. What has become known as liberal Romanticism was broadly rejected, especially in dramatic practice, and it was Schelegelian Romanticism which survived to dominate Spanish literature and ideas in the years immediately after 1837. As Alborg observed, the framework of ideas underlying Spanish Romanticism was firmly established during the reign of Ferdinand VII, before the return of the exiles.[32] Some scholars nevertheless still affirm that the efforts of Böhl impeded, rather than advanced, the diffusion of Romantic ideas in Spain. Ricardo Navas-Ruiz, for example, dismisses in a captious manner any possibility of the development of a conservative Romanticism, insisting that in each country the Romantic movement was inextricably linked to liberalism and its success directly proportionate to that of political reform. A conservative Romanticism, he doggedly reiterates, was an anachronism that could not hope to produce any kind of valid creative literature.[33] Instead, proof that Romanticism and liberal-ism went hand-in-hand was to be seen in the fact that the first traces of Romanticism in Spain could be dated to the constitutional period of 1820–3.[34] The valuable work of Böhl is, by implication, dismissed as irrelevant. José Luis Abellán has likewise claimed that the ideo-logical and overtly political elements of the Böhl–Mora polemic severely delayed the acceptance of Romantic ideas by Spanish writers.[35] Ironically, however, an implicit subordination of aesthetic considerations to political ones can be detected in Abellán's own study. It was owing to the reactionary stance of Böhl, he claims, that early-century Spanish liberals, 'existentially and politically Roman-tics', clung to neo-Classicism in their literary preferences.[36] This assertion surely has a distorting effect: Romanticism was more than a literary phenomenon, but an overly vigorous preoccupation with the movement's ideological associations leads Abellán to lose sight of its more important meaning. Hans Juretschke, in a more construc-tive assessment, has pointed to an aspect of the polemic which proved to be of significance in determining the whole character of Spanish Romanticism. As he noted, the application by Böhl via A. W. Schlegel of the ideas of Herder transcended the immediate argument over literary designations: Golden-Age drama and the *Romancero* were not just critical themes but a medium for the revitali-sation of national values. The application of Herder's framework of ideas, although indirect, was therefore of greater eventual sig-nificance than the Classical–Romantic polemic itself.[37]

Numerous modern critics have nevertheless defended a very different approach to Spanish Romanticism. Iris Zavala, viewing Böhl's work as destructive, argued that Romanticism came to Spain despite, rather than because of, the Böhl–Mora polemic.[38] She does not take fully into account the promotion of Romantic historicism, largely influenced by Böhl, during the 1820s; instead, Zavala claims that Romanticism lay dormant during the *ominosa década*, and was alive and well among Spanish intellectuals only in the cultural centres of London and Paris.[39] She further observes that within Spain the term 'Romantic' came to be seen as the opposite of *servil* (the name given to obedient followers of Ferdinand VII) and from around 1830 came to be identified with liberalism, a connection first made during the Cadiz parliament.[40] It is impossible to reconcile her perspective with that which emerges from the present study.

I would contend that the 'Romanticism equals liberalism' thesis has led inevitably to a misrepresentation of events. It is a problem that has long bedevilled our perception of the period and which continues to misdirect contemporary assessment of Spanish Romanticism. In a broader context, Marilyn Butler has recently provided a cogent rejoinder to approaches which see Romanticism as necessarily the literary manifestation of liberalism. Lamenting the 'facile equation' of one kind of revolution with another, she points to the determining factors of German Romanticism, which remained Catholic and counter-revolutionary until at least 1820. Meanwhile, Butler insists, in the same period it was the Classical or antique style that was commonly linked with republicanism, in England and France as well as in Germany. Even when Romantic taste began to gain ground in England after the end of the Napoleonic wars, it was first identified with the *anciens régimes* which had triumphed over France, and with their extreme political conservatism.[41] Butler's comments relate to a European context, but it must nevertheless be noted how closely they link with events in Spain. Only a handful of Spanish Romantic works can be seen to fit definitions which associate the movement with social and political revolution and with metaphysical crisis. Pointing to the shortcomings in the assessments of all those modern critics who have approached Spanish Romanticism burdened with a priori definitions of the term, Alborg sums up in words which I deliberately choose to echo. A sympathetic reading of the texts is the course that ought to be followed, he insists. The 'cross-examinations' made of Romanticism by so many modern critics put him in mind of Ortega y Gasset's reference to 'ideological imperialism', defined as a propensity for approaching the facts already requiring that they fit into a predetermined pattern.[42] In this study, I have endeavoured to adopt the kind of sympathetic, dare I say 'empathic', approach suggested by Alborg. A more open and less partisan consideration of developments in literary theory and criticism enables us both to perceive the dominance of Romantic historicism in Spain in the first half of the nineteenth century and to appreciate the marked traditionalism of the Romantic movement in the country. While Spanish Romantic critics derived their inspiration, in terms of literary theory, from abroad, especially from Germany, they effectively adapted such ideas to what they regarded as the character and needs of their own society. Spanish Romanticism was not merely derivative or superficial: it produced not only a revolution in aesthetics but also a recognisable movement with a coherent intellectual identity. If this identity does not accord with programmatic evaluations later superimposed upon the movement, it should in no way alter our reading of the original texts. Spanish Romanticism developed cohesively in its national context along lines broadly characteristic of the workings of the Romantic mind, while the essential reassurance felt to reside in its philosophical orientation meant that its conceptual framework remained consistent over a period of forty years.

Notes

Introduction

1 *Romanticism*, Methuen Critical Idiom Series, no. 2 (London, 1969).
2 *Historia de la literatura española. Vol. IV: El romanticismo* (Madrid, 1980), chapter 1, 'El romanticismo y sus problemas'.
3 *El romanticismo español: historia y crítica* (Salamanca, 1970), 21; retained in the revised edition of this work *El romanticismo español* (Madrid, 1982), 48.
4 *Historia crítica del pensamiento español. Vol. IV: Liberalismo y romanticismo (1808–1874)* (Madrid, 1984), 222.
5 *Historia crítica*, 251.
6 'Spanish Romanticism' in Roy Porter and Mikulás Teich (eds), *Romanticism in National Context* (Cambridge, 1988), 260–83.
7 'Spanish Romanticism', 262, 264, 266.
8 'The Concept of Romanticism in Literary History' in *Concepts of Criticism* (Yale, 1963), 128–98 (151–52).
9 'Towards a Theory of Romanticism', *PMLA* 66 (1951), 5–23.
10 'Towards a Theory of Romanticism', 5.
11 Northrop Frye (ed.), *Romanticism Reconsidered: Selected papers from the English Institute* (Columbia, 1963), 'Foreword', vi.

1 Böhl von Faber and the establishment of a traditionalist Romanticism

1 'Storm and Stress, and Herder' in *A History of Modern Criticism 1750–1950, Vol. I: The Later Eighteenth Century* (London, 1955), 176–200 (183).
2 I have consulted the English editions of these lectures: August Wilhelm Schlegel, *A Course of Lectures on Dramatic Art and Literature*, translated by John Black, 2 vols. (London, 1815); Friedrich Schlegel, *Lectures on the History of Literature, Ancient and Modern*, translated by John Gibson Lockhart, 2 vols. (Edinburgh, 1818). All future references in the text will be to these editions.
3 The piece was entitled 'Reflexiones sobre la poesía' and appeared on 12 July of that year: see J. García Mercadal, *Historia del romanticismo en España* (Barcelona, 1943), 110–11.
4 'Reflexiones de Schlegel sobre el teatro, traducidas del alemán', *El Mercurio Gaditano*, 16 September 1814.
5 Menéndez y Pelayo was thus led to view Romea y Tapia as Böhl's forgotten predecessor: see *Historia de las ideas estéticas en España*, 5 vols. (Santander, 1946–7), III, 280.
6 *El escritor sin título* (1763); cited by Menéndez y Pelayo, *Ideas estéticas*, III, 280.
7 *La Poética, o reglas de la poesía en general y de sus principales especies*, segunda edición (Madrid, 1789), II, 174–82.

8 For a full discussion see I. L. McClelland, *The Origins of the Romantic Movement in Spain* (Liverpool, 1937), 7–157.

9 Cited by Hans Juretschke, *Vida, obra y pensamiento de Alberto Lista* (Madrid, 1951), 231.

10 Cited by Pitollet, *La Querelle* (Paris, 1909), xxxi.

11 'Introducción del romanticismo en España', *La Revista Contemporánea*, 7 (1877), 79–98, 184–98.

12 *La Querelle*, xxxvi.

13 *Los orígenes del romanticismo reaccionario español: el matrimonio Böhl de Faber* (Valencia, 1978).

14 *Los orígenes*, 19.

15 See Juan Luis Alborg, *Historia*, 84–5n.

16 'Breve resumen de la historiografía sobre el Romanticismo', *Los orígenes del Romanticismo en Europa. Textos del simposio celebrado en el Instituto Germano-Español de Investigación de la Sociedad Goerres en noviembre de 1980* (Madrid, 1982), 9–26 (13).

17 'La presencia del ideario romántico alemán en la estructura y evolución teórica del romanticismo español' in *Romanticismo 1 – Atti del II congresso sul romanticismo spagnolo e ispanoamericano. Aspetti e problemi del teatro romantico* (Genoa, 1982), 11–24 (14).

18 All reference to Böhl's articles will be from his *Vindicaciones de Calderón y del Teatro Antiguo Español contra los Afrancesados en Literatura* (Cadiz, 1820). This volume contains virtually all of those articles by Böhl which featured in the polemic; the pamphlets, including the three *Pasatiempos críticos*, are each paginated separately. The above quotation is from p. 2.

19 *Vindicaciones*, 5–6.

20 *Vindicaciones*, 4–5.

21 *Vindicaciones*, 10.

22 As Pitollet commented, Mora would not have expressed himself as he did had he known Schlegel's original text in its entirety (*La Querelle*, 97).

23 'Crítica de las reflexiones de Schlegel sobre el teatro', cited by Pitollet, *La Querelle*, 94.

24 Cited by Pitollet, *La Querelle*, 95.

25 See Pitollet, *La Querelle*, 126.

26 Cited by Pitollet, *La Querelle*, 97.

27 *De la Littérature du Midi de l'Europe*, 3rd edn, 4 vols. (Paris, 1829), IV, 120.

28 See Carnero, *Los orígenes*, 142.

29 *Tercera parte del Pasatiempo crítico en defensa de Calderón y del teatro antiguo español; Apéndice de algunas lecciones al editor de la Crónica sobre unos cuantos disparates que afean su periódico en el año de 1819* (Cadiz, 1819).

30 *Tercera parte del Pasatiempo crítico*, 1–38. The first piece is a summary of Jean-Pierre-Frédéric Ancillon's 'Analyse de l'idée de littérature nationale' in his *Essais philosophiques, ou nouveaux mélanges de littérature et de philosophie*, 2 vols. (Paris–Geneva, 1817), I, 39–81. See Pitollet, *La Querelle*, 237–8 and note.

31 'La presencia del ideario romántico alemán', 13.

32 *Sämtliche Werke*, ed. B. Suphan (Berlin, 1877–1913), XVIII, 137; given in English by Isaiah Berlin. *Vico and Herder: Two Studies in the History of Ideas* (London, 1976), 169.

33 *Sämtliche Werke*, XVIII, 58; Berlin, *Vico and Herder*, 181.

34 Published in three volumes in Hamburg between 1821 and 1825.

35 'Artículo remitido', *Crónica Científica y Literaria*, 8 April 1817.

36 Letter to Navarrete dated 15 November 1821. See Carnero, *Los orígenes*, 147.

37 'Noticias literarias originales', *Diario Mercantil*, Cadiz, no. 703; *Vindicaciones*, 68.

38 'La presencia del ideario romántico alemán', 11–12.
39 *Donde las dan, las toman: en contestación a lo que escribieron Mirtilo y el Imparcial en el Mercurio Gaditano, contra Schlegel y su traductor* (Cadiz, 1814), 12; reproduced with minor changes in *Vindicaciones*.
40 *Liberales y románticos. Una emigración española en Inglaterra (1823–1834)* (El Colegio de México, 1954), 352.
41 *Liberales y románticos*, 354.
42 *Ibid.*, 354.
43 *La Revista Contemporánea*, 7, 94.
44 D. L. Shaw (ed.), Agustín Durán, *Discurso*, Exeter Hispanic Texts, IV (Exeter, 1973), xi.
45 Alfonso Par, *Shakespeare en la literatura española*, 2 vols (Madrid–Barcelona, 1935), I, 161–91; Juretschke, *Origen doctrinal y génesis del romanticismo español* (Madrid, 1954), 16–19.
46 See Carnero, *Los orígenes*, 171–2.
47 *Pasatiempo crítico*, 11.
48 Cited by Carnero, *Los orígenes*, 81.
49 'Friedrich Schlegel' in *A History of Modern Criticism 1750–1950. Vol. II: The Romantic Age* (London, 1955), 5–35 (24).
50 'La autointerpretación del romanticismo español' in *Los orígenes del Romanticismo en Europa* (Madrid, 1982), 123–36 (129).
51 Carnero, *Los orígenes*; Javier Herrero, *Los orígenes del pensamiento reaccionario español* (Madrid, 1971).
52 Cited by Pitollet, *La Querelle*, 79.
53 Cited by Pitollet, *La Querelle*, 80.
54 *Pasatiempo crítico*, 12.
55 *El Constitucional*, 16 August 1820; cited by María Teresa Cattaneo, 'Gli esordi del romanticismo in Ispagna e *El Europeo*' in *Tre studi sulla cultura spagnola* (Milan, 1967), 75–137 (87).
56 *Discurso*, xi.
57 'Two Sources of López Soler's Articles in *El Europeo*', *St. Rom.*, 5 (1965–6), 44–50.

2 The consolidation of Romantic ideas: 1820–1833

1 See Juretschke, *Origen doctrinal*, 20.
2 *Obras completas del Excmo. Sr. D. Manuel José Quintana*, BAE XIX (Madrid, 1867), 81.
3 'Reflexiones sobre la dramática española en los siglos XVI y XVII', *El Censor*, 7, 131–41 (135–6); cited by Hans Juretschke, *Vida, obra y pensamiento*, 281–2. When reworking this article in *El Europeo*, Ramón López Soler would suppress condemnation of the new aesthetic; see p. 30 above.
4 *Campagne du général Mina en Catalogne* (Paris, 1831); cited by Cattaneo, 'Gli esordi', 88.
5 See Cattaneo, 'Gli esordi', 86–8.
6 As Vicente Llorens reminds us, the ideas of A. W. Schlegel had been favourably received by the liberals of northern Italy, as they had served to support aspirations towards national unity: *El romanticismo español* (Madrid, 1979), 26.
7 *El Europeo*, I, 48–56. It appears that the only surviving collection of the issues of the periodical is that belonging to the Biblioteca del Ateneo de Barcelona. A selection of the articles published in *El Europeo* are reproduced in Luis Guarner, *El Europeo (Barcelona, 1823–1834)*, CIPP XVI (Madrid, 1953). Monteggia's article

is similarly included in *El romanticismo español. Documentos*, ed. Ricardo Navas-Ruiz (Salamanca, 1971), 33–42; page references in the text will be to this latter edition.

8 'Spain Romántico-Romanticismo ...', 347.

9 Madame de Staël's words bear some comparison with the evocation made by Monteggia: 'leur imagination se plaît dans les vieilles tours, dans les créneaux, au milieu des guerriers, des sorcières et des revenants; et les mystères d'une nature rêveuse et solitaire forment le principal charme de leurs poésies': *De l'Allemagne*, 3 vols. (London, 1813), 'Observations générales', I, 3.

10 See Juretschke's 'El problema de los orígenes del romanticismo español' in the Ramón Menéndez Pidal *Historia de España. XXXV: La época del romanticismo (1808–1874). Vol. I: Orígenes, religión, filosofía, ciencia* (Madrid, 1989), 5–209 (14).

11 *El Europeo*, I, 207–14, 254–9; reprinted in *Documentos*, 42–53. Page references in the text will again be to this edition.

12 See Schlegel's *A Course of Lectures*, II, 94. The section on 'organic' poetry was translated by Böhl for his first article of 1814.

13 See Ermanno Caldera, *Primi manifesti del romanticismo spagnolo* (Pisa, 1962), 27–35.

14 'Two sources', 45–6.

15 'Two sources', 50.

16 *El Europeo*, I, 193–200; Guarner, 71–5.

17 Guarner, *El Europeo*, 72.

18 See the passage from Böhl's article cited on p. 15 above.

19 Guarner, *El Europeo*, 74.

20 'Sobre la historia filosófica de la poesía española', *El Europeo*, I, 342–9; Guarner, 81–4.

21 *El Europeo*, II, 109–18; Guarner, 84–9.

22 *Primi manifesti*, 43–4.

23 *El Vapor*, 22 March 1833, 1.

24 *Ibid.*, 22 March 1833, 2.

25 See Cattaneo, 'Gli esordi', 121–2.

26 *Primi manifesti*, 41.

27 'Gli esordi', 100–1.

28 *Historia*, 92.

29 *Arte de hablar en prosa y verso*, 2 vols. (Madrid, 1826).

30 *Arte de hablar*, I, iii, 20. Cited by E. Allison Peers, *A History of the Romantic Movement in Spain*, 2 vols. (Cambridge, 1940), I, 182.

31 *La literatura española en el siglo XIX*, 3 vols. (Madrid, 1891–4) I, 399–400.

32 *Ideas estéticas*, III, 468.

33 *Obras de D. Francisco Martínez de la Rosa*, ed. Carlos Seco Serrano, 8 vols. BAE CXLVIII–CLV (Madrid, 1962), II, 227, 252. References in the text will be to this edition.

34 On this point, see particularly the opening chapter of Jorge Campos, *Teatro y sociedad en España (1780–1820)* (Madrid, 1969).

35 D. T. Gies, in his admirable study *Agustín Durán: A Biography and Literary Appreciation* (London, 1975), furnishes convincing evidence to suggest that Durán was born in 1789, and not in 1793, as stated in many sources. I have drawn freely on a great deal of helpful evidence provided by Professor Gies.

36 Published semi-anonymously (the title page bore the inscription 'Por D. A. D., con licencia') in Madrid in 1828; reprinted in *Documentos*, 54–100. Page references in the text will be to this edition.

37 As D. L. Shaw observed, the crux of the *Discurso* is Durán's assessment of the

Spanish national character and, by extension, that of its literature: see Shaw's lucid presentation of the ideas expounded by Durán in his edition of the *Discurso*, xv–xxi.

38 See Gies, *Agustín Durán*, 72.

39 On this point, see Shaw's well-chosen comments: *Discurso*, xxi.

40 *Primi manifesti*, 53.

41 *Agustín Durán*, 76ff.

42 The review appeared on 26 December 1828, and was unsigned.

43 See Pedro Sáinz Rodríguez, 'Documentos para la historia de la crítica literaria en España. Un epistolario erudito del siglo XIX', *BBMP* 3 (1921), 27–43, 87–101, 155–65, 251–62 and 4 (1922), 153–70; cited by Gies, *Agustín Durán*, 77.

44 'The Drama of Spain. *Discurso sobre el Influjo que ha tenido la crítica moderna en la decadencia del teatro antiguo español, y sobre el modo con que debe ser considerado para juzgar convenientemente de su mérito peculiar. Por D. A. D. Con licencia. Madrid, 1828', The Athenaeum*, 11 March 1829, 146–7 (146).

45 *Discurso*, xxvii.

46 See Shaw, *Discurso*, xxiv.

47 *Agustín Durán*, 81.

48 *El Correo*, 9 July 1832.

49 *Agustín Durán* 81.

50 Durán's first *Romancero* was published in five volumes between 1828 and 1832; a new and more extensive *Romancero* was published between 1849 and 1851 by Rivadeneyra (BAE vols. x and xvi).

51 *Romancero de romances caballerescos e históricos anteriores al siglo XVIII, que contiene los de Amor, los de la Tabla Redonda, los de Carlo Magno y de los Doce pares, los de Bernardo del Carpio, del Cid Campeador, de los infantes de Lara, etc.*, 2 vols. (Madrid, 1832), 'Discurso preliminar', 1, xvii.

52 *Boletín de Comercio*, 15 February 1833.

53 Documented by Sáinz Rodríguez, 'Un epistolario', *passim*.

54 See Gies, *Agustín Durán*, 103.

55 See Sáinz Rodríguez, 'Un epistolario', 30–1.

56 See Gies, *Agustín Durán*, 104.

57 See *Documentos*, 55–6.

58 See Gies, *Agustín Durán*, 12–13.

59 *Vida, obra y pensamiento*, 268–9.

60 *Ibid.*, 269–70.

61 *Discurso sobre la importancia de nuestra historia literaria, leído en la Real academia de la Historia por D. Alberto Lista* (Madrid, 1828).

62 Letter to Reinoso, dated Bayonne, 1829; reproduced by Juretschke, *Vida, obra y pensamiento*, 581–3.

63 '*Colección general de comedias escogidas*', *Gaceta de Bayona*, 7 November 1828.

64 Gies furnishes important evidence on this point: see *Agustín Durán*, 16–17.

65 *Primi manifesti*, 51.

66 *Gaceta de Bayona*, 3 October 1828 and 26 July 1830.

67 See Sáinz Rodríguez, 'Un epistolario', 89–90.

68 *Ibid.* 154–5.

69 *Ibid.* 159.

70 See *Orígenes del teatro español* (Paris, 1838), 15n, 55.

71 See Juretschke, *Origen doctrinal*, 24.

72 See Sáinz Rodríguez, 'Un epistolario', 30.

73 The speech is included in the *Obras completas de don Juan Donoso Cortés, Marqués de*

Valdegamas, ed. Hans Juretschke, 2 vols. (Madrid, 1946), I, 23–46. References in the text will be to this edition.

74 *Los bandos de Castilla, o el Caballero del Cisne* (Valencia, 1830).
75 See José F. Montesinos, *Introducción a una historia de la novela en España en el siglo XIX* (Madrid, 1966), 239–40.
76 Cited by E. Allison Peers, 'Studies in the Influence of Sir Walter Scott in Spain', *RH*, 68 (1926), 1–161 (145).
77 *El Vapor*, 9 November 1833; cited by I. M. Zavala, *Ideología y política en la novela española del siglo XIX* (Salamanca, 1971), 35.
78 *Cartas Españolas*, IV, 197–201, 373–6.
79 *Ibid.* 201.
80 *Cartas Españolas*, V, 31–6 (31).
81 *Ibid.* 32.
82 *Ibid.* 32n.
83 *Agustín Durán*, 77.

3 The exiles, liberal Romanticism and developments in criticism

1 *Shakespeare en la literatura española*, I, 174.
2 'Spanish Poetry' in *The European Review*, 1824, 373–83; 'Spanish Poetry: First Period' (1824, 535–41); 'Spanish Poetry: Moorish Romances' (1825, 292–7).
3 *The European Review*, 1824, 535.
4 *Ibid.* 374.
5 *Ibid.* 375.
6 *Ibid.* 383.
7 *The European Review*, 1825, 536.
8 *El romanticismo español*, 60.
9 See p. 21 above.
10 See *El romanticismo español*, 55–61, 70–4, 77–8.
11 *Introductory Lecture Delivered at the Opening of the University of London*, 2nd edn (London, 1829), 19.
12 *Introductory Lecture*, 24.
13 *El moro expósito* (Paris, 1834); reprinted in *El romanticismo español. Documentos*, ed. Navas-Ruiz, 107–28. Page references in the text will be to this edition.
14 As Carlos García Barrón points out, Alcalá Galiano had, during his stay in London *en route* to Sweden in 1814, been introduced to Madame de Staël, who asked him to take twelve copies of *De l'Allemagne* for distribution to her Swedish friends: *La obra crítica y literaria de don Antonio Alcalá Galiano* (Madrid, 1970), 95.
15 See Juretschke, *Origen doctrinal*, 28.
16 *El romanticismo español*, 147–8.
17 See pp. 97–8 above.
18 'Literature of the Nineteenth Century: Spain', a series of five articles published in *The Athenaeum* between 19 April and 14 June 1834.
19 *The Athenaeum*, 1834, 450.
20 *Ibid.* 414.
21 'Romanticism in Spain and Spanish Romanticism: A Critical Survey', *BSS*, 16 (1939), 3–37 (19).
22 *Spain 1808–1939* (Oxford, 1966), 157.
23 'Una comedia moderna: Treinta años o la vida de un jugador', *El Duende Satírico del Día*, 31 March 1828; *Obras de D. Mariano José de Larra (Fígaro)*, ed. Carlos Seco Serrano, 4 vols., BAE CXXVII–CXXX (Madrid, 1960), I, 16–22. All references in the text will be to this edition.

24 *Rev. Esp.*, 2 April 1833.
25 *Rev. Esp.*, 3 September 1833.
26 *Rev. Esp.*, 24 April 1834.
27 *Rev. Esp.*, 25 April 1834.
28 *El Español*, 12 June 1836.
29 *Larra y España* (Madrid, 1983), 189.
30 'El pastor Clasiquino', *El Artista*, I, 251–2.
31 'Literatura. Poesías de don Juan Bautista Alonso', *Rev. Esp.*, 19 February 1835.
32 'Literatura. Rápida ojeada sobre la historia e índole de la nuestra. Su estado actual. Su porvenir. Profesión de fe', *El Español*, 18 January 1836 (II, 130–4).
33 See D. G. Charlton, 'The French Romantic Movement' in *The French Romantics*, ed. Charlton, 2 vols. (Cambridge, 1984), I, 1–32 (22).
34 *Théâtre*, 4 vols. (Paris, 1873), II, 4.
35 See *Larra: el laberinto inextricable de un romántico liberal* (Madrid, 1977), 115.
36 *El Español*, 5 October 1836.
37 *El Español*, 29 February 1836.
38 *El Español*, 23, 25 June 1836.
39 *Poesías* (Madrid, 1834), 'Prólogo', ix–x.
40 *Ibid.*, 'Prólogo', x.
41 *Ibid.*, 'Prólogo', xii.
42 'Una visita a Víctor Hugo', *El Artista*, II, 294–6.
43 *Poesías*, 'Prólogo', xiii.
44 Pablo Alonso de la Avecilla, *Poética trágica* (Madrid, 1834).
45 *Ibid.* 6.
46 *Ibid.* 8.
47 *Ibid.* 58–65. The passage in question is taken from vol. II, chapter 11 of *De l'Allemagne*.
48 *Poética trágica*, 11.
49 'Introducción', *El Artista*, I, 1–2; reprinted in José Simón Díaz, *El Artista (Madrid, 1835–1836)*, CIPP I (Madrid, 1946), 118–19 (118).
50 *El Artista*, I, 2; Simón Díaz, 119.
51 See pp. 135–46 above.
52 'Un Romántico', *El Artista*, I, 36; Simón Díaz, 130–1.
53 *El Artista*, I, 36; Simón Díaz, 131.
54 *El Artista*, I, 34–5; not reproduced by Simón Díaz.
55 'Calderón', *El Artista*, I, 49–52; Simón Díaz, 112–16.
56 'Teatro', *El Artista*, I, 52–5 and 67–71 (53); not reproduced by Simón Díaz.
57 *El Artista*, I, 53.
58 'Literatura', *El Artista*, I, 86–90 (89); not reproduced by Simón Díaz.
59 *El Artista*, I, 89.
60 *El Artista*, 3 vols. (Madrid, 1981), 'Estudio preliminar', I, xvii.
61 'Teatro del Príncipe. *Don Alvaro o La fuerza del sino*, drama en cinco jornadas de don Angel Saavedra, Duque de Rivas', *El Artista*, I, 153–6; Simón Díaz, 103–6 (103).
62 'Examen del *Don Alvaro o La fuerza del sino*', *El Artista*, III, 106–8, 110–14; reproduced in full as 'Spanish Romanticism: Some Notes and Documents – I', *BSS*, 7 (1930), 3–13 (5).
63 *BSS*, 7 (1930), 5.
64 *Ibid.* 12.
65 'Sobre el estreno del *Don Alvaro*' in *Homenaje a Juan López-Morillas* (Madrid, 1982), 63–86 (82).
66 *Ideología y política*, 51–4.

67 *El Artista*, II, 47–8 (47): author's italics. Not reproduced by Simón Díaz.
68 'Clasicismo y romanticismo', *Obras completas del Doctor D. Manuel Milá y Fontanals*, ed. Marcelino Menéndez y Pelayo, 8 vols. (Barcelona, 1888–96), IV, 1–5 (5).
69 *Ibid.* 5.
70 'Two Barcelona Periodicals: *El Vapor; El Guardia Nacional*', *Liverpool Studies in Spanish Literature. First Series: from Cadalso to Rubén Darío*, ed. E. Allison Peers (Liverpool, 1940), 80–100 (84). Andrés Fontcuberta assumed editorship of the newspaper in 1836.
71 'Anuncio literario', *El Criticón*, no. 4 (Madrid, 1836); reprinted in *Obras escogidas de Bartolomé José Gallardo*, ed. Pedro Sáinz y Rodríguez, 2 vols (Madrid, 1928), II, 7–36 (17–18).
72 See p. 10 above.
73 See *El Artista*, I, 251–2; Simón Díaz, 66.
74 First read at the Ateneo in September of 1837, and later published in *Escenas matritenses*.

4 Condemnation and clarification in the literary debate

1 See *A History*, II, 1–159.
2 'Teatros', *Sem. Pint.*, I, 15–16 (16); cited by Peers, *A History*, II, 101.
3 These are all taken from the *Semanario Pintoresco Español* between 1836 and 1840, and are as follows: an unsigned critique of Bretón's *Muérete . . . y verás!*, II, 41–2; a critique of García Gutiérrez's *El paje* by 'M.', II, 166; a critique of Escosura's *Bárbara Blomberg* by 'S. el E.', II, 388; an unsigned prefatory note to an article by Lista, 2a serie, I, 102–3; a review of Campoamor's poems by Ramón de Navarrete, 2a serie, II, 247–8. See *A History*, II, 102–3.
4 *Sem. Pint.*, I, p. 16.
5 Peers likewise considered Ramón López Soler's 'Análisis' of 1823 as a straightforward attempt at reconciliation: see *A History*, II, 77–8.
6 *La Estrella*, 18 January 1834; see Juretschke, *Vida, obra y pensamiento*, 323.
7 *La Estrella*, 25 January 1834; cited by Juretschke, *Vida, obra y pensamiento*, 324.
8 *Lecciones de literatura española, explicadas en el Ateneo Científico Literario y Artístico*, 2 vols. (Madrid, 1853), 'Introducción', viii.
9 They bore the following titles: 'Del romanticismo'; 'De lo que hoy se llama romanticismo'; 'Resumen de los artículos anteriores sobre el romanticismo'. The articles were published first in *El Tiempo* at Cadiz and later in the *Gaceta de Madrid*. They also appear in Lista's *Ensayos literarios y críticos*, ed. José Joaquín de Mora, 2 vols. (Seville, 1844). II, 34–43. Subsequent references appearing in the text will be to this collection.
10 'Crónica teatral. *Marie Tudor*. Artículo primero', *El Vapor*, 14 January 1834.
11 'Crónica teatral. *Catalina Howard*', *El Vapor*, 1 July 1834.
12 'Del drama moderno. Artículo primero', *El Vapor*, 15 July 1834.
13 'Del drama moderno. Artículo segundo', *El Vapor*, 18 July 1834; italics mine.
14 'Two Barcelona Periodicals', 89.
15 'La Alemania literaria. Artículo primero', *Prop. Lib.*, I, 331–5 (332): author's italics.
16 'La Alemania literaria. Artículo cuarto', *Prop. Lib.*, II, 212–17 (214).
17 'Del romanticismo liberal en Cataluña', *Rev. Lit.*, 11–12 (1954), 9–30 (26–7).
18 *Ibid.* 24.
19 'Teatro', *El Vapor*, 5 July 1836.
20 *La Abeja*, 25 May 1835 (I, 167–79).

21 See p. o above.
22 *Antoni* [*sic*], *Eco del Comercio*, 24 June 1836.
23 *Eco del Comercio*, 24 June 1836: author's italics.
24 *No me olvides, periódico de literatura y bellas artes*, 7 May 1837, 1–2; reproduced in Pablo Cabañas, *No me olvides (Madrid, 1837–8)*, CIPP II (Madrid, 1946), 98.
25 *No me olvides*, 2; Cabañas, 98.
26 See pp. 115–16, 136–7 above.
27 *No me olvides*, 14 May 1837; 3–4 (4); Cabañas, p. 130.
28 'Acerca del estado actual de nuestra poesía', *No me olvides*, 12 December 1837, 3–4 (3); Cabañas, 46–7 (47).
29 'Moral literaria. Contraste entre la escuela escéptica y Walter Scott', *Obras* IV, 6–10 (8). The article was not published until 1842, in the *Album Pintoresco Universal*.
30 *Obras*, I, 351.
31 'Alemania en la obra de Milá y Fontanals', *RABL Barc.*, 35 (1973–4), 5–67 (29).
32 See Thomas A. Gabbert, 'Notes on the Popularity of the Dramas of Victor Hugo in Spain during the Years 1835–1845', *HR*, 4 (1936), 176–8.
33 See Peers, *A History*, I, 241.
34 'Literatura. Movimiento dramático', artículo 3°, *El Iris*, 1841, I, 109–14 (111).
35 'Juicio crítico de las tragedias y comedias de D. Antonio Gil y Zárate', *Rev. Esp. Ext.*, 1842, II, 90–6, 185–92 (189), 203–24.
36 'Juicio crítico de los dramas de D. Juan Eugenio Hartzenbusch', *Rev. Esp. Ext.*, II, 276–87, III, 83–96, 130–9 (136).
37 See p. 105 above.
38 The speech is reprinted in *Memorias de la Academia Española*, II (1870), 5–15.
39 *Ibid.* 7.
40 *Ibid.* 8–9.
41 *Ibid.* 9.
42 *Ibid.* 7. See Balmes's *Obras completas*, 8 vols., ed. P. Casanovas (Madrid, 1948–50), VIII, 226–41 (229).
43 *Memorias*, II, 12.
44 *Memorias*, II, 14.
45 'Victor Hugo y su escuela literaria', *Sem. Pint.*, 1840, 2a serie, II, 189–92 (189).
46 See Cardwell's '*Don Alvaro* or the Force of Cosmic Injustice', *St. Rom.*, 12 (1973), 559–79; also the broadly based introduction to his critical edition *El estudiante de Salamanca and Other Poems*, Tamesis texts (London, 1980).
47 See pp. 117–18 above.
48 *Las ideas literarias en España entre 1840 y 1850* (Berkeley, 1971), 5.
49 See *The Romantic Dramas of García Gutiérrez* (New York, 1922), 103–16.
50 'French Influence on the Madrid Theatre in 1837' in *Estudios dedicados a Menéndez Pidal* (Madrid, 1950), VII, 135–51 (143).
51 *Ibid.* 144.
52 *Obras completas*, ed. Narciso Alonso Cortés, 2 vols. (Valladolid, 1943), II, 2207.

5 Reaffirmation of Schlegelian principles in literary criticism

1 Angel del Río, 'Una historia del movimiento romántico en España', *RHM*, 9 (1943), 209–22; 'Present Trends in the Conception and Criticism of Spanish Romanticism', *RR*, 39 (1948), 229–48.
2 'Present Trends', 239.
3 'Towards the Understanding of Spanish Romanticism', *MLR*, 58 (1963), 190–5; 'The Anti-Romantic Reaction in Spain', *MLR*, 63 (1968), 606–11.

4 'The Anti-Romantic Reaction', 608.
5 *Ibid*. 606.
6 *Ibid*. 607–8.
7 *Las ideas literarias*, 5. See p. 88.
8 'Análisis crítico del drama de Tirso de Molina, intitulado *El Condenado por desconfiado*', *Rev. Mad.*, 3a serie, II, 109–34 (109–10).
9 *Emancipación literaria didáctica* (Barcelona, 1837), 82.
10 *Ibid*. 234.
11 'Teatro antiguo y teatro moderno', *Rev. Mad.*, 3a serie, I, 112–24 (114); the article is reprinted under the heading 'Spanish Romanticism: Some Notes and Documents – II' in *BSS*, 7 (1930), 55–64 (57).
12 'Literatura española. Poema del Cid. Crónica del Cid. Romancero del Cid', *Rev. Mad.*, 2a serie, III, 306–44 (306–7).
13 'De la literatura contemporánea. Artículo II', *El Pensamiento*, 226–32.
14 'Literatura dramática contemporánea. Juicio crítico de las tragedias y comedias de D. Antonio Gil y Zárate', *Rev. Esp. Ext.*, II, 90–6, 185–92, 203–24.
15 'Reflexiones sobre Homero y la tragedia griega. Caracteres distinctivos de la literatura antigua y moderna', *El Iris*, I, 385–8 (387).
16 *Rev. Esp. Ext.*, II, 186–7.
17 'Ensayo histórico-filosófico sobre el antiguo teatro español', *Rev. Esp. Ext.*, IV, 132–44 (133–4).
18 Enrique Gil's biographer, Jean-Louis Picoche, describes him as Spain's principal Romantic theorist: *Un romántico español: Enrique Gil y Carrasco (1815–1846)* (Madrid, 1978), 275.
19 'Poesías de don José Zorrilla', *Sem. Pint.*, 3 March 1839; in *Obras completas de D. Enrique Gil y Carrasco*, ed. Jorge Campos, BAE LXXIV (Madrid, 1954), 481–5 (481). Future page references in the text will be to this edition.
20 *A Course of Lectures ...*, II, 94; see also p. 11.
21 *El Correo Nacional*, 19, 20 December 1838.
22 'Cuentos de E. T. A. Hoffmann, vertidos al castellano por don Cayetano Cortés', *El Correo Nacional*, 16 April 1839.
23 'Revista Teatral', *Sem. Pint.*, 27 October, 5 November 1839.
24 See *Documentos*, ed. Navas-Ruiz, 117–18.
25 '*Romances históricos*, por don Angel Saavedra, Duque de Rivas', *El Pensamiento*, 1841.
26 Review of *Pablo el marino*, *El Correo Nacional*, 14 June 1839.
27 *Sem. Pint.*, II, 387–90 (387).
28 'De la novela histórica', *El Tiempo*, 1840; *Ensayos*, I, 156–63 (158).
29 *Introducción a la historia moderna, o examen de los diferentes elementos que han entrado a constituir la civilización de los actuales pueblos europeos* (Madrid, 1841), 12. As the title suggests, the work was directly inspired by Guizot, and the passage to which I refer was translated from the *Histoire de la Civilisation en France depuis la chute de l'Empire Romain*. This is an issue which I hope to investigate further in a forthcoming article.
30 See Ramón Carnicer, *Vida y obra de Pablo Piferrer* (Madrid, 1963), 162.
31 *Historiografía romántica española; introducción al estudio de la historia en el siglo XIX* (Seville, 1979).
32 See N. B. Adams, '*Siglo de Oro* Plays in Madrid, 1820–1850', *HR*, 4 (1936), 342–57.
33 *El Correo Nacional*, 23 May 1839.
34 'Galería Dramática. Teatro escogido del maestro Tirso de Molina', *El Correo Nacional*, 19 July 1839.

35 'Poesía Popular. Drama Novelesco. Lope de Vega', *Rev. Mad.*, 2a serie, II, 62-75 (62).
36 'Análisis', *Rev. Mad.*, 3a serie, II, 110.
37 'Literatura. Movimiento dramático. Artículo 1°', *El Iris*, I, 77-82 (81).
38 'Discurso sobre el teatro', *El Panorama*, 3a época, 131-4, 137-9 (138).
39 'Segundo discurso sobre el teatro', *El Panorama*, 3a época, 153-7 (155), 161-3.
40 *El Panorama*, 3a época, 157: author's italics.
41 'Literatura dramática', *Rev. Esp. Ext.*, II, 92.
42 'Literatura', *Rev. Mad.*, 1a serie, I, 41-55. Alcalá Galiano was to repeat these same sentiments in 1847: see 'Del estado de las doctrinas críticas en España en lo relativo a la composición poética', *Rev. Cient. Lit.*, I, 241-55 (245).
43 'Teatro antiguo', *Rev. Mad.*, 3a serie, I, 117; *BSS*, 7 (1930), 59.
44 'Movimiento dramático. Artículo 3°', *El Iris*, I, 112-13.
45 *Ibid.* 113.
46 'J. del P.' [?Joaquín del Pino], 'Reforma Teatral', *Rev. Teat.*, 1841, I, 1-2.
47 *Rev. Teat.*, I, 11.
48 *Observatorio Pintoresco*, 30 July 1837, 99-101.
49 *El Iris*, I, 225-7.
50 'Literatura dramática', *Rev. Esp. Ext.*, II, 190.
51 Some examples are *Rosmunda* (1839); *Don Alvaro de Luna* (1840); *Un monarca y su privado* (1841); *Guzmán el Bueno* (1842); *El Gran Capitán* (1843).
52 These included *El zapatero y el rey* (1840 and 1842); *El eco del torrente* (1842); *El puñal del godo* (1842); *Sancho García* (1842); *El molino de Guadalajara* (1843); *El caballo del Rey Don Sancho* (1843); *Don Juan Tenorio* (1844); *Traidor, inconfeso y mártir* (1849).
53 'Análisis crítico', *Rev. Mad.*, 3a serie, II, 123-4.
54 *Rev. Mad.*, 3a serie, II, 124-5.
55 'Rápida ojeada sobre la historia del teatro español. Epoca actual', *Sem. Pint.*, 1842, 2a serie, IV, 397-400 (399).
56 See *El Panorama*, I, 10-12.
57 'Literatura dramática contemporánea. Juicio crítico de los dramas de D. Juan Eugenio Hartzenbusch', *Rev. Esp. Ext.*, II, 276-87 (278).
58 'Agustín Durán, *Tesoro de los romanceros y cancioneros históricos, caballerescos, moriscos y otros, adicionado con el poema del Cid*, Barcelona, 1841', *El Iris*, II, 154-8 (154-5).
59 *Romances*, ed. Cipriano Rivas Cherif, 2 vols., Clásicos Castellanos (Madrid, 1911-12), 'Prólogo del autor', I, 23-47 (24).
60 *Romances*, I, 34.
61 Prologue to the first edition of Zorrilla's poetry, dated 14 October 1837; *Obras completas de Don Nicomedes-Pastor Díaz*, ed. José María Castro y Calvo, 3 vols, BAE CCXXVII, CCXXVIII, CCXLI (Madrid, 1969-70), I, 105-14 (112). References made in subsequent chapters to articles by Díaz will be to this edition.
62 *Obras*, II, 2207. See also p. 91 above.
63 See *El Iris*, I, 135-6.
64 *A Dream of Order: The Mediaeval Ideal in Nineteenth-Century Literature* (London, 1971), 5.
65 *Diario de Barcelona*, 29 March 1842; cited by Carnicer, *Vida y obra*, 260.
66 'Diferencias esenciales', *Manual de Literatura* (Madrid, 1842), I, 138-58.
67 'Unidades dramáticas', *Manual*, I, 289-303 (298).
68 *Manual de Literatura. Segunda parte. Resumen histórico de la literatura española*, I, 14.
69 *Ibid.* 15.
70 *Resumen histórico de la literatura española. Segunda parte de Manual de literatura, por D. A. Gil de Zárate*, cuarta edición, corregida y aumentada (Madrid, 1851),

312–15. I have found it impossible to consult the 1844 edition of this part of the *Manual*.

71 *Ibid.* 420. Gil y Zárate quotes from the Spanish translation of Sismondi's *De la Littérature du Midi de l'Europe*, a work which reproduced A. W. Schlegel's long passage in praise of Calderón. In Gil y Zárate's own work, the passage occupies 420–5.

6 The religious spirit in literary ideas and the influence of Chateaubriand

1 *Las ideas literarias*, 3–4.
2 'The Anti-Romantic Reaction', 606–7.
3 *Ibid.* 608.
4 See p. 84 above.
5 *No me olvides*, 12 November 1837, 6–8 (6); not reproduced by Cabañas.
6 Reprinted in Donoso's *Obras*, I, 537–72.
7 *No me olvides*, 10 December 1837, 1; not reproduced by Cabañas.
8 Cited by Picoche, *Un romántico español*, 46n.
9 'Sobre la poesía dramática, discurso leído por su autor en la Academia española para su admisión en ella', *Rev. Mad.*, I serie, III, 147–57.
10 *Rev. Mad.*, Iª serie, III, 153. The same remarks were repeated verbatim in Gil y Zárate's later *Manual de literatura*; see pp. oo above.
11 *Rev. Mad.*, Ia serie, III, 156.
12 'De la literatura contemporánea. Artículo III', *El Pensamiento*, 241–7 (241).
13 *ibid.* 242.
14 *Ensayos poéticos*, (Madrid, 1840), 'Al que leyere'.
15 *Ibid.*
16 *Ibid.*
17 Cited by I. M. Zavala, 'La literatura: romanticismo y costumbrismo' in the Ramón Menéndez Pidal *Historia de España. XXXV: La época del romanticismo (1808–1874). Vol. II: Las letras, las artes, la vida cotidiana* (Madrid, 1989), 5–183 (148).
18 *Vol. III: The Nineteenth Century* in *Life and Letters in France*, ed. Austin Gill (London, 1965), 12.
19 *Le Génie du Christianisme. Première Partie: dogmes et doctrines, introduction*; *Oeuvres Complètes*, 5 vols. (Paris, 1843), III, 4.
20 'Apuntes sobre Chateaubriand' (VIII, 475–9).
21 The passage reads as follows: 'La política, las ciencias, las artes, todo se puso en juego para arrancar de cuajo la creencia cristiana, y colocado el poeta filósofo a la cabeza de la conspiración más nefanda que jamás concibiera la insensatez y el orgullo, seguido de un brillante cortejo en que la corrupción de costumbres, la ambición y el desvanecimiento del falso saber, andaban disfrazados con ostentosos nombres y atavíos deslumbrantes, acaudillando siempre la empresa con increíble obstinación, con encarnizamiento inconcebible; llevó tan adelante su obra de iniquidad que, merced a sus sátiras indecentes y sarcasmos crueles, la religión quedó en Francia cubierta de ridículo y la turba de fanáticos, prosélitos del filósofo de Ferney, no reparaba en declararla a voz en grito como irreconciliable enemiga de la civilización y cultura' (VIII, 476).
22 *Life and Letters*, p. 12.
23 *El protestantismo comparado con el catolicismo en sus relaciones con la civilización europea*, 4 vols. (Barcelona, 1842–4), I, 156–7.
24 'Influencia de la sociedad en la poesía' (VIII, 462).
25 *El Pensamiento de la Nación, periódico religioso, político y literario* (Madrid, 1844–6).

26 'J. G', 'Ojeada religiosa', *El Pensamiento de la Nación*, 7 February 1844.
27 *El Pensamiento de la Nación*, 6 March 1844.
28 Cited on p. 134 above.
29 'Literatura religiosa', *El Arpa del Creyente*, 2, 9-10; José Simón Díaz, *El Arpa del Creyente (Madrid, 1842)*, CIPP VII (Madrid, 1947), 3-5 (4).
30 *El Arpa del Creyente*, 2, 9; Simón Díaz, 4.
31 'Chateaubriand', *El Laberinto*, I, 295-8 (296).
32 See p. 137 above.
33 See *Enrique Gil y Carrasco: A Study in Spanish Romanticism* (New York, 1939), 149-52.
34 *El concepto de la muerte en la poesía romántica española* (Madrid, 1959), 221.
35 *Galería de la literatura española*, (Madrid, 1846), 281-82.
36 *Obras completas* (Madrid, 1969), 669, 671.
37 See Raymond Carr, *Spain 1808-1939*, 169-72.
38 *Ibid.* 174.

7 The perception of literature's rôle in society

1 See 'Spain. Romántico-romanticismo', 364.
2 This was one of a series of articles on Romanticism published in Cadiz and Madrid: see pp. 78-9 above.
3 'Revista de la quincena', *El Pensamiento*, 236.
4 *No me olvides*, 14 May 1837, 3-4; Cabañas, 129.
5 See p. o above.
6 'De la literatura contemporánea. Artículo II', *El Pensamiento*, 227.
7 *Ibid.* 230.
8 'Discurso tercero sobre el teatro español, pronunciado por el Excmo. Sr. D. Javier de Burgos, en el Liceo de Granada, el viernes 16 de abril', *Rev. Teat.*, 13 June 1841, 81.
9 'Literatura dramática ... Artículo 2º.', *Rev. Esp. Ext.*, II, 187.
10 *Ibid.* 188.
11 *Ibid.* 189. These comments coincide with others already made by Enrique Gil y Carrasco and Agustín Durán; see pp. 98, 105 above.
12 In the same article, Gonzalo Morón enthusiastically outlined several major features of Schlegelian literary commentary; see p. 95 above.
13 *No me olvides*, 'Prospecto'; Cabañas, 25.
14 *Ibid.*
15 *No me olvides*, 7.v.1837, 2-3; Cabañas, 97-98.
16 *No me olvides*, 7.v.1837, 3; Cabañas, 98.
17 *No me olvides*, 7.v.1837, 2; Cabañas, 98. The tendency, in *No me olvides*, to regard literature as a potential means of promoting Christian morality and virtue in society at large has been noted by Robert Marrast: see *José de Espronceda et son temps. Littérature, société, politique au temps du romantisme* (Paris, 1974), 622-6.
18 Eamonn Rodgers, in a richly suggestive article, has recently investigated the influence of Herder on Sanz del Río and Giner; see 'Teoría literaria y filosofía de la historia en el primer Galdós' in Peter A. Bly (ed.), *Galdós y la historia*, Ottawa Hispanic Studies 7 (Ottawa, 1988), 35-47. For indications of a further linkage, between Romantic critics and Spanish writers of succeeding generations, see my own 'La misión regeneradora de la literatura: del romanticismo al modernismo pasando por Krause' in Richard A. Cardwell (ed.), *¿Qué es el modernismo? Nueva encuesta, nuevas lecturas* (University of Colorado at Boulder, in press). Professor Cardwell has himself analysed, in a series of penetrating articles, the idealistic prescriptions of Spanish intellectuals at the turn of the century.

19 *Ideal de la humanidad para la vida* (Madrid, 1860), 41.

20 'Tierras solares. En Barcelona', cited by Patricia O'Riordan, '*Helios*, revista del modernismo', *Abaco*, 4 (1973), 57–150 (79).

21 *The Mirror and the Lamp: Romantic Theory and the Critical Tradition* (Oxford, 1953), 218–19.

22 'Reflections on Romanticism in France' in David Thorburn and Geoffrey Hartman (eds.), *Romanticism: Vistas, Instances, Continuities* (Cornell, 1974), 38–61 (41).

23 *Ibid.* 42.

24 'Influencia de la literatura en las costumbres', *No me olvides*, 21 May 1837, 1; not reproduced by Cabañas.

25 These reviews all appeared in *No me olvides*: that of *El paje*, 28 May 1837, 8; that of *Fray Luis de León*, 20 August 1837, 7–8; that of *Carlos II el hechizado*, 12 November 1837, 6–8 (see the passage quoted on p. 115 above); that of *El rey monje*, 24 December 1837, 7–8. Cabañas reproduces the review of *El rey monje* (101–2).

26 '*El Rey monje*, drama de don Antonio García Gutiérrez, representado en el teatro del Príncipe', *No me olvides*, 24 December 1837, 7; Cabañas, 101.

27 *No me olvides*, 7. He insists that 'La popularidad que gozó en su tiempo el *No me olvides* es incuestionable' (19).

28 'Salas y Quiroga, *El Dios del siglo: novela original de costumbres contemporáneas* (Madrid, 1848)', *BHS*, 30 (1953), 32–40 (37).

29 *Historia del periodismo en España*, ed. Ma. Dolores Sáiz and Ma. Cruz Seoane, *Vol. II: El siglo XIX* (Madrid, 1983), 170.

30 See p. 16 above.

31 See Isaiah Berlin, *Vico and Herder*, 65.

32 *Poesías* (Madrid, 1840), 'Prólogo'; (III, 329).

33 *Memorias de una campaña periodística*, *Obras*, II, 9–33 (17).

34 Simón Díaz, *El Artista*, 118.

35 *Poesías*, 'Prólogo'; (III, 329).

36 See pp. 115, 117, 119, 131–2 above.

37 See D. L. Shaw, '*Armonismo*: The Failure of an Illusion' in Clara E. Lida and Iris M. Zavala (eds.), *La revolución de 1868. Historia, pensamiento, literatura* (New York, 1970), 351–61.

38 *La Préface de Cromwell*, ed. M. Souriau (Paris, undated), 214.

39 See pp. 136–7 above.

40 See *Life and Letters*, xv.

41 *Rev. Mad.*, 1843, 4a serie, I, 485.

42 'What is Spanish Romanticism?', *St. Rom.* II (1962–3), 1–11 (8).

43 For a broadly based and lucid analysis of Romantic conceptions of poetic rôle, see chapter 1, 'The Artist in Isolation' in Frank Kermode's *Romantic Image*, new edition (London, 1986), 1–29.

44 'Dos generaciones' in *Obras completas*, 9 vols. (Madrid, 1947–1954), IX, 1138.

45 See p. 126 above.

46 In this context, see particularly the comments of Enrique Gil and Salvador Bermúdez de Castro quoted on pp. 103–4 above.

47 See *The Classic: Literary Images of Permanence and Change* (Harvard, 1983).

8 Romantic traditionalism in the work of Fernán Caballero

1 They appeared as follows: *La gaviota. Novela original de costumbres españolas*, *El Heraldo*, 9 May–9 July; *Peso de un poco de paja. Leyenda piadosa*, *Sem. Pint.*, 3 June; *La hija del sol. Novela original*, *La Ilustración*, 18 July; *Los dos amigos*, *Sem. Pint.*, 22

July; *La familia Alvareda* [sic], *El Heraldo*, 7–26 September; *Una en otra*, *El Heraldo*, 28 September–14 November; *Sola*, *Sem. Pint.*, 28 October–4 November; *La Suegra del diablo. Cuento popular*, *Sem. Pint.*, 25 November; *Elia*, *La España*, December. These details immediately suggest the impact which Fernán Caballero must have created in that year.

2 See E. Herman Hespelt, 'The Genesis of *La familia de Alvareda*', *HR*, 2 (1934), 179–201. Chronological as well as bibliographical details relating to Fernán Caballero's entire output are provided by José F. Montesinos, *Fernán Caballero. Ensayo de justificación* (El Colegio de México, 1959), 143–78.

3 *Fernán Caballero*, 317–32; 'El naranjo romántico: la esencia del costumbrismo', *HR*, 46 (1978), 343–54.

4 'El naranjo romántico', 345.

5 *Fernán Caballero*, 317.

6 See Santiago Montoto, 'Cartas inéditas de Fernán Caballero', *BRAE*, 35 (1955), 383–414; 36 (1956), 29–64; 37 (1957), 85–134, 299–308, 469–83; 38 (1958), 117–34; 39 (1959), 295–331, 463–85; 40 (1960), 401–539. The passages referred to in the text are in vol. 37, 111 and 122.

7 See Theodor Heinermann, *Cecilia Böhl de Faber (Fernán Caballero) y Juan Eugenio Hartzenbusch. Una correspondencia inédita* (Madrid, 1944), Carta 2 (27 April 1849), 82.

8 *Ibid.* Carta 49 (30 May 1860), 205.

9 *Obras de Fernán Caballero*, ed. José María Castro y Calvo, 5 vols., BAE XCCCVI–CXL (Madrid, 1961), II, 255. Future references will be to this edition.

10 The first manuscript of *La familia de Alvareda* probably dates from 1828–9: see Hespelt, 'The Genesis'.

11 See E. Herman Hespelt and Stanley T. Williams, 'Two Unpublished Anecdotes by Fernán Caballero Preserved by Washington Irving', *MLN*, 49 (1934), 25–31.

12 *Ensayo de justificación*, 12.

13 'Fernán Caballero y el *Volksgeist*', *Arbor*, 97 (1977), 327–42 (329).

14 Heinermann, *Cecilia Böhl*, Carta 42 (26 February 1859), 186.

15 *Clemencia*, ed. Julio Rodríguez-Luis (Madrid, 1975), 370. I refer to this edition since the Rivadeneyra edition of *Clemencia* inexplicably fails to include the third part of the novel.

16 'Prólogo', x; quoted by Herrero, *Fernán Caballero*, 318.

17 'Respuesta de Fernán Caballero al Sr. D. Vicente Barrantes', *La Ilustración*, v, 33–4; cited by Montesinos, *Ensayo de justificación*, 35.

18 Heinermann, *Cecilia Böhl*, Carta 46 (1 October 1859), 197.

19 Montoto, 'Cartas inéditas', 37, 129–30.

20 *Ibid.* 36, 56. The letter is undated, but Montoto groups it with those dating from 1858.

21 Cited by D. A. Randolph, *Don Manuel Cañete, cronista literario del romanticismo y del posromanticismo en España* (Chapel Hill, 1972), 183.

22 Alberto López Argüello, *Epistolario de Fernán Caballero. Una colección de cartas inéditas de la novelista* (Barcelona, 1922), 125.

23 See pp. 10–11 above.

24 See p. 58 above.

25 Heinermann, *Cecilia Böhl*, Carta 10 (15 February 1850), 112–13.

26 See p. 108 above.

27 'Les premiers essais littéraires de Fernán Caballero', *BH*, 9 (1907), 286–92.

28 'Towards the Understanding', 194; 'The Anti-Romantic Reaction', 608–9.

29 López Argüello, *Epistolario*, 178.

30 Montoto, 'Cartas inéditas', 37, 470.
31 López Argüello, *Epistolario*, 92.
32 *Ibid.* 105.
33 *Ensayo de justificación*, 18.
34 *Clemencia*, ed. Rodríguez-Luis, 323.
35 See E. Herman Hespelt and Stanley T. Williams, 'Washington Irving's Notes on Fernán Caballero's Stories', *PMLA*, 49 (1934), 1129–39.
36 See Heinermann, *Cecilia Böhl*, Carta 37 (24 November 1856), 172.
37 See, for example, David Brown, *Walter Scott and the Historical Imagination* (London, 1979).
38 See Graham McMaster, *Scott and Society* (Cambridge, 1981).
39 *Novels and Tales of the Author of Waverley*, 12 vols. (Edinburgh, 1822), I, 13.
40 'Juicio crítico de *La gaviota*', *La España*, August, 1849; reprinted in Fernán Caballero's *Obras*, v, 433–41.
41 'On the Threshold of the Realist Novel: Gender and Genre in *La gaviota*', *PMLA*, 98 (1983), 323–40 (328).
42 See p. o above.
43 'Revista de Madrid. Cartas al director de la *Revista Peninsular*', Carta III, 31 July 1856; in *Obras completas*, ed. Luis Araujo Costa, 3rd edn, 3 vols. (Madrid, 1947), II, 85–6.
44 See Fernán Caballero's letter to Cañete: López Argüello, *Epistolario*, 92.
45 *Ibid.*
46 See José María Castro y Calvo's introduction to Fernán Caballero's *Obras*, I, cxiv.
47 See *Ideología y política*, 126–43.
48 Reprinted in Fernán Caballero's *Obras*, IV, 283.
49 '*Obras completas de Fernán Caballero. 13 vols. Madrid: 1856–1859*', *Edinburgh Review*, 114 (1861), 99–129.
50 See Heinermann, *Cecilia Böhl*, 182.

9 Conclusions: The mid-century

1 'Biografía. El Conde de Aranda', *El Laberinto*, II (1845), 17–20; 'Poesía popular', *El Laberinto*, II, 134–6 (135).
2 'Poesía dramática', *El Laberinto*, II, 201–3 (202), 214–15, 222–3.
3 *Ibid.* 202–3.
4 *Ibid.* 222.
5 'De la crítica contemporánea', *ibid.* 238–40 (239).
6 'Escritores contemporáneos. El Duque de Rivas', *El Siglo Pintoresco*, I (1845), 220–6 (225).
7 'Del estado de las doctrinas críticas en España en lo relativo a la composición poética', *Rev. Cient. Lit.*, I, 241–55.
8 *Ibid.* 249.
9 *Ibid.* 249–53.
10 *Ibid.* 251.
11 *Ibid.* 254.
12 'Curso de literatura dramática, o examen crítico del teatro español desde 1833 a 1847', *Rev. Cient. Lit.*, II, 9–21 (12), 49–63, 93–105.
13 *Ibid.* 97.
14 *Ibid.* 58.
15 *Ibid.* 105.
16 'Curso de literatura dramática. Examen crítico del teatro español desde 1834 hasta nuestros días. Introducción', *El País*, 12 September 1849.

17 *Obras completas de D. Angel Saavedra, Duque de Rivas, de la Real Academia Española, corregidas por él mismo*, 5 vols. (Madrid, 1854–5), I, xx.

18 *Ibid.* xx–xxi.

19 *Ibid.* xxix.

20 'Crítica literaria. Del neo-culteranismo en la poesía española. Zorrilla y su escuela', *Revista de Ciencias, Literatura y Artes*, 1855, I, 34–46 (36).

21 *Revista de Ciencias, Literatura y Artes*, I, 35.

22 *Revista Española de Ambos Mundos*, II, 801–42; reprinted in *Documentos*, ed. Navas-Ruiz, 150–207. References in the text will be to this edition.

23 Lista's article was entitled 'De lo que hoy se llama romanticismo' and published in *El Tiempo* in March 1839. It was reprinted in the *Gaceta de Madrid* in the same year and was later included in his *Ensayos*, II, 38–41.

24 See *ibid.* 38.

25 *Obras*, II, 7–19.

26 'Sobre la historia de la literatura española en la edad media', II, 148–53 (149).

27 'La poesía popular de Manuel Milá y Fontanals', II, 201–10 (204). This year of 1861 had seen the publication, in the Rivadeneyra collection Biblioteca de Autores Españoles, of a second edition of the *Romancero general* prepared by Durán, which had first appeared in 1849–51.

28 M. Ovilo y Otero, 'Necrología. Don Agustín Durán', *Museo Universal*, 1862, VI, 398–9.

29 *Memorias de la Academia Española*, II, 280–336 (281).

30 Published in the Granada newspaper *La Alhambra*, 24 January 1861. I am grateful to Professor Eamonn Rodgers for drawing my attention to this piece.

31 *Historia del periodismo*, II, 16.

32 *Ibid.* 57.

33 *El romanticismo español. Historia y crítica*, 14.

34 *Ibid.* 37.

35 *Historia crítica*, IV, 242.

36 *Ibid.* 223.

37 'La recepción de la cultura y ciencia alemana en España durante la época romántica' in *Estudios románticos* (Valladolid, 1975), 63–120 (71).

38 *Vol. V: romanticismo y realismo*, ed. I. M. Zavala in *Historia y crítica de la literatura española*, ed. Francisco Rico (Barcelona, 1982), Part 1: 'Románticos y liberales, Introducción', 7–16 (8).

39 *Ibid.* 8.

40 *Ibid.* 9.

41 *Romantics, Rebels and Reactionaries: English Literature and its Background 1760–1830* (Oxford, 1981), 5.

42 *Historia*, 61.

Select bibliography of works consulted

A Spanish newspapers and periodicals of the Romantic period

La Abeja, diario universal (Madrid, 1834–6).
El Alba (Madrid, 1838–9).
Antología española. Revista de ciencias, literatura, bellas artes y crítica de El Siglo (Madrid, 1848).
El Arpa del Creyente (Madrid, 1842).
El Artista (Madrid, 1835–6).
El Bibliotecario y El Trovador Español. Colección de documentos interesantes sobre nuestra historia nacional, y de poesías inéditas de nuestros poetas antiguos y modernos, acompañada de artículos de costumbres antiguas españolas escritos por D. Basilio Sebastián Castellanos, Anticuario de la Biblioteca Nacional (Madrid, 1841).
Cartas Españolas, o sea revista histórica, científica, teatral, artística, crítica y literaria (Madrid, 1831–2).
La Civilización. Revista religiosa, filosófica, política y literaria de Barcelona (Barcelona, 1841–2).
Crónica Científica y Literaria (Madrid, 1817–20).
Eco del Comercio (Madrid, 1834–49).
Eco Literario de Europa (Madrid, 1851–2).
El Iris, semanario enciclopédico (Madrid, 1841).
El Laberinto, periódico universal (Madrid, 1843–5).
Liceo Artístico y Literario (Madrid, 1838).
El Museo de Familias (Barcelona, 1838–41).
Museo de las Familias. Periódico mensual (Madrid, 1843–67).
No me olvides, periódico de literatura y bellas artes (Madrid, 1837–8).
El Observatorio Pintoresco (Madrid, 1837).
El País (Madrid, 1849–50).
El Panorama, periódico de literatura y artes (Madrid, 1838–41).
El Paraíso. Periódico semanal de filosofía, historia, literatura y bellas artes (Seville, 1838).
El Pensamiento, periódico de literatura y artes (Madrid, 1841).
El Pensamiento de la Nación, periódico religioso, político y literario (Madrid, 1844–6).
El Propagador de la Libertad (Barcelona, 1835–6).

El Reflejo, revista semanal (Madrid, 1843).
El Renacimiento (Madrid, 1847).
Revista de Ciencias, Literatura y Artes (Seville, 1855–60).
Revista Científica y Literaria, periódico quincenal (Madrid, 1847–8).
Revista de España y del Extranjero (Madrid, 1842–8).
La Revista Española, periódico dedicado a la Reina Ntra. Sra. (Madrid, 1832–3).
Revista Española de Ambos Mundos (Madrid, 1853–5).
Revista de Europa, periódico quincenal de ciencias, literatura y artes (Madrid, 1846).
Revista de Madrid (Madrid, 1838–45).
Revista del Progreso (Madrid, 1841).
Revista de Teatros, periódico semanal de literatura, sátira y bellas artes (Madrid, 1841–2).
Semanario Pintoresco Español (Madrid, 1836–57).
El Siglo Pintoresco (Madrid, 1845–8).
El Vapor, periódico mercantil, político y literario de Cataluña (Barcelona, 1833–6).

B Sources

Alcalá Galiano, A. *Introductory Lecture Delivered at the Opening of the University of London*, second edn (London, 1829).
'Literature of the Nineteenth Century. Spain', *The Athenaeum*, 1834, 290–5, 329–33, 370–4, 411–14, 450–4.
Prologue to Angel Saavedra, Duque de Rivas, *El moro expósito* (Paris, 1834); reprinted in *El romanticismo español. Documentos*, ed. Ricardo Navas-Ruiz (Salamanca, 1971), 107–28. Henceforth Navas-Ruiz.
'Literatura', *Rev. Mad.*, 1838, 1, 41–55.
'Del estado de las doctrinas críticas en España en lo relativo a la composición poética', *Rev. Cient. Lit.*, 1847, 1, 241–55.
Amador de los Ríos, J. *Oración pronunciada en la solemne apertura del curso académico de 1850 a 1851, de la Universidad de Madrid* (Madrid, 1850).
Athenaeum, The. 'The Drama of Spain. *Discurso sobre el influjo que ha tenido la crítica moderna en la decadencia del teatro antiguo español, y sobre el modo con que debe ser considerado para juzgar convenientemente de su mérito peculiar.* Por D.A.D. Con licencia. Madrid, 1828', *The Athenaeum*, 1829, 146–7.
Avecilla, P. A. de la. *Poética trágica* (Madrid, 1834).
Balmes, J. *Obras completas*, ed. P. Casanovas, 8 vols., BAC (Madrid, 1948–50).
(ed.) *La Civilización. Revista religiosa, filosófica, política y literaria de Barcelona* (Barcelona, 1841–2).
(ed.) *El Pensamiento de la Nación, periódico religioso, político y literario* (Madrid, 1844–6).
Bermúdez de Castro, S. *Ensayos poéticos* (Madrid, 1840).
(ed.) *El Iris, Semanario enciclopédico* (Madrid, 1841).
Böhl von Faber, J. N. *Vindicaciones de Calderón y del Teatro Antiguo Español contra los Afrancesados en Literatura* (Cadiz, 1820).

Borao, J. 'El romanticismo', *Revista Española de Ambos Mundos*, 1854, II, 801–42; reprinted in Navas-Ruiz, 150–207.

Burgos, J. de. 'Discurso sobre el teatro'; 'Segundo discurso sobre el teatro español'; 'Discurso tercero', *El Panorama*, 1841, 3a época, 131–4, 137–9, 153–7, 161–3, 170–3, 180–3.

Caballero, Fernán (pseud.) *Obras de Fernán Caballero*, ed. José María Castro y Calvo, 5 vols., BAE, CXXXVI–CXL (Madrid, 1961).

Campoamor, R. de. 'Acerca del estado actual de nuestra poesía', *No me olvides*, 1837, 32, 3–4; Pablo Cabañas, *No me olvides (Madrid, 1837–1838)*, CIPP II (Madrid, 1946), 46–7.

Cañete, M. 'Curso de literatura dramática o examen crítico del teatro español desde 1833 a 1847', *Rev. Cient. Lit.*, 1848, II, 9–21, 49–63, 93–105.

'Estudios críticos. Rápida ojeada acerca del rumbo que ha seguido la literatura dramática española en 1847', *Antología Española*, 1848, I, 97–108; III, 1–8.

'Curso de literatura dramática. Examen crítico del teatro español desde 1834 hasta nuestros días. Introducción', *El País*, 12 September 1849.

Prologue to *Obras completas de D. Angel Saavedra, Duque de Rivas, de la Real Academia Española, corregidas por él mismo*, 5 vols. (Madrid, 1854–5), I, v–li.

'Crítica literaria. Del neo-culteranismo en la poesía española. Zorrilla y su escuela', *Revista de Ciencias, Literatura y Artes*, 1855, I, 34–46.

Carabantes, J. V. 'Literatura religiosa', *El Arpa del Creyente*, 1842, II, 9–10; José Simón Díaz, *El Arpa del Creyente (Madrid, 1842)*, CIPP VII (Madrid, 1947), 3–5.

Carnerero, J. M. (ed.) *Cartas Españolas, o sea revista histórica, científica, teatral, artística, crítica y literaria* (Madrid, 1831–2).

Chateaubriand, F. R., Vicomte de. *Le Génie du christianisme, Oeuvres complètes*, 5 vols. (Paris, 1843), vol. III.

'Consabido, el'. 'Sobre clásicos y románticos', *Cartas Españolas*, 1832, V, 31–6.

Cortés, C. 'De la literatura contemporánea', *El Pensamiento*, 1841, 226–32, 241–7.

Cueto, L. A. 'Examen del "Don Alvaro o La fuerza del sino"', *El Artista*, III, 106–8, 110–14; reprinted as 'Spanish Romanticism: Some Notes and Documents – I', *BSS*, 7 (1930), 3–13.

Díaz, N-P. *Obras completas de D. Nicomedes-Pastor Díaz*, ed. José María Castro y Calvo, 3 vols., BAE CCXXVII, CCXXVIII, CCXLI (Madrid, 1969–70).

Donoso Cortés, J. *Obras completas de don Juan Donoso Cortés, Marqués de Valdegamas*, ed. Hans Juretschke, 2 vols., BAC (Madrid, 1946).

Durán, A. *Discurso sobre el influjo que ha tenido la crítica moderna en la decadencia del teatro antiguo español y sobre el modo con que debe ser considerado para juzgar convenientemente de su mérito peculiar* (Madrid, 1828); reprinted in Navas-Ruiz, 54–100.

Romancero de romances caballerescos e históricos anteriores al siglo XVIII, que contiene los de Amor, los de la Tabla Redonda, los de Carlo Magno y de los Doce Pares, los de Bernardo del Carpio, del Cid Campeador, de los infantes de Lara, etc., 2 vols. (Madrid, 1832), 'Discurso preliminar'.

Talía española, o colección de dramas del antiguo teatro español, recogidas y ordenadas por don Agustín Durán (Madrid, 1834), 'Prospecto'.

'Poesía popular. Drama novelesco. Lope de Vega', *Rev. Mad.*, 1839, 2a serie, II, 62–75.

'Análisis crítico del drama de Tirso de Molina, intitulado *El condenado por desconfiado*', *Rev. Mad.*, 1841, 3a serie, II, 109–34.

Romancero general o colección de romances castellanos anteriores al siglo XVIII, recogidos, ordenados, clasificados y anotados por don Agustín Durán, 2 vols., BAE x, xvi (Madrid, 1849–51), 'Prólogo'.

Edinburgh Review. 'Obras completas de Fernán Caballero. 13 vols. Madrid: 1856–1869', *Edinburgh Review*, 114 (1861), 99–129.

Espronceda, J. de. 'El pastor Clasiquino', *El Artista*, I, 251–2; Simón Díaz, 66.

Fernández de Moratín, L. *Orígenes del teatro español, seguidos de una colección escogida de piezas dramáticas anteriores a Lope de Vega* (Paris, 1838).

Ferrer del Río, A. 'Chateaubriand', *El Laberinto*, 1844, I, 295–8.

Galería de la literatura española (Madrid, 1846).

Fontcuberta, A. (ed.) *El Propagador de la Libertad* (Barcelona, 1835–8).

(ed.) *El Vapor, periódico mercantil, político y literario de Cataluña* (Barcelona, 1836–8).

Gallardo, B. J. *Obras escogidas de Bartolomé José Gallardo*, ed. Pedro Sáinz y Rodríguez, 2 vols. (Madrid, 1928).

Gil y Carrasco, E. *Obras completas de don Enrique Gil y Carrasco*, ed. Jorge Campos, BAE LXXIV (Madrid, 1954).

Gil y Zárate, A. 'Sobre la poesía dramática, discurso leído por su autor en la Academia española para su admisión en ella', *Rev. Mad.*, 1839, 1a serie, III, 147–57.

Introducción a la historia moderna, o examen de los diferentes elementos que han entrado a constituir la civilización de los actuales pueblos europeos (Madrid, 1841).

'Teatro antiguo y teatro moderno', *Rev. Mad.*, 1841, 3a serie, I, 112–24; reprinted under the heading 'Spanish Romanticism: Some Notes and Documents – II', *BSS*, 7 (1930), 55–64.

Manual de literatura (Madrid, 1842).

Manual de literatura. Segunda parte. Resumen histórico de la literatura española (Madrid, 1844).

Resumen histórico de la literatura española. Segunda parte de Manual de literatura, cuarta edición, corregida y aumentada (Madrid, 1851).

Gómez Hermosilla, J. *Arte de hablar en prosa y verso*, 2 vols. (Madrid, 1826).

Gonzalo Morón, F. 'Reflexiones sobre Homero y la tragedia griega. Caracteres distintivos de la literatura antigua y moderna', *El Iris*, 1841, I, pp. 385–8.

(ed.) *Revista de España y del Extranjero. Director y redactor principal, D. Fermín Gonzalo Morón* (Madrid, 1842–8).

Hartzenbusch, J. E. (ed.) *Revista de Teatros, periódico semanal de literatura, sátira y bellas artes* (Madrid, 1841–2).

Hugo, V. M. Preface to *Hernani* (1829) in *Théâtre*, 4 vols. (Paris, 1873), II, 3–9. Preface to *Cromwell* (1827) in *La Préface de Cromwell*, ed. M. Souriau (Paris, undated).

'J. G.' 'Ojeada religiosa', *El Pensamiento de la Nación*, 7 February 1844.

'J. del P.' [?Joaquín del Pino], 'Reforma teatral', *Rev. Teat.*, 1841, I, 1–2.

Larra, M. J. de. *Obras de D. Mariano José de Larra (Fígaro)*, ed. Carlos Seco Serrano, 4 vols., BAE CXXVII–CXXX (Madrid, 1960).

Lista, A. *Discurso sobre la importancia de nuestra historia literaria, leído en la Real Academia de la Historia por D. Alberto Lista* (Madrid, 1828).

Ensayos literarios y críticos, ed. José Joaquín de Mora, 2 vols. (Seville, 1844).

Lecciones de literatura española, explicadas en el Ateneo científico, literario y artístico de Madrid, 2 vols. (Madrid, 1853).

'Literato rancio, el'. 'Sobre clásicos y románticos', *Cartas Españolas*, 1832, IV, 197–201, 373–6.

López Soler, R. 'Examen sobre el carácter superficial de nuestro siglo', *El Europeo*, 1823, I, 193–200; reprinted in Luis Guarner, *El Europeo (Barcelona, 1823–1824)*, CIPP XVI (Madrid, 1953), 71–5. Henceforth Guarner.

'Análisis de la cuestión agitada entre románticos y clasicistas', *El Europeo*, I, 207–14, 254–9; reprinted in Navas-Ruiz, 42–53.

'Sobre la historia filosófica de la poesía española', *El Europeo*, I, 342–9; reprinted in Guarner, 81–4.

'Perjuicios que acarrea el olvido de las costumbres nacionales', *El Europeo*, II, 109–18; reprinted in Guarner, 84–9.

Los bandos de Castilla, o el Caballero del Cisne (Valencia, 1830), 'Prólogo'; reprinted in Navas-Ruiz, 101–7.

(ed.) *El Vapor, periódico mercantil, político y literario de Cataluña* (Barcelona, 1833–5).

Luzán, I. de. *La Poética, o reglas de la poesía en general y de sus principales especies*, 2nd edn, 2 vols. (Madrid, 1789).

'M.' [?Mesonero Romanos] 'Teatros, *El paje*. Drama en cuatro jornadas; su autor, don Antonio García Gutiérrez', *Sem. Pint.*, 1837, II, 165–6.

Martínez de la Rosa, F. *Obras de D. Francisco Martínez de la Rosa*, ed. Carlos Seco Serrano, 8 vols., BAE CXLVIII–CLV (Madrid, 1962).

Mesonero Romanos, R. de. *Obras completas de D. Ramón de Mesonero Romanos*, ed. Carlos Seco Serrano, 5 vols., BAE CIC–CCIII (Madrid, 1967).

(ed.) *Semanario Pintoresco Español* (Madrid, 1836–42).

Milá y Fontanals, M. *Obras completas del Doctor D. Manuel Milá y Fontanals*, ed. Marcelino Menéndez y Pelayo, 8 vols. (Barcelona, 1888–96).

Monteggia, L. 'Romanticismo', *El Europeo*, 1823, I, 48–56; reprinted in Navas-Ruiz, 33–42.

Mora, José Joaquín de. 'Spanish Poetry'; 'Spanish Poetry: First Period'; 'Spanish Poetry: Moorish Romances', *The European Review*, 1824, 373–83; 1824, 535–41; 1825, 292–7.

(ed.) *Crónica Científica y Literaria* (Madrid, 1817–20).

(ed.) Alberto Lista, *Ensayos literarios y críticos*, 2 vols. (Seville, 1844).

Muñoz Maldonado, J. 'Doña María de Molina', *El Panorama*, 1838, I, 10–12.

Navarro Villoslada, F. (ed.) *El Arpa del Creyente* (Madrid, 1842).

(ed.) *El Siglo Pintoresco* (Madrid, 1845–8).

Negrete, J., Conde de Campo Alange. 'Teatro', *El Artista*, 1835, I, 52–5, 67–71.

'Teatro del Príncipe. "Don Alvaro o La fuerza del sino", drama en cinco jornadas de don Angel Saavedra, Duque de Rivas', *El Artista*, I, 153–6; Simón Díaz, 103–6.

Ochoa, E. de. 'Juicio crítico de *La gaviota*', *La España*, 1849; reprinted in *Obras de Fernán Caballero*, ed. José María Castro y Calvo, 5 vols., BAE CXXXVI–CXL (Madrid, 1961), V, 433–41.

(ed.) *El Artista* (Madrid, 1835–6).

Ovilo y Otero, M. 'Necrología. Don Agustín Durán', *Museo Universal*, 1862, VI, 398–9.

Pidal, P. J. 'Literatura española. Poema del Cid. Crónica del Cid. Romancero del Cid', *Rev. Mad.*, 1840, 2a serie, III, 306–44.

Quadrado, J. M. 'Víctor Hugo y su escuela literaria', *Sem. Pint.*, 1840, 2a serie, II, 189–92.

Quintana, M. J. *Obras completas del Excmo. Sr. D. Manuel José Quintana*, BAE XIX (Madrid, 1867).

Revilla, J. de la. 'Teatros', *Sem. Pint.*, 1836, I, 15–16.

Ribot y Fontseré, A. *Emancipación literaria didáctica* (Barcelona, 1837).

Saavedra, A., Duque de Rivas. Prologue to *Romances históricos* (1841) in *Romances*, ed. Cipriano Rivas Cherif, 2 vols., Clásicos Castellanos (Madrid, 1911–12), I, 23–47.

Salas y Quiroga, J. de. *Poesías* (Madrid, 1834).

(ed.) *No me olvides, periódico de literatura y bellas artes* (Madrid, 1837–8).

(ed.) *El Paraíso. Periódico semanal de filosofía, historia, literatura y bellas artes* (Seville, 1838).

(ed.) *Revista del Progreso* (Madrid, 1841).

Sanz del Río, J. *Ideal de la humanidad para la vida* (Madrid, 1860).

Schlegel, A. W. *A Course of Lectures on Dramatic Art and Literature*, tr. John Black, 2 vols. (London, 1815).

Schlegel, F. *Lectures on the History of Literature, Ancient and Modern*, tr. John Gibson Lockhart, 2 vols. (Edinburgh, 1818).

Scott, Sir W. *Novels and Tales of the Author of Waverley*, 12 vols. (Edinburgh, 1822).

Simonde de Sismondi, J. C. L. *De la Littérature du Midi de l'Europe*, 3rd edn, 4 vols. (Paris, 1829).

Staël-Holstein, G. L. Necker, Baronne de. *De l'Allemagne*, 3 vols. (London, 1813).

Tejado, Gabino, 'Biografía. El Conde de Aranda', *El Laberinto*, II (1845), 17–20.

'Poesía popular', *El Laberinto*, II, 134–6.

'Poesía dramática', *El Laberinto*, II, 201–3, 214–15, 222–3.
'De la crítica contemporánea', *El Laberinto*, II, 238–40.
'Escritores contemporáneos. El Duque de Rivas', *El Siglo Pintoresco*, I (1845), 220–6.
Valera, J. *Obras completas*, ed. Luis Araujo Costa, 3rd edn, 3 vols. (Madrid, 1947).
Vega, V. de la. *Discurso que leyó don Ventura de la Vega, al tomar asiento en la Academia* in *Memorias de la Academia Española*, II (1870), 5–15.
Vera e Isla, F. de la. 'Verdadera poesía', *No me olvides*, 14 May 1837, 3–4; Pablo Cabañas, *No me olvides (Madrid, 1837–1838)*, CIPP II (Madrid, 1946), 129.
Zorrilla, J. *Obras completas*, ed. Narciso Alonso Cortés, 2 vols. (Valladolid, 1943).

C *Secondary literature*

Abellán, J. L. *Historia crítica del pensamiento español. Vol. IV: Liberalismo y romanticismo (1808–1874)* (Madrid, 1984).
Abrams, M. H. *The Mirror and the Lamp: Romantic Theory and the Critical Tradition* (Oxford, 1953).
Adams, N. B. *The Romantic Dramas of García Gutiérrez* (New York, 1922).
'*Siglo de Oro* Plays in Madrid, 1820–1850', *HR*, 4 (1936), 342–57.
'French Influence on the Madrid Theatre in 1837' in *Estudios dedicados a Menéndez Pidal* (Madrid, 1950), VII, 135–51.
Alborg, J. L. *Historia de la literatura española. Vol. IV: El romanticismo* (Madrid, 1980).
Alonso Cortés, N. *Zorrilla, su vida y sus obras*, 3 vols. (Valladolid, 1916).
(ed.) José Zorrilla, *Obras completas*, 2 vols. (Valladolid, 1943).
Andioc, R. 'Sobre el estreno del *Don Alvaro*' in *Homenaje a Juan López-Morillas* (Madrid, 1982), 63–86.
Ayuso Rivera, J. *El concepto de la muerte en la poesía romántica española* (Madrid, 1959).
Berlin, Sir I. *Vico and Herder: Two Studies in the History of Ideas* (London, 1976).
Blanco García, P. Celso. *La literatura española en el siglo XIX*, 3 vols. (Madrid, 1891–4).
Brown, D. *Walter Scott and the Historical Imagination* (London, 1979).
Brown, R. F. 'Three Madrid Periodicals: *La Abeja*; *Eco del Comercio*; *El Español*' in E. Allison Peers (ed.), *Liverpool Studies in Spanish Literature. First Series: From Cadalso to Rubén Darío* (Liverpool, 1940), 44–79.
'Salas y Quiroga, *El Dios del siglo. Novela original de costumbres contemporáneas*, Madrid, 1848', *BHS*, 30 (1953), 32–40.
Butler, M. *Romantics, Rebels and Reactionaries: English Literature and its Background, 1760–1830* (Oxford, 1981).
Cabañas, P. *No me olvides (Madrid, 1837–1838)*, CIPP II (Madrid, 1946).
Caldera, E. *Primi manifesti del romanticismo spagnolo* (Pisa, 1962).
Callahan, W. J. *Church, Politics and Society in Spain, 1750–1874* (Harvard, 1984).

Calvo Sanz, R. *Don Salvador Bermúdez de Castro y Díez. Su vida y su obra* (Valladolid, 1974).

Campos, J. *Teatro y sociedad en España (1780–1820)* (Madrid, 1969).

Cardwell, R. A. '*Don Alvaro* or the Force of Cosmic Injustice', *St. Rom.*, XII (1973), 559–79.

(ed.) José de Espronceda, *El estudiante de Salamanca and Other Poems*, Tamesis Texts (London, 1980).

Carnero, G. 'El lenguaje del reaccionarismo fernandino en boca de Juan Nicolás Böhl de Faber', *BH*, 76 (1974), 265–85.

Los orígenes del romanticismo reaccionario español: el matrimonio Böhl de Faber (Valencia, 1978).

Carnicer, R. *Vida y obra de Pablo Piferrer* (Madrid, 1963).

Carr, R. *Spain, 1808–1939* (Oxford, 1966).

Castro y Calvo, J. M. (ed.) *Obras de Fernán Caballero*, 5 vols., BAE CXXXVI–CXL (Madrid, 1961).

Cattaneo, M. T. 'Gli esordi del romanticismo in Ispagna e *El Europeo*' in *Tre studi sulla cultura spagnola* (Milan, 1967), 75–137.

Chandler, A. *A Dream of Order: The Mediaeval Ideal in Nineteenth-Century Literature* (London, 1971).

Chao Espina, E. *Pastor Díaz dentro del romanticismo*, *RFE* Anejo XLVI (Madrid, 1949).

Charlton, D. G. (ed.), *The French Romantics*, 2 vols. (Cambridge, 1984).

Correa Calderón, E. (ed.) *Costumbristas españoles*, 2 vols. (Madrid, 1950).

Dendle, B. J. 'Two Sources of López Soler's Articles in *El Europeo*', *St. Rom.*, V (1965–6), 44–50.

Díaz-Plaja, G. *Introducción al estudio del romanticismo español* (Madrid, 1942).

Eichner, H. (ed.) '*Romantic*' and its Cognates: The European History of a Word (Toronto, 1972).

Estudios románticos (Valladolid, 1975).

Fernández González, F. *Historia de la crítica literaria en España desde Luzán hasta nuestros días, con exclusión de los autores que aún viven* (Madrid, 1867).

Flitter, D. W. 'La misión regeneradora de la literatura: del romanticismo al modernismo pasando por Krause' in Richard A. Cardwell (ed.), *¿Qué es el modernismo? Nueva encuesta, nuevas lecturas* (University of Colorado at Boulder, in press).

Frye, N. (ed.) *Romanticism Reconsidered: Selected Papers from the English Institute* (Columbia, 1963).

Furst, L. R. *Romanticism*, Methuen Critical Idiom Series, no. 2 (London, 1969).

Gabbert, T. A. 'Notes on the Popularity of the Dramas of Victor Hugo in Spain during the Years 1835–1845', *HR*, 4 (1936), 176–8.

Galindo Herrero, S. 'Donoso Cortés en su paralelo con Balmes y Pastor Díaz', *Revista de Estudios Políticos*, 69 (1953), 111–39.

García, S. *Las ideas literarias en España entre 1840 y 1850* (Berkeley, 1971).

García Barrón, C. *La obra crítica y literaria de don Antonio Alcalá Galiano* (Madrid, 1970).

García Mercadal, J. *Historia del romanticismo en España* (Barcelona, 1943).

Gies, D. T. *Agustín Durán: A Biography and Literary Appreciation* (London, 1975).

Guarner, L. *El Europeo (Barcelona, 1823–1834)*, CIPP XVI (Madrid, 1953).

Hartman, G. 'Reflections on Romanticism in France' in David Thorburn and Geoffrey Hartman (eds.), *Romanticism: Vistas, Instances, Continuities* (Cornell, 1974), 38–61.

Heinermann, T. *Cecilia Böhl de Faber (Fernán Caballero) y Juan Eugenio Hartzenbusch. Una correspondencia inédita* (Madrid, 1944).

Herrero, J. *Fernán Caballero: un nuevo planteamiento* (Madrid, 1963).

Los orígenes del pensamiento reaccionario español (Madrid, 1971).

'El naranjo romántico: esencia del costumbrismo', *HR*, 46 (1978), 343–54.

Hespelt, E. H. 'The Genesis of *La familia de Alvareda*', *HR*, 2 (1934), 179–201.

(with Stanley T. Williams), 'Two Unpublished Anecdotes by Fernán Caballero Preserved by Washington Irving', *MLN*, 49 (1934), 25–31.

(with Stanley T. Williams), 'Washington Irving's Notes on Fernán Caballero's Stories', *PMLA*, 49 (1934), 1129–39.

Juretschke, H. 'Las revistas románticas españolas y su valor historio-biográfico', *Arbor*, 10 (1948), 409–21.

Vida, obra y pensamiento de Alberto Lista (Madrid, 1951).

Origen doctrinal y génesis del romanticismo español (Madrid, 1954).

'Del romanticismo liberal en Cataluña', *Rev. Lit.*, 11–12 (1954), 9–30.

'Alemania en la obra de Milá y Fontanals', *Bol. RABL Barc.*, 35 (1973–4), 5–67.

'La recepción de la cultura y ciencia alemana en España durante la época romántica' in *Estudios románticos* (Valladolid, 1975), 63–120.

'La presencia del ideario romántico alemán en la estructura y evolución teórica del romanticismo español' in *Romanticismo 1 – Atti del II congresso sul romanticismo spagnolo e ispanoamericano. Aspetti e problemi del teatro romántico* (Genoa, 1982), 11–24.

'El problema de los orígenes del romanticismo español' in the Ramón Menéndez Pidal *Historia de España. XXXV: La época del romanticismo (1808–1874). Vol. I: Orígenes, religión, filosofía, ciencia* (Madrid, 1989).

(ed.) *Obras completas de don Juan Donoso Cortés, Marqués de Valdegamas*, 2 vols., BAC (Madrid, 1946).

Kermode, F. *The Classic: Literary Images of Permanence and Change* (Harvard, 1983).

Romantic Image, new edn (London, 1986).

King, E. L. 'What is Spanish Romanticism?', *St. Rom.* II (1962–3), 1–11.

Kirkpatrick, S. *Larra: el laberinto inextricable de un romántico liberal* (Madrid, 1977).

'On the Threshold of the Realist Novel: Gender and Genre in *La gaviota*', *PMLA*, 98 (1983), 323–40.

'Spanish Romanticism' in Roy Porter and Mikulás Teich (eds.), *Romanticism in National Context* (Cambridge, 1988), 260–83.

Le Gentil, G. *Les Revues littéraires de l'Espagne pendant la première moitié du XIXe siècle* (Paris, 1909).

Llorens, V. *Liberales y románticos. Una emigración española en Inglaterra (1823–1834)* (El Colegio de México, 1954).

El romanticismo español (Madrid, 1979).

López Argüello, A. *Epistolario de Fernán Caballero. Una colección de cartas inéditas de la novelista* (Barcelona, 1922).

Lovejoy, A. O. 'On the Discrimination of Romanticisms', *PMLA*, 39 (1924), 229–53.

McClelland, I. L. *The Origins of the Romantic Movement in Spain* (Liverpool, 1937).

McMaster, G. *Scott and Society* (Cambridge, 1981).

Marrast, R. *José de Espronceda et son temps. Littérature, société, politique au temps du romantisme* (Paris, 1974).

Menéndez y Pelayo, M. *Estudios y discursos de crítica histórica y literaria*, 7 vols. (Santander, 1941–2).

Historia de las ideas estéticas en España, 5 vols. (Santander, 1946–7).

(ed.) *Obras completas del doctor D. Manuel Milá y Fontanals*, 8 vols. (Barcelona, 1888–96).

Montesinos, J. F. *Fernán Caballero. Ensayo de justificación* (El Colegio de México, 1959).

Costumbrismo y novela. Ensayo sobre el redescubrimiento de la realidad española. 2nd edn (Madrid, 1965).

Introducción a una historia de la novela en España en el siglo XIX, 2nd edn (Madrid, 1966).

Montoto, S. 'Cartas inéditas de Fernán Caballero', *BRAE*, 35 (1955), 383–414; 36 (1956), 29–64; 37 (1957), 85–134, 299–308, 469–83; 38 (1958), 117–34; 39 (1959), 295–331, 463–85; 40 (1960), 401–539.

Moreno Alonso, M. *Historiografía romántica española; introducción al estudio de la historia en el siglo XIX* (Seville, 1979).

Navas-Ruiz, R. *El romanticismo español: historia y crítica* (Salamanca, 1970).

El romanticismo español, 3rd edn (Madrid, 1982).

(ed.) *El romanticismo español. Documentos* (Salamanca, 1971).

Los orígenes del Romanticismo en Europa. Textos del simposio celebrado en el Instituto Germano-Español de Investigación de la Sociedad Goerres en noviembre de 1980 (Madrid, 1982).

O'Riordan, P. '*Helios, revista del modernismo*', *Abaco*, 4 (1973), 57–150.

Par, A. *Shakespeare en la literatura española*, 2 vols. (Madrid–Barcelona, 1935).

Peckham, M. 'Towards a Theory of Romanticism', *PMLA* 66 (1951), 5–23.

'Towards a Theory of Romanticism: II. Reconsiderations', *St. Rom.* 1 (1961–2), 1–8.

Peers, E. A. 'Later Spanish Conceptions of Romanticism', *MLR*, 18 (1923), 37–50.

'La influencia de Chateaubriand en España', *RFE*, 11 (1924), 351–82.

'Studies in the Influence of Sir Walter Scott in Spain', *RH*, 68 (1926), 1–161.

A History of the Romantic Movement in Spain, 2 vols. (Cambridge, 1940).

(ed.) *Liverpool Studies in Spanish Literature. First Series: From Cadalso to Rubén Darío* (Liverpool, 1940).

Picoche, J. L. *Un romántico español: Enrique Gil y Carrasco* (Madrid, 1978).

Pitollet, C. 'Les Premiers Essais littéraires de Fernán Caballero', *BH*, 9 (1907), 67–86, 286–302, 10 (1908), 286–305, 378–96.

La Querelle calderonienne de Johan Nikolas Böhl von Faber et José Joaquín de Mora, reconstituée d'après les documents originaux (Paris, 1909).

Raitt, A. W. *Vol. III: The Nineteenth Century* in Austin Gill (ed.), *Life and Letters in France* (London, 1965).

Randolph, D. A. *Eugenio de Ochoa y el romanticismo español* (Berkeley, 1966).

Don Manuel Cañete, cronista literario del romanticismo y del posromanticismo en España (Chapel Hill, 1972).

Río A. del. 'Una historia del movimiento romántico en España', *RHM*, 9 (1943), 209–22.

'Present Trends in the Conception and Criticism of Spanish Romanticism', *RR*, 39 (1948), 229–48.

Rodgers, E. 'Teoría literaria y filosofía de la historia en el primer Galdós' in Peter A. Bly (ed.), *Galdós y la historia*, Ottawa Hispanic Studies 7 (Ottawa, 1988), 35–47.

Rodríguez-Luis, J. '*La gaviota*: Fernán Caballero entre romanticismo y realismo', *Anales Galdosianos* 8 (1973), 125–35.

(ed.) Fernán Caballero, *Clemencia*, Ediciones Cátedra (Madrid, 1975).

Romanticismo 1 – Atti del II congresso sul romanticismo spagnolo e ispanoamericano. Aspetti e problemi del teatro romántico (Genoa, 1982).

Sáinz Rodríguez, P. 'Estudios sobre la historia de la crítica literaria en España. Don Bartolomé José Gallardo y la crítica literaria de su tiempo', *RH*, 51 (1921), 211–304, 305–595.

'Documentos para la historia de la crítica literaria en España. Un epistolario erudito del siglo XIX', *BBMP*, 3 (1921), 27–43, 87–101, 155–65, 251–62, 4 (1922), 153–70.

(ed.) *Obras escogidas de Bartolomé José Gallardo*, 2 vols. (Madrid, 1928).

Samuels, D. G. *Enrique Gil y Carrasco: A Study in Spanish Romanticism* (New York, 1939).

Seoane, M. C. *Vol. II: El siglo XIX* in Ma Dolores Sáiz and Ma. Cruz Seoane (eds.) *Historia del periodismo en España* (Madrid, 1983).

Shaw, D. L. 'Towards the Understanding of Spanish Romanticism', *MLR*, 58 (1963), 190–5.

'The Anti-Romantic Reaction in Spain', *MLR*, 63 (1968), 606–11.

'*Armonismo*: The Failure of an Illusion' in Clara E. Lida and Iris M. Zavala (eds.), *La revolución de 1868. Historia, pensamiento, literatura* (New York, 1970), 351–61.

The Nineteenth Century in R. O. Jones (ed.), *A Literary History of Spain* (London, 1971).

'Spain. Romántico-Romanticismo-Romancesco-Romanesco-Romancista-Románico' in Hans Eichner (ed.), '*Romantic*' and its Cognates: The European History of a Word* (Toronto, 1972), 341–71.

(ed.) Agustín Durán, *Discurso*, Exeter Hispanic Texts, IV (Exeter, 1973).

(ed.) Duque de Rivas, *Don Alvaro o La fuerza del sino*, Clásicos Castalia (Madrid, 1986).

Silva, R. 'Two Barcelona Periodicals: *El Vapor*; *El Guardia Nacional*' in E. Allison Peers (ed.), *Liverpool Studies in Spanish Literature. First Series: From Cadalso to Rubén Darío* (Liverpool, 1940), 80–100.

Simón Díaz, J. *El Artista (1835–1836)*, CIPP I (Madrid, 1946).

El Alba (Madrid, 1838–1839), CIPP III (Madrid, 1946).

Liceo Artístico y Literario (Madrid, 1838) CIPP VI (Madrid, 1947).

El Arpa del Creyente (Madrid, 1842), CIPP VII (Madrid, 1947).

Souriau, M. (ed.) *La préface de Cromwell* (Paris, undated).

Sullivan, H. W. *Calderón in the German Lands and the Low Countries: His Reception and Influence, 1654–1980* (Cambridge, 1983).

Tarr, F. C. 'Romanticism in Spain and Spanish Romanticism: A Critical Survey', *BSS*, 16 (1939), 3–37.

Tubino, F. M. 'Introducción del romanticismo en España', *La Revista Contemporanea*, 1877, 7, 79–98, 184–98.

Varela, J. L. 'Fernán Caballero y el *Volksgeist*', *Arbor*, 97 (1977), 327–42.

'La autointerpretación del romanticismo español' in *Los orígenes del Romanticismo en Europa. Textos del simposio celebrado en el Instituto Germano-Español de Investigación de la Sociedad Goerres en noviembre de 1980* (Madrid, 1982), 123–36.

Larra y España (Madrid, 1983).

Wellek. R. *A History of Modern Criticism 1750–1950. Vol. I: The Later Eighteenth Century; Vol. II: The Romantic Age* (London, 1955).

'The Concept of Romanticism in Literary History' in *Concepts of Criticism* (Yale, 1963), 128–98.

Williams, S. T., *see* Hespelt, E. H.

Zavala, I. M. *Ideología y política en la novela española del siglo XIX* (Salamanca, 1971).

'La literatura: romanticismo y costumbrismo' in the Ramón Menéndez Pidal *Historia de España. XXXV: La época del romanticismo (1808–1874). Vol. II: Las letras, las artes, la vida cotidiana* (Madrid, 1989).

(ed.) *Vol. V: Romanticismo y realismo* in Francisco Rico (ed.), *Historia y crítica de la literatura española* (Barcelona, 1982).

Index